IMMINENT COMMONS: LIVE FROM SEOUL

SEOUL BIENNALE
OF ARCHITECTURE
AND URBANISM
2017

EDITED BY HYUNGMIN PAI

CONTENTS

WELCOME TO THE SEOUL BIENNALE OF ARCHITECTURE AND URBANISM

The Seoul Biennale of Architecture and Urbanism is taking its first step. Long dormant as a seed at the heart of our city, after two years of preparation, the Seoul Biennale has finally come to fruition as a new cultural event based in Seoul. Throughout the city's central role in the dazzling cultural growth of the past half-century, architecture has served as the primary instrument of development. Now, people are becoming the center of urban development. Architecture as a means to create a just and sustainable city for its people is not a dream of the distant future, but a reality that stands alongside our citizens. Since my inauguration as the Mayor of Seoul, I have implemented a robust range of policies such as regeneration-centered urban renovation, Seoul the Walking City, promotion of urban manufacturing and agricultural businesses, revitalization of local communities, and youth start-up support projects. These initiatives have brought about the birth of a new architectural paradigm, which had been inherent as potential in the minds of our citizens and everyday life in the city. The Seoul Biennale will present a milestone for the new role taken on by the architecture of the city.

The Seoul Metropolitan Government announced the Seoul Architecture Manifesto in 2013. It starts with the following resolution: "Every work of architecture in Seoul is public property that belongs to all citizens. We will transform Seoul into a shining example of sharing architecture and a city of commons that everyone can enjoy and toward which they can feel a sense of pride." We have selected "Imminent Commons" as the theme for the first Seoul Biennale of Architecture and Urbanism, based on the belief that this idea of consistent civic administration presents the philosophy and methodology of addressing impending issues of cities worldwide. This event will show the essentials of the city of commons as to what and how the city is sharing by expanding policies relevant to the sharing city.

Along with Dongdaemun Design Plaza and Donuimun Museum Village, where major exhibitions are scheduled to be held, the historical downtown areas of Seoul will serve as a venue for hands-on experiences and a laboratory for policy discovery. Sharing brings blessings and happiness for all. The Seoul Biennale 2017 will offer people the opportunity to enjoy the exhibitions together, participate in various projects, and engage in in-depth discussions on the future of the city. The Seoul Biennale will continue to create a place where cities of the world can learn from Seoul and Seoul can learn from them in return.

Won-Soon Park, Mayor of Seoul

SEOUL BIENNALE, OR THE MAKING OF PLACE

Hyungmin Pai
Director of Seoul Biennale of Architecture and Urbanism 2017; professor, University of Seoul

Imminent Commons: Live from Seoul is the last volume in the publication series of the Seoul Biennale of Architecture and Urbanism 2017. While additional books based on the vast curatorial and research work of the biennale will be published in the coming months, *Imminent Commons: Live from Seoul* provides an overview of the sites, exhibition spaces, events, performances, as well as the thoughts and work of the many people that comprised the two-year process that was the Seoul Biennale. Centered on the Live Projects and the diverse array of public programs, the volume sets itself in Seoul as a place enabled by its locality to become part of a global network of urban communities. It is a book that focuses less on individual installations and more on the biennale as a specific set of places. It assumes that the character of these places is an integral part of the Biennale's cosmopolitan, transnational gaze. The practice and theory of the Seoul Biennale as an act of place-making within a global world was, in effect, my answer to the question of how an exhibition on urbanism, a biennale on the city, should be curated; a rejoinder to the issue of whether the Seoul Biennale should assume an audience of expert communities or the wider general public. In other words, the organization of the Seoul Biennale—centered on the three major curatorial sections of the *Thematic*, the *Cities Exhibition*, and the *Live Projects*—is best explained by the way each section sets up a particular relation with its immediate physical and social context as well as the global network of places in which it participates.

The *Cities Exhibition*, first of all, sought to bring an array of places, mediated as objects and images, into a singular space. In the Design Exhibition Hall and Design Pathway of the Dongdaemun Design Plaza (DDP), the most traditional exhibition space of the Seoul Biennale, fifty-five installations, including contributions from fifty cities around the world, presented a set of issues, policies, or projects related to the commons. For sixty-six days, the DDP was a place of gathering: a global gathering of places, communities, and ideas about the present and future of the city. The scale of each installation varied but they were all relatively small, from objects to rooms that generally occupied less than thirty square meters. In contrast to most DDP exhibitions that create their own cocoon-like gallery environment—totally separated from the conditions of Zaha Hadid's undulating interior, forcing visitors along a fixed movement sequence—the *Cities Exhibition* sought to open the gallery space up to the audience. Through enfilades, a terrace overlooking the gallery, open views toward the ceiling, and multiple adjacencies, each installation was considered part of an expansive network of undetermined connections. The point was to create a large congregation of objects, images, drawings, ideas brought together as an open-ended experience.

In this sense, it was extremely important for Pyongyang to be one of the fifty cities gathered within the gallery. Though created without any direct North Korean involvement, appropriating support from the Seoul Metropolitan Government's South/North Korea Exchange Fund, *Pyongyang Sallim* became even more important as tensions around the Korean Peninsula escalated during the very period in which the Seoul Biennale was going up. Stirring some controversy in the media, it became the most visited installation in the DDP. The special docents of *Pyongyang Sallim*, refugees of North Korea who have now settled in Seoul, reported several incidents where visitors came to the gallery to communicate their anger at the very existence of an exhibition related to North Korea. From my perspective, the point of recreating a Pyongyang apartment in Seoul was clear. It was a simple but essential reminder that there are ordinary people living ordinary lives in Pyongyang. Other visitors of the DDP will make different connections and reach different conclusions. Though deliberately placed next to *Sectioning Seoul* and linked to Seoul by the *Letters to the Mayor* project, there was no intent to compare Seoul and Pyongyang. Whatever intellectual, emotional, or practical relation was to be drawn from this mediated gathering, it was left primarily to the visitor's own commitments and imagination.

If the Cities Exhibition brought places into Seoul, the Live Projects were direct engagements into the urban fabric of the city. Production City, Urban Foodshed, and Walking the Commons, each with its peculiar thematic thread and

Dongwoo Yim & Calvin Chua, *Pyongyang Sallim*, DDP Exhibition Hall. Photo: Kyungsub Shin Studio.

method of intervention, appropriated a series of spaces in the everyday fabric of central Seoul. Some were ephemeral and performative, as with the *Musicity* and *Playable City* programs of the Walking the Commons; some took the form of temporary residencies, as with the Biennale café and restaurant; and as in the Sewoon Basement and *Project Seoul Apparel*'s Changsin-dong Spin-off Gallery, some created new spaces that extend beyond the exhibition time frame of the Seoul Biennale. This intervention into the urban everyday was possible because the Live Projects engaged with the on-going work of a wide range of local stake-holders: residents, workers, owners, shopkeepers, community activists, the district office, and of course the municipality of Seoul. Though some of the work of the Biennale curators, participants, staff, and officials has been documented in this volume, it is but a small recording of their vast collaborative work. The people and their places are of course what matter. The Seoul Biennale was merely a moment in their history—a brief musical experience, playful game in a familiar neighborhood, or a trigger for a more extended engagement. The purpose is for that moment, however transient, to be transformative, to be part of the evolution of the place.

The *Thematic*, comprised mostly of projects that were non-place in nature (machines, projects, technologies, and ideas applicable to any city) was installed within the Donuimun Museum Village, a site seeking to re-establish its sense of place. The site, adjacent to Donuimun (the West Gate of the walled city of Hanyang, the only unrestored gate out of the four main gates of the capital of the Joseon Dynasty) and Gyeonghee Palace, is part of an important historical neighborhood. Mostly built up between the 1930s and 1970s as a mixture of traditional hanoks, jerry-built houses, small office buildings, and back-alleys, the neighborhood was a busy eatery and motel district before it was turned over to the municipality as contributed acceptance. Rather than creating a park, the typical form of contributed acceptance in Korean redevelopment projects, the site was renovated (maintaining many of the existing houses and buildings) with the idea of creating a public cultural complex.

As an architectural environment, its residential grain, material texture, and spatial complexity stand at the very opposite of the DDP. As a public cultural facility, the Donuimun Village is a new kind of project that the city of Seoul must learn how to manage. Having vacated what had been a bustling private sector of the city, the challenge now is to balance public investment into culture and commercial ventures such as guest houses and rental shops. While the former would burden the municipality's budget, an overload of the latter would contradict the basic idea of the new initiative, perhaps even betray the public trust. With the thirty-eight installations of the *Thematic*, the *Common Library* and bookshop, the studio archives, and the interventions of the *Urban Foodshed* as the first occupants of the Donuimun Village, the Biennale tested its potential in becoming a space of the commons. While the restaurant, café, bookstore, library, and thematic installations such as the Eco-Village sought to reproduce the everyday environment of an urban neighborhood, many installations seemed strangely out of place—machines and objects in unfinished rooms; in buildings that are neither new nor old, neither house nor gallery. The Donuimun Village as a biennale experience, whether viewed positively or negatively, was simultaneously awkward, provocative, new, comfortable, and artificial. With several visitors who argued that the streets and plaza of the Village should be open free to the public, this multiple identity, or confusion, manifested itself in the practical matter of admission ticket control. While the biennale installations in the Donuimun Village have been taken down, its ownership, management, and programming is being discussed and contested among various stakeholders.

Finally, the *Public Programs* constituted an array of mechanisms—conferences, studios, workshops, tours, and lectures that brought in a wide range of participants into the intellectual and local framework of the biennale. In this vein, there was no question that the audience of the Seoul Biennale were as much the citizens of Seoul as the global architectural community. It is an arrangement that can be contrasted with the Venice Biennale, which occupies an urban area of less than 270,000 residents. Unlike Seoul, a city of 10 million people, Venice is mostly occupied by tourists. Tourism, as Venice so well knows, opens itself up to occupation without commitment. The question is whether a biennale audience, a biennale community can be different. As a site for the Biennale, Venice is visited primarily by the global, expert community. It is a beautiful paradox when Venice becomes a unique non-place, a historic international hub where people fly in to "Meet in Architecture" (2009), find "Common Ground" (2011), and talk about "Fundamentals" (2014). If we know that places are created not by conjured-up authenticity but by human commitment, then can an international biennale be a part of place-making? I respond by first stating that commitment to a place is not confined to those who take permanent residence. As an ethical stance, it separates itself from both universalism and parochialism. Commitment is a sense of responsibility to others, wherever they may reside. That is why an international biennale can be committed to the making of places. Indeed, the commons shares with the idea of commitment an understanding that each person's well-being is contingent on a wider set of human and non-human relations. Whatever success or failure may be deemed of the commitments garnered within the Seoul Biennale, I reaffirm that its ambition was to be part of a place-making process.

In these different ways, the Seoul Biennale enters into the fray of the political economy of place: a star architect's spectacle of a gallery, the live sites of urban production, and a new type of public space. Through its curatorial engagements, it sought to demonstrate that space and place are central to workings of capitalism and governance. As a theoretical statement, it was David Harvey who most clearly articulated this dynamic between location and mobility with the notion of "the spatial fix": "capitalism has to fix space (in immoveable structures of transport and communication networks, as well as in built environments of factories, roads, houses, water supplies, and other physical infrastructures) in order to overcome space (achieve a liberty of movement through low transport and communication costs)."[1] In as much as the commons can be understood as part of a critical transformation of capitalism and the public body, the Seoul Biennale was not only an exhibition about the fixed spaces of the contemporary city but was also a testing ground for the commons. It was not only about the commons as an entity but also a small but intricate part of the process of "commoning." Presented in a city undergoing major transformation not, as in previous decades, in its redevelopment and physical expansion but in its culture and social fabric, the Seoul Biennale was specific to its moment and location. In times when all over the world nationalistic impulses and identity politics are taking on fascist forms, a biennale of the city requires a commitment to the here and now; that is, to a global sense of place.

1. David Harvey, "Globalization and the 'Spatial Fix'," *Geographische Revue*, 2/2001: 23–30.

Terreform ONE (Mitchell Joachim) &
DJ Spooky, *Plug-In-Ecology: Urban
Farm Pod*, Donuimun Museum Village.
Photo: Kyungsub Shin Studio.

Donuimun Museum Village. Photo: Kyungsub Shin Studio.

국민의 비상벨
더 빨리 달려가겠습니다
112

Donuimun Museum Village. Photo: Kyungsub Shin Studio.

SHARABLE
CITY
SHARABLE CITY
EXHIBITION 2017.
9.2 — 11.5
URBAN TERRAIN LAB
CITY PROFILER
ZERO BOUNDARY

The Living, *Twin Mirror*, Donuimun Museum Village. Photo: Kyungsub Shin Studio.

Nikolaus Hirsch, Michel Müller, and Rirkrit Tiravanija, *Do We Dream Under the Same Sky*. Donuimun Museum Village. Photo: Kyungsub Shin Studio.

Dirk E. Hebel and Philippe Block,
Beyond Mining: Urban Growth.
Donuimun Museum Village.
Photo: Kyungsub Shin Studio.

Donuimun Museum Village. Photo: Kyungsub Shin Studio.

Two guerrilla farmers, Seongbuk-dong, Seoul, 2017. Photo: Suyeon Yun.

URBAN
FOODSHED

URBAN FOODSHED: EATING, DRINKING, AND BREATHING IN SEOUL

Hyewon Lee
Curator, Seoul Biennale 2017; professor, Division of Visual Arts, Daejin University

There are nearly 7,000 professional farmers in Seoul, and the city produces 630 tons of grain, 175 tons of potatoes, 1,160 tons of cucumbers, 411 tons of tomatoes, and 311 tons of pears every year (http://kosis.kr). Because of Seoul's guerilla farmers, largely composed of senior citizens, it is common to see sesame leaves and zucchini plants growing along the well-maintained landscapes of city apartment blocks. In addition, due to the growing interest in urban farming by Seoul's younger residents, as well as local government support, the total area of urban farms has increased 5.6 times just in the last five years. However, the total foodstuffs produced by these professional, guerilla, and recreational farmers can only support 0.001 percent of Seoul's megacity population of over 10 million people.

Many inhabitants of the city take it for granted that Seoul is a food-consuming rather than food-producing city, and that 3.67 million tons of food is brought into Seoul, circulated, and consumed every year, with 1/3 of this amount thrown away. Not only that, many may wonder why we even need to talk about food and farming in Seoul today. However, food disasters occurring all over the world for the last 10 years indicate that our vague optimism about the food crisis must be reconsidered. The bee colony collapse sweeping across the U.S., Europe, and Asia since 2006 set off alarm bells for the future of food production worldwide. The serial wheat crop failure in the world's major wheat producing countries—Ukraine and Russia from 2007–2009, followed by China in 2010–11—due to extreme heat wave and drought conditions led to rising bread prices in the top grain importing countries of the Middle East and North Africa, heightening existing tensions that led to the Arab Spring from 2010–12. At the same time, the effects of the same heat wave and drought in the "Fertile Crescent" region, the main breadbasket of the Middle East, uprooted much of its rural population, further exacerbating social instability in the region. And most recently, the global avian flu outbreak in 2016, which resulted in the culling of 27 million birds in South Korea alone, has led to a sharp decline in poultry production as well as hike in egg prices.

The food crisis is further compounded by global water insecurity, as not only climate change but also corporate greed endangers access to water, which is a critical resource for food production. The so-called "water barons," top multinational investment banks and individual billionaires, are buying up land that holds major aquifers across the globe as well as buying operating rights to tap water in South America, Asia, and parts of Europe, taking advantage of economic crises or corrupt regimes, and low public awareness. Furthermore, corporations that manufacture chemical fertilizers and pesticides, that is, companies that have been the backbone of the green revolution that has exhausted the regeneration capacity of water and soil, are now advancing into the seed industry. And in 2013, the Food and Agriculture Organization of the United Nations predicted an impending food shortage by the year 2030 that will be difficult for humanity to withstand, and identified insects as a future food resource.

The impacts of climate change that can no longer be denied and the political climate of the international community that is becoming increasingly difficult to predict day by day also make it hard to believe that what we now take for granted will continue. Springing forth from this sense of crisis, the 2017 Urban Architecture Biennale Live Project Urban Foodshed: Eating, Drinking, and Breathing in Seoul looks at the future of the city through issues related to food. The project began by imagining a failure, for whatever reason (environmental or political), in any of the processes of food flows in Seoul, and examines not only the city's food problems but also those that surround water, land, air, and energy, the key resources that underpin our food system.

The primary goal of this project is visitors' direct experience of the process of food production, distribution, consumption, and recycling in Seoul. Towards this purpose, the Urban Foodshed will be presented as a compressed system, consisting of a production system that is composed of a garden, an apiary, hydroponics, rainwater reservoirs, a seed library, etc.; a market, the most intimate space of distribution in the lives of urban residents; a restaurant and a café where food and drinks are consumed, and food waste either gets discarded or returned to the garden as compost. This system operates on the basis of farmers in Seoul as well as a domestic farming network. Borrowing the knowledge and experience of farmers practicing various farming methods in accordance with different topographical conditions, we grow vegetables, herbs, and fruit trees in the Donuimun Museum Village and use this produce in our restaurant and café.

By eating or drinking at the restaurant or café, visitors to the Urban Foodshed will not only be able to embody the vision of the Urban Foodshed, but will also encounter various issues and problems related to eating, drinking, and breathing that extend beyond the boundaries and scope of the restaurant and café to three exhibits focused on the privatization of water, Seoul's worsening air pollution, and the future of food in the city. Through these activities, visitors are invited to empathize with the urgency of the problems inherent in the closely intertwined global food system and join in finding coping mechanisms that traverse urban and national boundaries.

In addition, the project seeks to build a platform for information sharing that would bring together in one place the knowledge, alternatives, and practical models needed to address the food, water, land, air, and energy crises. To this end, we have joined up with individuals, organizations, and institutions in many parts of the world that are implementing alternatives across national boundaries. Representative examples include the Green Wall project by the Korean NGO Future Forest, which has planted nearly 10 million trees in the Inner Mongolia Kubuqi desert over the last 16 years; The Ocean Cleanup, a large-scale project initiated by Boyan Slat, a young Dutch entrepreneur, to clean up sea waste; and Rwanda's Environmental Management Authority, which has played a decisive role in the global spread of the campaign to reduce disposable plastics by prohibiting the use of plastic bags by law and enforcing this law for the past ten years.

During the course of the project, India, the Middle East, Africa, and the East Mediterranean region became important reference points. This is because these regions are already experiencing chronic water scarcity and the severe impact of climate change and extreme weather that Seoul may experience in the not too distant future. Alternative approaches to water, land, air, and energy that people in these regions have already initiated are important components of this project. Among these are a movement to restore the traditional water storage system, Eri, in Tamil Nadu, India; pest control research using natural insects at a research institute in the Egyptian desert; organic farming methods to cope with climate change pioneered by Nicolas Netien at the Atsas Farm in the Solea Valley of Cyprus, which produces olive oil that set the record for the highest total phenolic compounds; and a solar oven developed in order to reduce the amount of wood and fossil fuels used for cooking by inventor and civilian activist Savvas Hadjixenophontos.

In addition to the cross-border activities of these individuals and organizations, we have also invited numerous field experts who are active in their own locales: organic farmers who preserve seeds by increasing organic matter in soil; migratory beekeepers who chase after blooming flowers with beehives in tow in the face of climate conditions that are increasingly disadvantageous to the bees' survival; botanists who have dedicated their lives to the study of wild plants as the key to securing future food resources and soil regeneration; hydrologists, who cannot sleep on days of heavy rainfall because of potential flooding; activists fighting to defend the right to drink clean water; and young mothers who, in order to provide clean water and food for their children, find and share a tremendous amount of information about both resources. We hope that the information, knowledge, alternatives, and practical models collected by all of these people will form the basis for solving the problems that surround food, the resulting product of the proper interaction of four resources: water, land, air, and energy.

Lastly, I would like to add a few words about my own experience as the curator of this project who went from working on water-related projects for the last several years to expanding this interest into the current Urban Foodshed project. To be honest, this process has raised doubts for me as to whether mankind has ever shared food, water, land, and energy fairly and democratically at any point in history. This is a time that makes me doubt more than ever before whether an individual who was born, raised, and educated in a capitalist system, and has become accustomed to defining himself/herself through consumption would be able to suppress his/her desires in order

to "save the planet." However, it was important to meet various field experts from home and abroad, and to experience growing vegetables in the city center of Seoul, even if at a micro scale, and to refrain from unnecessary consumption.

This personal journey towards the Urban Foodshed helped make it clear to me that the city and the countryside are bound together in a single destiny and that they are companions heading towards an uncertain future. Not only that, it has helped identify what the growing ranks of amateur farmers, who are leading the sporadic but certain flow of urban farming spreading like fashion in many cities across the world, can do for the future of humankind. In other words, urban farming for the future is more than just restoring urban ecosystems, strengthening community awareness, and contributing a part of the production of food consumed by the city. It has to be an agriculture that takes into account the expected impacts of climate change and environmental hazards, an agriculture that produces and preserves healthy seeds, and an agriculture that more actively practices biodiversity. This challenging agriculture is a better choice for urban farmers rather than livelihood farmers,

and it will be easier to create the basis for this environment in the city. I am not talking about a scientific experiment that is possible at an agricultural research institute. Farming in a slightly drier or colder climate or more polluted air is possible through only slight changes to the current conditions of the city.

This kind of practice will still require the help of architects and urban planners. As the growth that seemed to be expanding infinitely eventually slowed down, Seoul has begun exhibiting signs of slumification. Rather than reviving the buildings whose future uses are being abandoned, it would be more effective to demolish them in order to expand both farmland and permeable land to prepare for the food and water problems that we may encounter in the future. The future architect may have to be the person who demolishes rather than builds, or someone who systematically restores nature in order to create a city in which it is less difficult to eat, drink, and breathe.

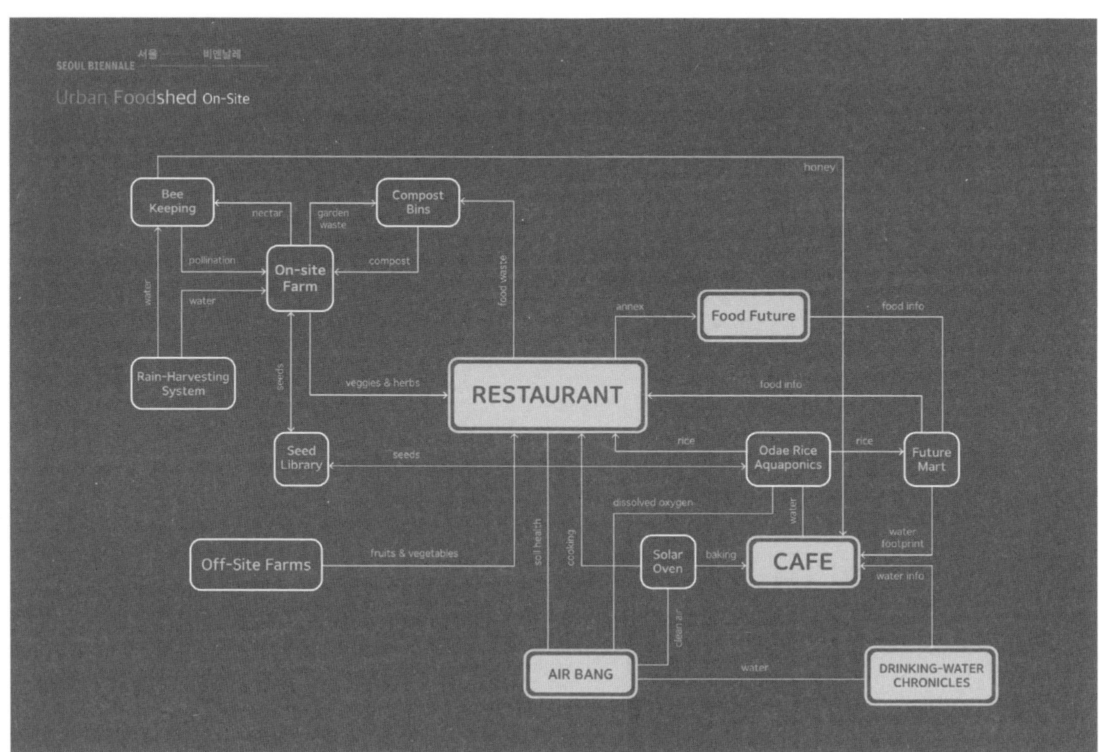

Diagram/network of the Urban Foodshed exhibition at Donuimun Museum Village

BIENNALE RESTAURANT

Seoul Biennale Opening Day: People lined up outside the Biennale Restaurant. Photo: Suyeon Yun.

Vegetarian Thali from South India
Rathi Jafer (InKo Centre)

For as long as we have existed, so has our food. Food alone however, does not define a particular cuisine or by extension, distinguish a specific culture. It is often the meaning and myths surrounding the ingredients, the preparation, the cooking, the combination of flavors, which determine the makings and particularities of a cuisine or reinforce a culinary tradition. It is no wonder then that cuisine is so often the focus of historical or anthropological studies. Cuisine, when viewed as a cultural signpost, is often what sets a culture apart and provides a common understanding of what it means to "belong" to that community. The South Indian vegetarian Thaali restaurant at the Urban Foodsehed section of the Seoul Biennale of Architecture and Urbanism aims to position cuisine from South India, particularly from Tamil Nadu, within the larger ambit of culture in order to understand its local characteristics but also to examine the intercultural connections and the transnational currents that have historically existed between this southern Indian region and the southern regions of South Korea.

In specific terms, the Thaali restaurant will be a South Indian vegetarian restaurant/kitchen which will serve the traditional thaali. A team of chefs from Eden restaurant in Chennai will be in Seoul to present the authentic thaali meal with key ingredients specially flown in from Chennai, India. A Thaali is a composite and wholesome meal which is basically a combination of various delicious dishes served on a single, usually round, plate. Although there are regional variations across India, we will focus on the thaali meal from Tamil Nadu. In Tamil Nadu, thaali meals are served on plates as well as on banana leaves. Considered to be the birthplace of the elaborate sappadu (meal), most restaurants in Tamil Nadu offer a vegetarian thaali that uses

Themed Dinner Lecture: "Wild Plants: Soil Regenerators and Future Food Resources." Food was prepared with beans, grass, and other plants from the wild. Photo: Suyeon Yun.

Thaali from South India. Photo: Suyeon Yun.

seasonal vegetables and traditional culinary traditions and techniques of the region that are several thousand years old. While presenting the traditional wisdom ingrained in such culinary traditions, especially the manner in which the cyclical nature of the seasons and the circadian rhythms of human beings dictate the making and consumption of food, we aim to examine the main concerns of the imminent commons of air, water, fire, earth, as well as the concept of making and sharing, which is central to the Seoul Biennale on Architecture and Urbanism. While presenting traditional cuisine from Tamil Nadu, we will also obliquely draw attention to the similarities and differences in traditional Korean cuisine with its variety of dishes like a thaali but differently arranged; seasonal variations, the concept of sharing and community identity and the preservation and dissemination of traditional knowledge systems.

The restaurant opens on 1 September 2017, with a special Indian Night—a reception co-hosted by the Ambassador of India and InKo Centre and a riveting multi-instrumental percussive performance by Taan, a talented quartet from Ahmedabad, India, followed by the screening of Lunchbox, an acclaimed film from India, and a discussion with one of India's foremost architects, Rahul Mehrotra. Following on from the opening, relevant discussion forums will be periodically presented at the restaurant, complementing the thaali meal service that will reinforce the themes of sustenance and sustainability that the Urban Foodshed aims to promote as an empathetic and well-informed choice.

With specific reference to the cities of Seoul and Chennai in particular, the restaurant aims to examine the relevance of traditional methods and practices in contemporary urban spaces.

Beehive on a hydroponic strawberry farm. Pocheon, Gyeonggi Province, Korea. Photo: Suyeon Yun.

Themed Dinner

Planting Apple Trees in Seoul
15 September 2017
Choi Yongsu, "Bees and the Future of Agriculture"

Seoul is a city with many green areas. However, because of the restricted focus on greening and landscaping, these areas do not help form a healthy ecosystem. For example, the white fringe-trees that many cities have planted to beautify their cityscapes are not useful for bees because they cannot make nectar.

Planting honey plants in the city is more important than urban beekeeping. Honey plants such as acacia, chestnut, and apple trees naturally brings back the bees, the insects that eat the fruit of the plants, and animals eating the insects. They produce food for bees, insects, and of course, people.

How to Boost the Immune System of a Plant
28 October 2017
Park Kyungbum, "Honey, Melon, and THAAD"

Go to a mountain near your farm, clear away the leaf cover, and collect about 2kg of soil from underneath. There are many indigenous microorganisms in this soil.

Community garden, Naegok-dong, Seoul, 2017. Photo: Suyeon Yun.

Put the soil in a large container, fill it with water, and plug up the air bubbles. This provides the oxygen necessary for the microorganisms to grow. If you want to cultivate a large number of microorganisms, mix rice and beans in a ratio of about 7 to 3, cook the mixture, and add it to the container. Keep the container in the shade for one week to ten days until a white film appears on the water. This is a sign that the microorganisms have been fully cultured.

If you add this cultured mixture to the water every time you water your plants, the immunity of the plants will improve. However, when making this mixture, you need to avoid very hot or cold weather. 20 degrees Celsius is good.

Recently, there are a lot of farmers who cultivate specific microorganisms. However, this is undesirable. It is almost impossible to manage good and bad microorganisms separately. The important thing is the balance between microorganisms. Aerobic and alkaline microorganisms must live together. Isn't this also the case with people?

Soil and Climate Change
3 September 2017
Nicolas Netien, "Going Beyond Sustainable: The Global Case for Agro-Ecology"

One way to actively cope with climate change is to increase the amount of organic matter in the soil. Because 50 to 58% of organic matter is carbon, the way to draw atmospheric carbon into the ground is to fertilize the land.

At Atsas farm, we do not till the soil. We do not mix the organic matter into the soil but just leave it on the ground. Organic matter is brought into the ground by microorganisms, and trees take it upon themselves to find their own food. In other words, we raise olive trees by imitating nature as much as possible.

We also use the minimum amount of water. When it is hot you have to pay particular attention to the water. If you give the trees a lot of water, then the temperature of the trees will be lower than the outside temperature, and olive flies will overrun the trees.

Themed Dinner Lecture: "Going Beyond Sustainable." Photo: Suyeon Yun.

Consumer Citizenship: Maggi Noodles and the Social Life of Industrial Foods in India

Amita Baviskar (Institute of Economic Growth, Delhi)

Noodle Mania

Walking along Chhatra Marg, the main road through the Delhi University campus, one comes across pavement vendors not selling time-honored Indian snacks such as peanuts or chaat, but Maggi noodles. College canteens and restaurants that students frequent may still have samosas but their popularity has been eclipsed by Maggi. Elsewhere in India, a scenic lookout point on the road to the hill resort of Mussoorie—known for decades as Sunset Point—has now been renamed Maggi Point because now that's why one goes there, to look at the sunset while eating Maggi. Talking to college students in cities as far apart as Guwahati, Chidambaram, and Allahabad, I am struck by how many said that Maggi was their favourite food. Some said that they can't go a day without eating Maggi. Restaurants serve Maggi dosai, Maggi sandwiches, Maggi milkshakes, indicating the emergence of a vibrant fusion cuisine.

In a survey of mid-day meals served in government-run primary schools in Delhi, children said that they did not want to eat rajma-chaaval (beans and rice) and chhole-chaaval (chickpeas and rice) the nutritious foods that they were usually served. They wanted noodles.

Unbranded noodles are popular across social classes in urban and rural India—rickshaw pullers in a busy retail market in Delhi crowd around a chow mein cart, twirling strands of noodles slippery with oil and soya sauce onto forks; workers at construction sites in Bihar and Odisha do the same. In urban bastis (squatter settlements) and in small rural towns, five-rupee packets of Maggi make it possible to occasionally—and for some, regularly—indulge in this treat, one that is advertised on television by no less a national icon than the mega-filmstar Amitabh Bachchan.

What is going on? How has a food, virtually unknown to the vast majority of Indians a generation ago, become so popular across the country? How has a particular brand of this food—Maggi is manufactured by Nestlé—managed to capture millions of Indians' imagination in terms of what they like to eat, what they eat, who they are, and who they want to be? How has Maggi become, as Mumbai-based advertising expert Kiran Khalap said, the "third staple" of Indian food after wheat and rice? What does the success of Maggi—a brand name synonymous with noodles in India—tell us about the changing contours of social inequality and aspirations in India?

I analyse the phenomenal popularity of instant noodles through the concept of "consumer citizenship" or how "the social life of things," of objects of consumption opens up unintended and unexpected political possibilities.

From the Producer Patriot to the Consumer Citizen

I examine citizenship, not as a purely political concept of relationships based on rights between the state and citizens, but as a social and economic concept focused on belonging within a nation, as expressed through practices, simultaneously material and symbolic.

Satish Deshpande has analysed how the idea of the nation and its citizens has been imagined as a state-led economy after Independence through the Soviet-inspired Five-Year Plans, with investment in capital-intensive infrastructure—dams, steel plants, nuclear reactors, and dedicated industrial towns where the citizen was meant to be a "producer-patriot." This analysis has mainly focused on production, not on the circulation and consumption of commodities. However, consumption, especially of industrially manufactured consumer goods, has emerged as an equally important mode of constituting citizenship, especially after the 1990s when policies of economic liberalization were instituted. From a public discourse of austerity and deferred consumption, we now have a celebration of consumerist gratification. As William Mazzarella observes, for globalizing societies, consumer practices and discourses have become an increasingly important axis of belonging for negotiating citizenship.

Maggi Noodles

How is social membership re-articulated though consumer citizenship, more specifically, through eating Maggi noodles? The first notable aspect of Maggi consumers in India is that they are young. They are children, adolescents, and young adults. Capturing this demographic slice of India is crucial for the manufacturers of consumer goods. As market analyst Rama Bijapurkar points out, "About 7 out of 10 households [in India] have a liberalization child who acts as a change agent in that household. [Children] are not just a very attractive niche market opportunity but are also critical to the mainstream."

The second striking feature of instant noodles consumers is that they are not confined to big cities. People who live in small towns and large villages eat noodles now. Rural India continues to

suffer from serious deprivation in terms of certain basic amenities: 45 per cent of Indian villages have no electricity, 70 per cent of rural households have no toilets. But they are growing consumers of manufactured goods, not only durables like mobile phones and motorbikes, but also processed and packaged foods. The share of these foods in the rural household's food basket is rising. Government data show that, although food still makes up 50 to 65 per cent of the total monthly expenditure of households in rural India, the category now includes larger outlays on tea, glucose biscuits, corn chips, bottled beverages, and noodles.

This spread into rural areas has not only been enabled by companies investing in their distribution networks, but by innovations in packaging technology. This link between changing technologies of organization and materials is a significant factor in the spread of industrial foods. For big brand producers of FMCG (fast-moving consumer goods such as snacks and cosmetics) like Nestlé, Unilever, ITC and Pepsi, the development of metallized polymer films allowed packaging to be eye-catching and airtight, enabling brands to deliver the guarantee of quality that they claim. Metallized polymer films also made it possible to sell small units of processed foods at low prices to large numbers of low-income customers, tapping what marketing guru C. K. Prahalad calls the "fortune at the bottom of the pyramid." These shiny packets of corn chips, instant coffee, chewing tobacco and other products are now ubiquitous in urban and rural markets.

In the case of Maggi noodles, the big breakthrough occurred in 2002 when, in response to emerging competition from brands like Nissin's Top Ramen, Nestlé decided to sell its instant noodles in 5-rupee packets of 50 grams and to aggressively expand their availability in small towns. Maggi now has a 75 per cent share of a 250 billion rupee (or 3.8 billion USD) market, growing at 20 per cent annually.

The consumers for this new food commodity thus include not only the so-called "new middle classes," but also working class people in rural and urban India who can now, in a small way, enjoy some of the same pleasures as the classes above them. In a nation still defined by sharp economic and social inequality, this convergence of consumption styles is celebrated in the media through numerous television advertisements that resonate with the aspirations of subaltern classes for upward mobility. These ads also signify that citizenship is about shared national belonging as constituted through the consumption of mass manufactured and marketed packaged goods. One Maggi ad, for instance, shows a fisherman in the sea off the coast in western India and young Tibetan monks in the northern Himalayas enjoying this national dish.

As the data show, processed and packaged foods are proliferating across the class and urban-rural divide among social groups for whom consuming products such as instant noodles and soups would have been previously unthinkable. The association of these foods with modernity is signalled not only by the snazzy packaging, but also by advertising campaigns that stress convenience and hygiene while also appealing to the premium placed on instant gratification in the present. But their appeal lies not only in their association with modernity.

The slogan "bas do minute!" (just two minutes!) is indeed about instant gratification but it is also about empowering a mother to immediately satisfy her child's hunger, an enduring cultural value across India and perhaps the world. Another ad shows a girl making Maggi, while her mother watches, bristling with disapproval. But the mother's worry is soon replaced by a gratified smile when she sees that her daughter has cooked Maggi exactly the way she does! So Maggi is now a way of transmitting family tradition, a bond between mother and daughter.

For Indian students abroad, the mouth-feel of Maggi noodles—that soft, curly form that you suck in and the unique flavour of the Masala "Tastemaker" that converts white flour, oil, sugar and assorted chemical additives into a veritable sensorium—is the stuff of nostalgia and longing, a cultural memory from which they are exiled unless they bring back packets of the stuff in their suitcases. Since 2008, 25 years after Maggi launched in India, the ad campaign about "Me and Mera Maggi." with its stories from Maggi eaters about how they personalize the dish, consolidates the sensual-sentimental association between the commodity and its consumers.

With its social emphasis on food, the bonding of families and friends, Nestlé has taken an unfamiliar food and domesticated it so thoroughly that producers and consumers have begun "blurring the boundaries between the global and the local, the new and the original," so that it is associated with trust, comfort and intimacy. If Maggi is a comfort food for millions of well-to-do young Indians, for even more millions it is a desired taste, a lifestyle aspiration, and even a measure of "distinction." Comfort and aspiration, need and want, belonging and striving are the cornerstones of consumer citizenship. However,

I want to emphasize that the locus of this noodle-shaped citizenship is national—a cosmopolitan national, but national nevertheless. Unlike Coke, McDonald's and KFC, the community that Maggi constructs doesn't have a global reference, it isn't held together by the cultural allure of America. Maggi's glamour is anchored in Indian icons and values. At the same time, the claim to represent national identity is a contested one. Maggi was challenged in 2015 by allegations of pesticide contamination in the Tastemaker flavouring packet, after which the yoga guru Baba Ramdev, who now runs a fast-growing packaged food, cosmetic, and medicine empire under the Patanjali brand, launched his own "natural noodles." So Nestlé's cosmopolitan Indian product is confronted by a business rival's claim to a more authentically Indian identity, on the rather ironic battleground of instant noodles.

Conclusion

One could argue that eating the same product across different social contexts creates a semblance of equality—a shared moment when you are as good as anyone else. In the context of sharp inequalities, this feeling may offer a moment of consolation. "We are all the same; we eat the same food" is not a sentiment that has had much success in Indian social life. The emergence of differentiation is already evident with Maggi: there is the more expensive whole-wheat "Atta Maggi with vegetables," marketed with the slogan "Tasty bhi aur healthy bhi" for consumers conscious of the low nutritive value of the product. The idea of "mera Maggi" is not just about difference as unity in diversity, but also about distinction and cultural dominance. Embedded as they firmly are in a multinational food industry, implicated in the explosive growth of obesity, diabetes, and heart disease among children and adolescents, the larger political economy of these products is deeply compromised.

One transformation of cultural politics with which we can certainly credit commodities like instant noodles is the decisive shift in the demographics of power, the creation and affirmation of a youth identity within the household and outside. Jitender Chhatar, the khap panchayat (traditional village council) leader from Haryana in north India, blamed noodles for causing hormonal imbalance in young men so that they become sexually violent. Everyone laughed at him, showing how thoroughly noodles have been incorporated into local diets. Old men may express a fear of foreign foods and frustration at rebellious youth who no longer listen to their elders, but for the younger generation, noodles are here to stay.

As the career of instant noodles demonstrates, food is not only to do with nutrition and biological needs, but cultural desires. Even as Right to Food activists strive to include the diversity of Indian foodways to some extent—promoting millets to end the monopoly of wheat and rice—they confront the challenge of a generational shift in what is considered "good to eat," moving away from local, more nutritious diets to branded industrial foods of low nutritional value—junk foods. At the same time, for poor people stigmatized by caste and rurality, eating these foods signifies participation in a desired modern lifestyle, of being as good as anyone else, so these foods play an important, yet contradictory, part in claiming social belonging and equality, which is an intrinsic element of social well-being.

Bibliography

Appadurai, Arjun. 1986. "Introduction: Commodities and the Politics of Value" in A. Appadurai (ed.), *The Social Life of Things: Commodities in Cultural Perspective*. Cambridge: Cambridge University Press.

———. 1996. *Modernity at Large: Cultural Dimensions of Globalization*. Minneapolis: University of Minnesota Press.

Bardhan, Pranab. 1991. *The Political Economy of Development in India*. New Delhi: Oxford University Press.

Baviskar, Amita. 2012. "Food and Agriculture" in VasudhaDalmia and Rashmi Sadana (eds.), *Cambridge Companion to Contemporary Indian Culture*, 49–66. Cambridge: Cambridge University Press.

Bijapurkar, Rama. 2007. *We Are Like That Only: Understanding the Logic of Consumer India*. New Delhi: Portfolio/Penguin.

Bobrow-Strain, Aaron. 2012. *White Bread: The Social History of the Store-Bought Loaf*. Boston: Beacon Press.

Caldwell, Melissa L. 2005. "Domesticating the French Fry: McDonald's and Consumerism in Moscow" in James L. Watson and Melissa L. Caldwell (eds.), *The Cultural Politics of Food and Eating*, 180–196. Malden, MA: Blackwell.

Collingham, Lizzie. 2007. *Curry: A Tale of Cooks and Conquerors*. New York: Oxford University Press.

Cross, Jamie. 2014. *Dream Zones: Capitalism and Development in India*. London: Pluto Press.

Shopping for *Theme Dinners*: "Consumer Citizenship" (Multinational Dinner) and "Honey, Melon, and THAAD" (SPAM Commons). Photo: Suyeon Yun.

Deshpande, Satish. 2003. *Contemporary India: A Sociological View*. New Delhi: Viking.

Doran, Assa and Robin Jeffrey. 2013. *Cell Phone Nation*. Gurgaon: Hachette.

Drèze, Jean. 2007. "Food and Nutrition" in KaushikBasu (ed.), *The Oxford Companion to the Indian Economy*. New Delhi: Oxford University Press.

Fuller, Chris J. and VéroniqueBénéï. 2001. *The Everyday State and Society in Modern India*. London: Hurst.

Gell, Alfred. 1986. "Newcomers to the World of Goods: Consumption among the MuriaGonds" in A. Appadurai (ed.), *The Social Life of Things: Commodities in Cultural Perspective*. Cambridge: Cambridge University Press.

Gupta, Akhil. 2012. *Red Tape: Bureaucracy, Structural Violence, and Poverty in India*. Durham, NC: Duke University Press.

Haynes, Douglas E., Abigail McGowan, Tirthankar Roy and Haruka Yanagisawa. 2010. *Towards a History of Consumption in South Asia*. New Delhi: Oxford University Press.

Jayal, NirajaGopal. 2013. *Citizenship and its Discontents: An Indian History*. New Delhi: Permanent Black.

Levien, Michael. 2013. "Regimes of Dispossession: From Steel Towns to Special Economic Zones" in Development and Change, 44(2): 381–407.

Lozada, Eriberto P. 2005. "Globalized Childhood?Kentucky Fried Chicken in Beijing" in James L. Watson and Melissa L. Caldwell (eds), *The Cultural Politics of Food and Eating*, 163–179. Malden, MA: Blackwell.

Ludden, David. 1992. "India's Development Regime" in N. Dirks (ed.), *Colonialism and Culture*, 247–283. Ann Arbor: University of Michigan Press.

Lukose, Ritty A. 2009. *Liberalization's Children: Gender, Youth, and Consumer Citizenship in India*. Durham, NC: Duke University Press.

Mander, Harsh. 2013. *Ash in the Belly: India's Unfinished Battle Against Hunger*. New Delhi: Penguin Books India.

Mazzarella, William. 2003. *Shoveling Smoke: Advertising and Globalization in Contemporary India*. Durham, NC: Duke University Press.

Mintz, Sidney W. 1985. *Sweetness and Power: The Place of Sugar in Modern History*. New York: Penguin Books.

Padel, Felix and Samarendra Das. 2010. *Out of This Earth: East India Adivasis and the Aluminium Cartel*. New Delhi: Orient Blackswan.

Patel, Raj. 2007. *Stuffed and Starved: What Lies Behind the World Food Crisis*. London: Portobello Books.

Prahalad, C. K. 2006. *The Fortune at the Bottom of the Pyramid: Eradicating Poverty through Profits*. London: Dorling Kindersley.

Rudolph, Lloyd and Susanne Hoeber Rudolph. 1987. *In Pursuit of Lakshmi: The Political Economy of the Indian State*. Chicago: University of Chicago Press.

Sanyal, Kalyan K. 2007. *Rethinking Capitalist Development: Primitive Accumulation, Governmentality and Post-Colonial Capitalism*. New Delhi: Routledge.

Snyder, Michael. 2015. "How Maggi Noodles Became India's Favourite Comfort Food" in *Scroll*, 29 January. http://scroll.in/article/701437/ How-Maggi-noodles-became-India%27s-favourite-comfort-food. Accessed on 29 January 2015.

Used Kitchen Supply Stores Thrive in Seoul
Large outlets selling used restaurant and café supplies have flourished in recent years in the suburbs of Seoul. A large number of their branches can be found in the Wangsimni and Euljiro areas of Seoul. This is a reflection of how many cafés, restaurants, and fried chicken shops are both starting up and closing down in Korea. It shows how many small, self-employed entrepreneurs, often referred to as the veins of the urban economy, are suffering from an unprecedented recession. The kitchen supplies, dishes, and cups used in the *Biennale Café* and the *Biennale Restaurant* were purchased or rented from several of these used kitchen supply stores.

A second-hand kitchen supply outlet. Anseong, Gyeonggi Province, Korea, 2017. Photo: Suyeon Yun.

미래식품 FUTURE MART

2017 Autumn

According to the Huffington Post, food prices for 12 items including fruits, rice, etc. in South Korea rank in the top 10% among 119 countries across the globe. Banana ranks in the world's top 3, apple/orange/tomato rank within the top 4, rice/potato rank in the top 5, onion/milk/cheese/beef rank in the top 6, and bread/cabbage in the top 11.

"It is known that the seeds of peppers, tomatoes, paprika, and spinach, which make up a large portion of the Korean vegetable market, remain Monsanto's right.
Korean farmers have to pay the patent fee for six newly patented items (reporter's note: strawberry, citrus, raspberry, blueberry, cherry and kelp)."

As the demand for avocados grows, forests are being destroyed in Mexico. CNN Money reported that Mexican farmers are destroying forests for avocado cultivation because of the popularity of avocados in the US. Maria Vargas, a researcher at the Mexican National Institute, said that, "the cultivation of avocados has a negative impact on the forest ecosyste m as a whole." In drought-stricken California, water from hydrants was stolen to water avocado fields.

The most widely sold banana variety today is the Cavendish banana. Bananas are originally seeded fruits, but the Cavendish banana is a genetic twin that is reproduced through planting rather than propagating through seeds. If there is no diversity of species, it may become extinct if exposed to fatal fungal disease.
The Fusarium oxysporum fungus, which wiped out the banana species called 'Gros Michel' in the 1950s, is threatening the Cavendish species as well.

Factory farming is one of the main causes of various diseases that result in the mass death of livestock. Due to the poor environment, animals are easily infected by diseases, which are then transmitted at a rapid rate leading to a high mortality rate. In factory cages, semen is artificially injected into the hen with a syringe to produce fertile eggs, while the cage lights are left on all night to increase the egg production rate. Forced molting is also utilized. If a chicken with low egg production is not fed for about a week or more, it loses most of its feathers. When you begin feeding the chicken again at that time, it begins to grow new feathers and the egg production rate increases to some degree.

The more the marbling, the better the meat?
Marbling is an artificially produced result by feeding cows a large amount of grains and restraining exercise. Therefore, the higher the marbling score, the worse the health of the cow. It is also not healthy for people because of the high level of neutral fats. For this reason, voices against the marbling score system is gradually increasing in Korea, especially among livestock specialists.

Pollack, a fish enjoyed by Koreans, has almost completely disappeared due to the rising temperature of the East Sea and overfishing of small/young pollack. In 2014, the Korean government set a 500,000 KRW reward for one live pollack and is now studying how to farm pollack. As a result, they secured 530,000 fertilized eggs from one mother pollack last year and succeeded in growing 39,000 pollack measuring up to 20cm. Currently, most people eat imported pollack from Russia.

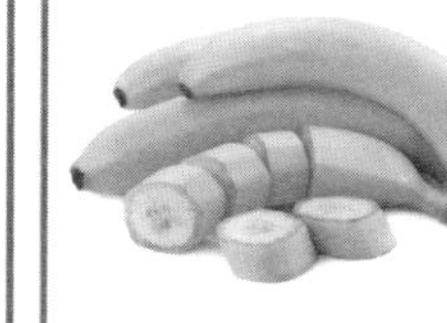

Last year, 40% of the salmon consumed in Korea was farmed salmon. As overfishing cuts down the number of wild salmon and demand continues to grow, South Korea is also starting to breed salmon. The color of salmon originally comes from krill shrimp, but the color of farmed salmon is chemically synthesized. Additionally, farmed salmon eat soybean meal and fishmeal made by grinding fish that people do not eat. Between imported Alaskan and Chilean salmon, Chilean salmon is bred with more pesticides, and they are fed byproducts of chicken and beef to gain weight.

Korea's soybean self-sufficiency rate is less than 10%, so the country depends on imported soybeans. However, since 83% of global soybean production is GMO soybeans, most of the imported soybeans are also GMO soybeans. "GMO soybeans imported into Korea are processed and sold as soybean oil," states Yoon Cheol-han, head of the Consumer Justice Center for Citizen's Coalition for Economic Justice. He also states "Most of the oil made from imported soybeans is a product made from GMO soybeans."

"Korea's wheat, soybean and corn self-sufficiency rate is estimated at only 1.6 percent.
According to the US Department of Agriculture's (USDA) recent estimates obtained by the Bank of Korea on August 25, Korea's self-sufficiency rate (including feed use) of wheat, soybean, and corn—among the 130 countries, whose production and demand estimates were researched—is 1.6 percent, the bottom 16th."

As you all know, soybeans occupy the largest proportion in setting the price of tofu.Tofu made from non-pesticide or organic certified domestic soybeans is twice as expensive as tofu made from ordinary domestic soybeans cultivated with pesticides or low-pesticides, based on weight per 100g.
Also, well-known brand tofu is more expensive than less-known cooperative brand tofu.

Controversial beer
There are some controversial beers that contain GM corn and corn syrup, high fructose corn syrup, fish bladder, propylene glycol, and MSG.
There are controversies surrounding the following beers: New Castle Brown regarding the use of caramel pigments made from ammonia; genetically modified corn used in Budweiser; GM corn syrup and propylene glycol in Corona Extra; GM corn syrup in Coors Light.

A leaflet distributed by the artist at the *Future Mart* contains information on heath issues of many of the ordinary consumer food products and on the impact these products have on the environment.

BIENNALE RESTAURANT

49 out of 1,239 poultry farms nationwide were found to contain pesticides that should not be used or should not be detected above acceptable levels. 31 farms among them were certified eco-friendly farms, making up 63% of the total.

Eggs have become a big issue in Europe too. This is not because of low egg production caused by avian influenza, as in Korea, but because of the insecticide, Fipronil, which kills insects such as ticks and cockroaches, found in eggs produced in Belgium and Holland.

In the US, a cow with mad cow disease has been found. In 2008, the South Korean government promised to "stop imports immediately if mad cow disease is found in the United States." A cow infected with mad cow disease has recently been found in Alabama, USA. However, the government is taking minimum measures saying that there are no slaughterhouses and processing factories in Alabama exporting beef to South Korea.

In order to extract the blood of pregnant mares, pharmaceutical companies put the mares through the repeated process of forced insemination and abortion until the mares pass out. They sell a particular hormone that is present in pregnant mares' blood to the livestock industry, which is then used on pigs and other livestock animals to induce pregnancy in the factory farming industry. Animal abuse begets more animal abuse.

Last November, South Korea ordered its biggest-ever cull of chickens and other poultry, amounting to 3,312,000 birds or 20% of the total number of domestic fowl, to fight an avian flu outbreak. This number is 1.7 times higher than that of poultry culled between 2014-2015.
This unprecedented level of destruction is caused by concentrated factory farming.

If the geologic layer of this era is examined in the future, it is likely to be recorded as the chicken age due to the massive amount of chicken bones. Following from the unprecedented high levels of chicken consumption worldwide, chickens have been improved to be a fast-growing species Compared with the year 1957, the size of a 56 day-old-chicken is about four times bigger now. Factory-produced chickens are usually grown in cages as small as A4 sized paper with their beaks mutilated.

Are pigs and cows raised with antibiotics environmentally friendly?
As people increasingly pay more attention to food safety, more people buy environmental-friendly agricultural products. However, the certification system turns out to be a mess. Pork and beef that were raised with antibiotics and agricultural products treated with pesticides received 'Environmentally-Friendly Agricultural Product' certification marks.

무항생제 (NON ANTIBIOTIC) 농림축산식품부   동물복지 (ANIMAL WELFARE) 농림축산식품부

This label indicates that the livestock feed does not contain antibiotics or antimicrobials, and that growth accelerators and growth hormones are not used. Products labeled 'Non-antibiotic livestock products' are produced according to these certification standards, using general feed without antibiotics, synthetic antimicrobials, and hormones.

무농약 (NON PESTICIDE) 농림축산식품부

Sows are artificially inseminated in stalls in a repeating cycle of pregnancy and birth. The stalls are made of metal cages that are 60cm wide and 210cm long. The pigs have to endure painful mutilations, having their tails and teeth cut off ("to relieve stress") and being castrated, with no pain relief. As the majority of these pigs are raised in over-crowded factory farms—where they are constantly fed antibiotics due to the high amount of disease from the concentrated method of production—prevention of infectious diseases seem a difficult task. When foot-and-mouth disease broke out in Korea in 2010-2011, it spread to 6,241 dairy farms across the country leading to the culling of 3.4 million cows and pigs.

The owner of the poultry farm, Kim, refuses animal welfare certification because the government's certification standards are insufficient. For example, if you raise 27 chickens in a 3.3m² room without cages, you will meet the criteria, but they will still not be able to move properly. On his farm he grows 8 or 9 chickens in the same sized space. Kim also refuses non-antibiotic agricultural product certification. Non-antibiotic certification can be obtained by feeding antibiotics-free feed. However, there is no restriction on the use of antibiotics for animal medicine. If antibiotics are given mixed with water they will not be detected after about 10 days. The non-antibiotic certification mark does not relieve the concerns of antibiotic misuse.

'Non Pesticide' labeled agricultural products do not use organosynthetic agricultural chemicals, and chemical fertilizers are used within 1/3 of the recommended amount.

More than 80% of the world's almond crop is grown in California, which has been experiencing its worst drought on record. As almond orchards comprise 10% of water consumption, the number of almond haters has been on the rise. Tom Philpott, who has detailed the environmental ravage of this crop in California, summed up the problem: almond farmers drilling thousands of feet down into aquifers to pump out water has resulted in subsidence of around 11inches a year, which "threatens vital infrastructure like bridges, roads, and irrigation canals" and could trigger earthquakes. Furthermore, insatiable demand for almonds is harming honeybees, already an embattled species. Bringing in 1.6 million honeybees to California every year, "into an area dripping with insecticides is a recipe for disaster" writes Philpott.

People need to be careful about almonds that have been fumigated with propylene oxide (PPO) gas, which is defined as a carcinogen. In 2007, after Salmonella was found in raw almonds, the sale of raw almonds was prohibited and the process of heat sterilization and sterilization with PPO was introduced in the US. PPO, however, is prohibited in Mexico, Canada and Europe. Organic almonds are mostly heat sterilized.

A genetically modified (GMO) apple that does not brown was developed in the United States in 2015. With the US Department of Agriculture approving the sale of genetically modified (GMO) apples for the first time, many controversies have arisen.

Gold (3.75g) = KRW 180,000
Paprika seeds (3.75g) = as much as KRW 450,000

A recent study reported that glyphosate residue was unexpectedly found in honey in the US. After investigating a grocery store in Philadelphia researchers found that over 62% of common honey on the market and 45% of organic honey had glyphosate above the accepted level. It also assessed that it would be difficult for honeybees carrying 250 pounds of honey a year to completely avoid toxic substances such as insecticides and pesticides.

Richard Robert, Chief Scientific Officer of New England Biolabs, is known to have organized the letter campaign of Nobel laureates vindicating GMO products. New England Biolabs is "a collective of scientists committed to developing innovative products for the life sciences industry, and a recognized world leader in the discovery, development and commercialization of recombinant and native enzymes for genomic research." Robert, however, argues that he has no financial interest in carrying out GMO research.
The second organizer behind this letter campaign, Phillip A. Sharp, works at MIT's Center for Cancer Research (now the Koch Institute). Sharp, who was awarded the 1993 Nobel Prize in Physiology, also runs a biotech business.

The major cause of pollution that leaks into the dead zone of the Gulf of Mexico is chemical fertilizers used in the United States. Phosphorus and Nitrogen reduce the amount of oxygen in the ocean, generating green tides and destroying marine ecosystems.

Certified organic strawberries may not be organic at all. Some organic strawberries are fumigated with toxic chemicals, including methyl bromide, at the beginning stages of their life cycle. Methyl bromide is used to sterilize the soil before strawberries are planted. It's not sprayed on the fruit. It's a soil fumigant that kills just about everything it touches. Many hybridized seed varieties have been created that can only grow in sterile soil.

"107 Nobel laureates sign letter blasting Greenpeace over GMOs"
The Washington Post reported that more than 100 Nobel laureates have signed a letter urging Greenpeace to end its opposition to genetically modified organisms (GMOs). These scientists say GMO crops and foods are as safe as those derived from any other method of production. They also highlight that there has never been a single confirmed case of a negative health outcome for humans or animals from their consumption.

U.S. First Lady Melania Trump banned Monsanto products from the White House after learning of the health effects associated with consuming genetically modified (GM) corn.

Cheongyang chili pepper is a crop developed in Korea, but every time you buy it, you have to pay royalties to a foreign company. This is because JoongAng Seed that originally had ownership of this crop was acquired by Monsanto.
At the time of the IMF crisis, four of the five largest seed companies in Korea were taken over by multinational corporations.

50% of native vegetable seeds such as daikon and cabbage have been transferred to foreign companies. Onion, carrot and tomato seeds have exceeded over 80%. From 2006 to 2015, the royalties paid by the ROK for overseas seeds amounted to 145.68 billion KRW

It has been confirmed that the Korean Rural Development Administration and LG Chemical's 'FarmHannong' is developing genetically modified rice that has resistance to certain herbicides.

The Korean Rural Development Administration is experimentally growing 142 species of 14 GMO crops including soybeans, potatoes, tomatoes, and rice across 7 regions in Korea. This news has been especially shocking because of the inclusion of rice, which is a staple food item in Korea. The first genetically modified rice in Korea is called 'Iksan 526,' known to have an anti-obesity effect. Patent applications are completed and it is now in the process of safety testing after going through animal testing.

MONSANTO

Monsanto Brands to Avoid

The following brands have the potential to be genetically modified and associated with the use of Monsanto materials.

Aunt Jemima, Aurora Foods, Banquet, Best Foods, Betty Crocker, Bisquick, Cadbury, Campbell's, Capri Sun, Carnation, Chef Boyardee, Coca Cola, ConAgra, Delicious Brand Cookies, Duncan Hines, Famous Amos, Frito Lay, General Mills, Green Giant, Healthy Choice, Heinz, Hellman's, Hershey's Nestle, Holsum, Hormel, Hungry Jack, Hunts, Interstate Bakeries, Jiffy, KC Masterpiece, Keebler/Flowers Industries, Kelloggs, Kid Cuisine, Knorr, Kool-Aid, Kraft/Phillip Morris, Lean Cuisine, Lipton, Loma Linda, Marie Callenders, Minute Maid, Morningstar, Butterworths, Nabisco, Nature Valley, Ocean Spray, Ore-Ida, Orville Redenbacher, Pasta- Roni, Pepperidge Farms, Pepsi, Pillsbury, Pop Secret, Post Cereals, Power Bar Brand, Prego Pasta Sauce, Pringles, Procter and Gamble, Quaker, Ragu Sauce, Rice-A-Roni, Smart Ones, Stouffers, Shweppes, Tombstone Pizza, Totinos, Uncle Ben's, Unilever, V8

BAYER

Bayer, a German chemical and pharmaceutical company, has reportedly pledged to invest US $8 billion (9.36 trillion won) in agricultural research and development (R & D) in the U.S. over the next six years to US President Donald Trump.

Source
Mainstream Media
Independent Media
Online Communities and Blogs
Books
ETC.

New York City (Steady) State: Home Grown
Michael Sorkin (Terreform)

New York City (Steady) State is a thought and design experiment that seeks to test the outer limits of urban self-sufficiency. Terreform—a non-profit urban research and advocacy center in New York City—has long been investigating how close our city can come to a completely internalized metabolic system, establishing its independence in a variety of key "respiratory" functions, including food, waste, air, water, climate, mobility, construction, manufacture, and energy. The goal is to reduce New York's ecological footprint to as closely co-terminus with its political boundaries as possible and to examine the morphologies, technologies, and behaviors that will enable this.

Our motive is compound. Recognizing that the planetary environment is in deep peril and that the competence and will of nation states—or multinational corporations—to take decisive constructive action cannot be relied upon, we believe that cities are urgently logical increments of organization, accountancy, resistance, and democracy and research is predicated on the belief that systems should be as locally distributed as possible. This is not to fly in the face of logical economies of scale but to seek the greatest systemic resiliency and to devolve responsibility on people and communities with a visibly direct relationship to the forces and issues at play.

We recognize that the first approach to questions of the environment must always be on the side of demand. Our project always looks first at questions of social organization, habit, and behavior. We know, for example, if New Yorkers were to adopt a largely vegetarian diet the city "foodprint" would shrink radically. We also know that approximately one-third of our food is wasted, mainly in the consumption stage, and that more sustainable behavior in our kitchens could have a transformative impact. Likewise, we know that if the city's neighborhoods are conceived as complete—with all the necessities of daily life including work, commerce, culture, education, recreation, etc. within easy walking compass of home—transportation requirements would be greatly reduced. And, we anticipate important social knock-on effects. If everyone in a neighborhood were able to walk to work then all the neighborhood's workers—from the banker to the barista—would find themselves living together as a community, helping redress our city's radical—and growing—spatial inequality.

Home Grown—the first part of the project to be completed—examines New York's food system.

It demonstrates the marginal possibility of producing 2.500 nutritious calories of food for our 8.5 million people within the city. Our initial analysis shows that the New York foodprint is approximately 150 times the area of the city and Home Grown proceeds via a sequence of iterations to look at the means by which this territory can be shrunk. Simply eliminating waste would get us down to 104 NYC equivalents. Vegetarianism would have an even more radical impact, reducing our food-print to a "mere" 16 New Yorks! And, by transforming the mode of production to the most efficient methods—a change from our industrial systems of mono-cropping to more bio-intensive techniques, including greenhouse hydroponic and aeroponic systems—yields can be multiplied by as much as 30 times! This combination of strategies gets us down to the area of a "mere" four additional New Yorks. Where might these be found in our densely built and crowded city?

Our initial design looks first at the most readily available sites, including vacant land, parking lots, community gardens, parks, rooftops, private yards, basements, streets, utility corridors, and a variety of derelict or underused infrastructure—such as rail yards and highways that might be overbuilt. By appropriating a reasonable proportion of this resource (half of the streets, a third of rail infrastructure, all the vacant lots) we are able to reduce the supplementary requirement for 100% production to 700,000 acres. Which brings us to that beloved magic bullet: vertical farms. Research suggests that a thirty story farm the size of a typical Manhattan block might feed approximately 50,000 people and that around 250 such giant structures (or 5,000 more neighborhood-scale versions) would do the job! But such towers are insanely inefficient, requiring enormous investment, huge embodied and recurrent energy inputs (we've estimated ten nuclear plants would be needed to power the system!), and place a demand on local water resources that would oblige the construction of 28 desalination plants with their own massive energy requirements and other deleterious environmental impacts! Not!

Our study does show two scenarios that demonstrate how such a 100% system might be installed but doesn't persuasively argue the ultimate benefit, short of siege conditions. Which leads us to the more important elements of the work: looking for and designing "sweet spots" to materially upgrade self-reliance, community participation, and nutrition and we've offered a complex scenario for producing around 30% of our food within our borders with the remainder provided either within a 100-mile hinterland or from a state-wide system focused on the old Erie Canal as a low-energy transport armature.

The core aim of the study is to compile an encyclopedia of possibilities for radically enlarging local autonomy that can be applied at every conceivable scale, from the kitchen to the apartment to the building to the block to the neighborhood to the borough to the city to the region. Each of these can have widespread application not simply in New York but in cities around the world striving to take responsibility both for the welfare of their citizens and for their planetary impacts. Looking at medium density urban blocks, for example, we investigate the very large amount of space devoted to individual kitchens (at a time when New Yorkers consume the majority of their meals away from home and when traditional nuclear families are an increasingly shrinking minority of our population) and propose various strategies for aggregating and using this space for food cultivation, preparation, and consumption. Blocks that opt into the highest intensity version of such cooperation could raise 100% of their vegetables at home.

Terreform hopes that this work—and the volumes to come—can be of value to cities around the world striving to take real responsibility for their planetary impacts and to deepen their collective polity.

Land Area Available

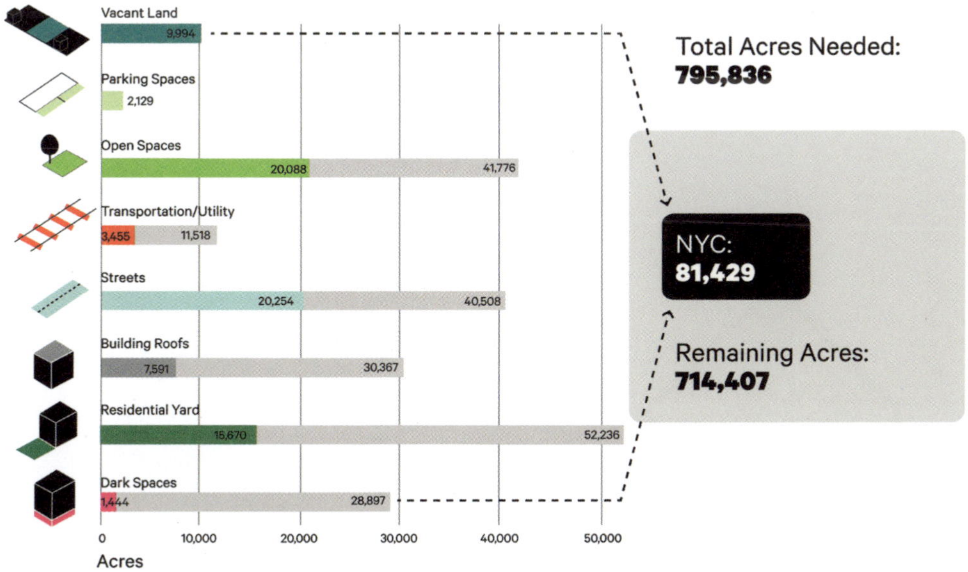

Available land area for farming in Manhattan.

Wheat cups and bamboo straws used at the Café.

Plastic Free Café

Last year, France passed a law banning all plastic plates, cups, and utensils by 2020, while the National Green Tribunal in India has introduced a ban on disposable plastic bags, cups, and other forms of single-use plastic items for its capital Delhi. African countries such as Kenya, Uganda, Cameroon, Ethiopia, and Tanzania have banned the use of plastic bags. In particular, Rwanda has set an example for the global plastic reduction campaign by confiscating all plastic bags at the airport, as well as enforcing laws related to the ban on plastic bags for over 10 years.

While there are no statistics that measure the environmental burden of using disposable waste by the 7.1 billion global population, just the number of disposable cups used by 25,086 Starbucks stores around the world is said to be about 40 billion a year. If the average weight of one cup is 10 grams, this amounts to 400,000 tons, and the yearly amount of disposable cup waste for one store adds up to 16 tons on average. There are more than 850 Starbucks stores in Korea, and Seoul has more cafés than any other city in the world.

In the hope of Seoul also joining in the international effort to reduce the burden of disposable products on the planet, this café does not use disposable cups and straws.

Discounts are given on drinks for customers who come with their own cup or tumbler.

On take-out orders, deposits are charged on the wheat cups. Deposits are returned upon return of the cups.

Refraining from the use of straw is recommended. For those who need one, we provide bamboo straws.

Café Menu

Wild Soybean Milk

The soybean, a crucial ingredient for Northeast Asian food items such as tofu, soymilk, and fermented soybean paste, is at the center of controversy over genetically modified foods. About 78 percent of the soybeans produced in the world are known as GMOs. South Korea, which has only 6.4 percent soybean self-sufficiency as of 2012, imports more than 9 million tons of soybeans a year. And about two million tons of this amount are used as food. Wild soybeans grow in all parts of the Korean peninsula, but because they are small, their yields are low compared to the effort that goes into picking them. However, according to Gyuhwa Chung, Professor of Agrobiology at Chonnam National University, who has studied wild beans for the past thirty years, wild beans are a big crop in terms of their significance as a genetic resource. This is because the soybean we eat is bred from wild beans. The wild soybeans and recipes used at this café will be provided by Professsor Chung.

Urban Mint Tea

As people's interest in urban agriculture and its support by local governments have grown over the past five to six years, the area of urban farms has increased sixfold. The mint tea served at this café uses fresh mint grown in the front yards of the *Biennale Café* and the *Biennale Restaurant*.

Mint tea has a deeper taste when taken with honey; a spoonful of honey harvested by urban beekeepers in Seoul will be provided for those who want it. As bee colony collapse has been ongoing around the world since 2006, accelerating the global food crisis, many countries have banned the use of pesticides and insecticides, mandated the greening of rooftops, and encouraged urban beekeeping in an effort to increase the bee population. This menu item was designed to expand interest in both urban farming and the plight of bees.

Bedouin Tea

The Bedouins, who have long carried on a nomadic existence in the deserts of the Middle East and North Africa, boil a strong concentration of tea leaves with sugar and herbs in a kettle and drink it in a glass the size of a shot glass. Optimized for water-deficient regions, this tea is said to help alleviate headaches associated with lengthy exposure to sunlight.

Solar Bread

Seoul produces an estimated 1.16 million tons of food waste a year. This apple bread was developed to participate in the city's efforts to tackle the twin goals of reducing food waste and energy conservation at the same time. Using the fiber left over after the apples are cored and juiced, the fibrous material is combined with flour and kneaded into bread and baked in a solar oven. This item will not be available on rainy days.

The apple bread is served with hydroponic strawberry jam. Hydroponic cultivation techniques have been widely used in Korea since their introduction from the Netherlands in the 1960s. Many farmers in Gyeonggi province, which is located closest to Seoul's fruit and vegetable wholesalers, use hydroponics to cultivate a variety of agricultural products. Among them, strawberries are a particularly popular hydroponic crop. This is because the soft flesh of the fruit makes it particularly vulnerable to harmful pesticide residues (which soak into the flesh), and pesticides are not necessary for this method since pest damage is considerably reduced in hydroponic cultivation.

DMZ Apple Juice

Korea's warming rate is more than double the global average. It has risen by 1.2 degrees in the past thirty years and is expected to rise further. As the Korean peninsula is shifting from a temperate to subtropical climate due to global warming, apples are at the forefront of agricultural crop cultivation that is moving northward. As such, apples are currently being grown in the vicinity near the civilian restricted area of Cheolwon, located at the northern end of South Korea. This item will be available from the middle of September when apple harvest begins, and made with "ugly apples," which do not sell well in order to contribute to reducing food waste.

Muggol Pear Juice

We make juice from Muggol pears, which are native to Seoul. Muggol pear fields made up a large area of the northeastern part of Seoul (from Mug-dong to Sinnae-dong, Junghwa-dong, and Sangbong-dong) until the mid 1980s when the area was swept up in the development craze ahead of the 1988 Seoul Olympics. The reason why Muggol pears are exceptionally juicy and sweet, compared to other varieties, is believed to be due to the soil composition of this area, which is mixed with lots of sand. Most of the land used to cultivate this breed of pears, which still carries the name Muggol (Mug-dong), has gradually been reduced and its production mostly moved to the cities of Guri and Namyangju in Geonggi province. Nonetheless, more than 300 tons of Muggol pears are still produced in Seoul every year.

Banana Almond Shake
Almond prices have recently surged. This is due to the drought in California that has been ongoing for several years. Almonds are a water-intensive crop and California produces about 80% of the world's almonds. In addition, as the reduction of the bee population has made the natural pollination of the almond flower impossible, farmers have also been hit with the additional cost of hiring migratory beekeepers to install beehives throughout almond plantations. For these reasons, the neologism, "almond hater," was recently coined in California.

There is a new Panama disease that attacks bananas of the Cavendish variety, which accounts for 95% of bananas consumed worldwide. Caused by the fungicide-resistant mold called TAR4, Panama disease causes the leaves to dry out, leading the plant to die of dehydration. This disease killed 70% of the bananas planted in Taiwan in the 1990s, and spread to the Middle East, Africa, and Australia. The Cavendish banana crisis is an example of how large-scale monoculture farming can aggravate rather than solve the food shortage. An international consortium called Banana Save has been organized in order to try to secure bananas as a food source for future generations.

Teardrops of Aphrodite Tea
Produced in the mountainous regions of the Mediterranean island nation of Cypress, which has been facing a chronic water shortage crisis, this organic herbal tea is said to be effective in healing wounds. Sprouting from the rust that fell from Achilles' sword, the herb is said to have been used by Achilles to treat wounded soldiers during the Trojan War. Referred to as "herba militaris" or "Achillaia" in ancient Greece, the current name for this herb originates from the tears shed by Aphrodite upon seeing Achilles dying from a poisoned arrow.

This herb is called topul, or saw weed, in Korean and grows in plains and mountains in central and northern regions. It is known as the "carpenter's herb" because of its ability to heal wounds from knives, sickles, and planes. It is also known to facilitate blood circulation and to have anti-allergic properties.

The Fornelia Portable Solar Oven invented by Savvas Hadjixenophontos. Photo: provided by the artist.

Environmental activist Chang Jien gives a talk at the *Biennale Café*. Photo: Suyeon Yun.

String Bean Tea

Native to Korea, the yard-long bean is a vine plant with thin string-shaped husks, which are mainly eaten as vegetables rather than the beans inside. According to the Compendium of Medical Herbs, a study on medicinal herbs compiled in 1596 Ming Dynasty China, these beans protect the kidneys, strengthen the stomach, promote blood circulation, and help with diabetes and osteoporosis. This tea is made from the string bean extract that Dongyoung Cho, a farmer, has been saving the heirloom bean in South Cholla province since the mid 1990s.

Chameleon Plant Tea

The Chameleon plant is indigenous to Korea, China, and Japan. It thrives in moist, shaded areas of mountains and its hardy nature naturally repels pests. Thus, it is unnecessary to use pesticides when cultivating it. As reflected in its Chinese/Korean name, the leaves of the plant are said to have a fishy smell. However, when brewed using the plant's extract, it has a deep flavor without any hint of a fishlike odor. Because the leaves resemble buckwheat leaves, it is also referred to as "medicinal buckwheat."

Coffee

There are about 17,000 coffee shops in Seoul (as of March, 2016), and on average one adult consumes about 340 cups of coffee a year (based on statistics for 2014, Korea Customs and Trace Development Institute). However, we are largely unaware of the immense costs associated with our coffee consumption habits. About 140 liters of water is needed to grow the amount of coffee beans for one cup of coffee and the pesticides used in coffee farming pollute the soil. In addition, the direct sunlight cultivation method introduced in the 1970s is destroying the rainforests and taking over the habitat of its flora and fauna. In order to minimize the damage to coffee growing nations, what we can do is to consume fairly traded coffee that is cultivated in the environmentally friendly farming method of shade cultivation. Currently, eco-friendly, fair trade certification systems like Bird-Friendly Coffee Certification and Rainforest Alliance Coffee Certification are being implemented internationally. Although these systems have not yet been established in Korea, a small number of social enterprises sell organic, shade cultivated, fair traded coffee. This café uses these imported coffee beans.

Drinking Water Chronology in Korea

1972   Diamond Pure Water Co. Ltd. founded for supply to U.S. military bases only. Sales prohibited to Korean citizens.

1988   Sale of bottled water is allowed temporarily for consumption by foreign visitors on the occasion of the 1988 Seoul Olympics but prohibited after the Olympics.

1991   16 March. The upstream of the Nakdong River is contaminated by phenol discharge from Doosan Electronics.

6 April. Incheon Water Works sets up Water Analysis Laboratory.

1992   The Water Analysis Laboratory of Incheon designated as a drinking water testing agency.

1993   ChungHo Nais, a water purifier manufacturing and distribution company, is established and becomes the leader in the industry.

1994   In response to the petition filed by water bottling companies and sellers, the Constitutional Court rules that the prohibition of selling bottled water in Korea violates people's "right to drink clean water (the right to pursue happiness)."

1995   "Drinking Water Management Act" is enacted, and sale of bottled water is allowed.

Woongjin Coway, a water treatment equipment and services company, reports monthly sales of ten billion won.

2000   July. Diamond Mountain Spring Water (Geumgangsan Saemmul) is imported from North Korea.

2006   "Drinking Water Management Act" is amended. The amended law prohibits the use of the terms saengsu (live water), yaksu (medicinal water), and ionsu (ionized water) and designates meongneun saemmul (drinking spring water) as the term to be used for commercially bottled water. Advertising "live waters" (the term used by the general population to refer to bottled water despite the law) on network television is prohibited as it may cause other types of water to be perceived as "dead water." Advertisement of bottled water on network television is prohibited.

2007   Seoul Metropolitan Government launched Arisu project aimed at providing high-quality tap water to its citizens (500 billion won invested).

2009   Busan Metropolitan City Office of Water Supply commissions Doosan Heavy Industries to build the "world's largest" seawater desalination plant in Gijang-gun, located eleven kilometers from the Gori nuclear plant.

Diamond Pure Water is acquired by LG Household and Healthcare and is sold as a Coca-Cola brand.

2010   Import of premium-brand bottled water increases.

At its Yeongdeungpo water purification facility, Seoul Metropolitan Government builds a bottling plant with a daily capacity of producing 80,000 bottles of Arisu water.

2010–2012   Seoul Metropolitan Government spends 3.4 billion won on promotion of Arisu.

2011   Dusan Heavy Industries builds seawater desalination plant in Gijang-gun.

2012   Problems with commercial water purifying equipment are reported on numerous news outlets.

Regulatory Reform Committee, a committee working directly under the supervision of the Prime Minister, votes for the revision of the Enforcement Regulation of the Drinking Water Management Act to allow commercial advertisement of bottled water on network television stations.

2013   Woongjin Coway is acquired by MBK Partners.

Seoul Metropolitan Government considers exporting Arisu, bottled tap water.

Advertisement of bottled water allowed on Korea's three major network televisions.

Coca-Cola Korea sales reach over one trillion won.

2014   Seoul Metropolitan Government announces it will provide "highly purified tap water" to 100% of the Seoul area by 2015.

Leakage of phenol from Posco magnesium refining factory in Gangneung, Gangwon Province, is reported.

Carbonated drinks market grows by 40% annually on average.

2015   Doosan Heavy Industries completes Seawater Desalination Plant in Gijang.

Protests held against using desalinated water for tap water supply.

2016   Court orders Busan Metropolitan Government to "stop the supply of desalinated tap water" as 90% of Gijang-gun residents oppose the supply.

2017   News media have reported that Busan Metropolitan Government has distributed 400,000 bottles of the desalinated tap water bottled at the Gijang plant to the socially disadvantaged population in the city in two years.

Greek public water companies on the way to being privatized despite citizen's opposition and the Supreme Court. EU dmocracy?
23 September, 2016 @EU Water Movement

Water services enter the Superfund @IMFNews @ecb @EU_Commission EQUALLY RESPONSIBLE WITH GREEK GOV FOR THE VIOLATION OF THE CONSTITUTION.
23 September, 2016, @SAVEGREEKWATER

#EDAP #ETAH are privatised despite Supreme Court decision more than 50% is transferred to Superfund. @EU_Commission must disclose correspondence.
26 September, 2016 @SAVEGREEKWATER

3.3 million emails/24h sent to MPs to vote down the #EDAP #ETAH transfer to Superfund. @euwm
2 October, 2016 @SAVEGREEKWATER

Twitter tags: SNS tags opposing the Greek government move to privatize tap water.

The Zayandrud, or the River of Life, is the largest river of the Iranian Plateau in central Iran. It flows 400 kilometers and passes through Siosepol, or Bridge of 33 Arches, in the city of Isfahan. In recent years the water dried up completely before reaching Isfahan due to water extraction up river by farming irrigation. Photo by M.A. Lange, 2016

**I have not held back the water
when it should flow.
I have not diverted the running water
in a canal.
I have not polluted the water.
I have given bread to the hungry man,
and water to the thirsty man.**
Book of the Dead, Egypt, c. 1250 BC

EM/MENA Project Going Beyond Sustainable: Water. Soil. Land. Food.
Melina Nicolaides (Cyprus-based curator and activist)

EM/MENA refers to the broad geographical area that encompasses the Eastern Mediterranean, Middle East and North Africa, a region in which 14 of the world's 33 most water stressed countries are located. Despite sub-regional differences, this area is confronted with many similar but interconnected challenges, such as growing resource demand, soil degradation, desertification, and biodiversity loss, which endanger the future availability of water, food, and energy to communities across this region.

At the Seoul Biennale, the EM/MENA Project will contribute to the vision of the *Urban Foodshed* by bringing an introduction to the concerns of and solutions for this geographical region, as a counterpart to the issues raised regarding current Korean food systems and other future resource challenges. Examples from this region of the world can serve as evidence-based and adaptable models to establish that "beyond sustainable" change and remediation can occur in any location, and in any climate of the planet. To achieve this goal, the collective effort must focus on regenerating living systems—water, soil, and food production—as a basis to long-term transformation, resource management, and protection from the ongoing effects of climate change.

The EM/MENA Project originated from the intention of wanting to contribute to the effort of connecting the knowledge of institutions and researchers working towards finding regionally-applicable and resilient solutions for the future, through an exchange not only between countries, but with people engaged "on the ground." To achieve this, the EM/MENA Project is working with a series of experts from academia and science research centers, and with practicing agro-ecologists of the region. The long-term objective of this approach is to link current scientific studies to the real-world experiences of innovative individuals and small farming communities using creative nature-based solutions to deal with current challenges of food, energy, and water security for the projected climatic conditions of the region.

At the *Urban Foodshed*, the EM/MENA project will bring a solutions-oriented perspective with documentary material and live presentations. It will present practical knowledge and innovative examples from several countries of this region that discard conventional and industrial farming practices, and use agro-ecological principles which can empower people anywhere to restore their natural environments, to collect rainwater, to sequester carbon, increase soil organic matter, re-establish biodiversity, mitigate against flooding, and increase drought resistance. These methods not only create productive food systems that will ensure both future water and food security, but can also ultimately reverse the effects of climate change.

Invited guests at the Urban Foodshed acknowledge the need to combine scientific strategy + real world action in order to face the enormity of the challenges ahead, and the wisdom of bringing together diverse knowledge systems and worldviews in global climate policy and decision-making regarding solutions for water, food, and energy. At the Foodshed, they will personally exchange experiences, hands-on knowledge, and practices with their Korean counterparts—scientists and farmers—and with the general public of Seoul.

<u>The EM/MENA Project's Live Presentations</u>
Nicolas Netien of Atsas Organic Farm, environmental engineer, soil biologist, and authority on regenerative farming and dryland "integrated agro-ecology" systems, shares his knowledge on topics such as biomimicry, and how the agro-ecological system has a very crucial role to play in our future. These methods not only bring diversity to ecosystems, protect soil, water, and seeds, create food abundance for self-sufficiency, grow nutrient-dense food, but can also reverse the effects of climate change. Netien demonstrates how these methods can be applied and integrated into the dense urban environment and fabric of the city of Seoul. Additionally, Netien presents the science and biological strategies behind high phenolic olive oil, and reveals how, through his use of the farm's limited water resources, its soil quality, and geology, he has produced the world's most nutritious olive oil.

Savvas Hadjixenophontos, electronics engineer and inventor, shares his experiences with renewable energies, and the promise of the world's next energy systems that will help deal with the world's growing energy consumption. An ongoing project in the Foodshed, will be a demonstration of his innovative "Fornelia" Portable Solar Oven, which requires only the energy of the sun to cook meat, vegetables, even bread, through a process that is a much healthier cooking method than traditional ovens, wood burning or coal. The energy-efficient Fornelia, aims to contribute to the global energy transition to a future without carbon-based fossil fuels, whose over-use is

causing devastating deforestation, land and air-quality degradation, and increasingly adverse impacts on our climate across the globe.

Dr. Salah A. Soliman of the Bibliotheca Alexandrina addresses the ongoing environmental threats to the fertile farmlands of the Nile Delta, a low-lying zone on the northern coast of Egypt where climate change and the rising level of the Mediterranean have affected vegetation, threatened freshwater resources, agricultural activity, and coastal zone populations. He will explain how agricultural practices of local farmers have been changing since the early 20th century as a result of saltwater intrusion into the Delta area. Dr. Soliman will also address the current food crisis in Egypt, where food insecurity is epitomized in the rising prices for even the government-subsidized "balady" bread.

Dr. Manfred A. Lange of the Future Earth MENA Regional Center discusses the multiple impacts of climate change on water availability in the countries of this region, which are particularly sensitive to changes in the water balance, and to water scarcity as caused by altered climate conditions. He will also put into context the distinct challenges faced by the arid and semi-arid regions of the EM/MENA area, the interconnected nature of water, energy, and food (WEF Nexus), and how these pose a threat to the futures of people living in urban and rural areas of this region.

Other introductory regional examples will bring highlights from Greece, Cyprus, Egypt, Lebanon, Yemen, Saudi Arabia, Iran and other locations, and touch upon issues such as: permaculture-based soil-restoration ecosystem restoration; aquaponics and soil-less farming techniques; regional composting methods, seed saving and beekeeping practices; traditional climate-based water harvesting methods; reversal of desertification and growing food in desert conditions.

AIR BANG: SEOUL-BEIJING-KUBUQI

Air pollution in Seoul viewed from Namsan, Seoul. Spring 2017. Photo: Suyeon Yun.

Entrance to *Air Bang*. Donuimun Museum Village. Photo: Suyeon Yun.

Mangwon-dong Community-based Fine Dust Particles Sensor 107 Project
Hojun Song & 1px Gardening

At present, there are 39 fine dust particles measuring stations in Seoul, with 1 to 2 in operation in every district. If one of these stations stops operating or the sensor is not properly maintained, the lives of the residents in the said district will inevitably be affected. Even if the sensor works properly, people who live at the outer limits of the station are in an adverse position. For these reasons, many people have taken to directly purchasing fine dust particles sensors and sharing the measurements through Internet communities. However, the variability in the purchased sensors makes it difficult to compare measured values, and the way that the measurements are shared online by posting to bulletin boards makes it difficult to find the posted information. This community-based dust sensor project was initiated by the voluntary participation of local communities to propose a new model to measure and monitor fine dust particles as well as microclimate changes, such as temperature and humidity.

107
In order to measure the fine dust particles of an appropriate sized area of the community, the relatively small neighborhood of Mangwon (37.5556942 N, 126.891392 E) is divided into 107 zones based on the area of actual roads, excluding the Han river area, and a fine dust particles sensor is installed in the representative space of each zone. Considering the fact that there are only two official measuring stations in all of Mapo district (measuring 23.87 km2), of which the Mangwon neighborhood (measuring 1.81 km2) is a part, the 107 sensors installed in the Mangwon neighborhood can measure fine dust particles up to 700 times more precisely than the current existing standard. Of course the sensors are less expensive sensors than those used by the city monitoring stations. However, it is possible to obtain a meaningful value by averaging the measurements from several locations. Moreover, since the fine dust particles concentration can be measured at a radius of 100 meters, we are better able to infer the causes of fine dust particles that cannot be obtained from the macroscopic measurements.

Playful Environmental Monitoring
In order to encourage the representative spaces in each zone to buy and operate sensors, a brief introduction and location of these spaces are promoted on the project website, and the sensors to be installed outside these spaces are produced as cute fine dust character designs. We also have plans to develop various goods and contents related to the fine dust character design so that the representative spaces and area residents can experience environmental monitoring as a kind of play rather than a struggle.

Fine Dust Particles Sensor App
These private fine dust particles sensors will connect to the Internet via Wi-Fi and relay data collected in the cloud to residents in real-time through a website (https://msmg.today), and Android and iPhone applications. The fine dust data and total average values of each of the 107 sites are updated every minute, and push notification service through the application will also be provided in order to design a system where residents can grasp at a glance the concentration of fine dust at all times.

Fine Dust Big Data
If we continuously collect the values of fine dust data that is measured every minute from each of the 107 sensor stations in Mangwon every day for one year, 526,600 points of dust data can be obtained from each sensor station. If we analyze the correlation between this data with the more macroscopic climate data from the area provided by public institutions over the same period using deep-learning algorithms, we hope to be able to grasp new and unexpected causes of fine dust.

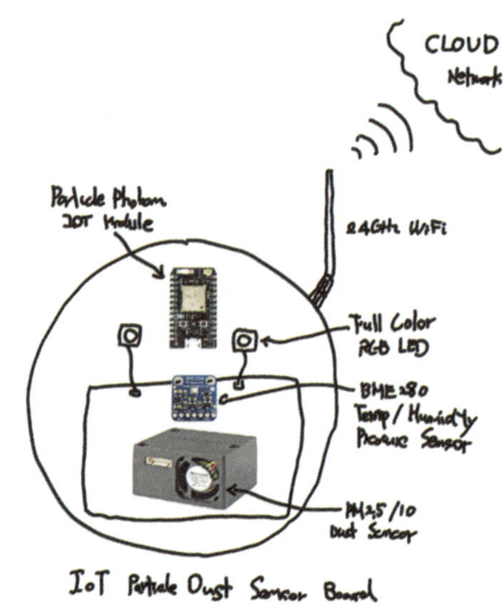

A drawing of a Mangwon-dong dust sensor.

Asia's Climate Refugees Mr. Guo and Mr. Lee
Suyeon Yun

In this video, the story of the Guo couple, who lived through the desertification of Inner Mongolia beginning in the 1970s and have been resettled in the Kubuqi desert, is juxtaposed with the environmental problems of North Korea discussed by Lee, who escaped from the North in order to avoid the famine that ravaged North Korea in the mid-nineties. Lee's testimony alerts us to the fact that most of the North Korean refugees, who are generally seen as political refugees, are food refugees/climate refugees, namely, people who have had to leave their homes in response to agricultural failures due to climate change.

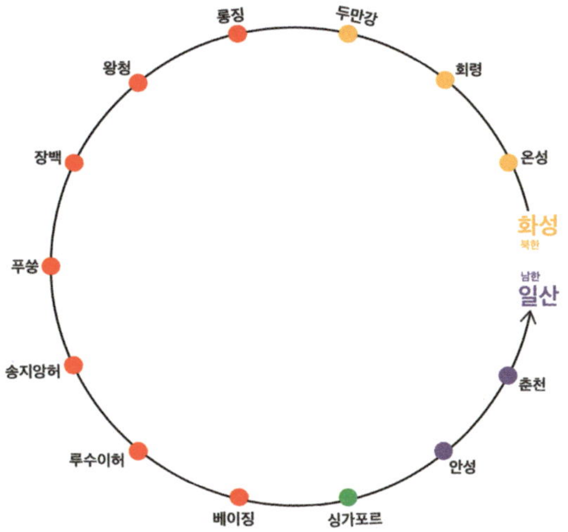

A North Korean climate refugee, Mr. Lee's migration route, 1991–2002.

Mr. Guo has re-settled in Kubuqi Desert, Inner Mongolia, China. Photo: Suyeon Yun.

Desert Sandstorm: Kubuqi-Beijing-Seoul

After planting trees for two days in the Kubuqi desert with 100 members of the 5th Green Corps, we were scheduled to leave on 8 April 2006, for Beijing, but we got hit with a severe sandstorm in Kubuqi. We took the night train that evening and arrived in Beijing the following morning, to find the sky covered with yellow dust. Our party departed Beijing that day for Tianjin, and we traveled from Tianjin to Seoul. The bus from Beijing to Tianjin continuously wiped the sand off the windshield, and traveled with the headlights on even though it was daytime. When we arrived in Seoul the next day, 10 April, the government had shut down the schools. Schools remained closed for two days due to yellow dust. This is the yellow dust that our group, Future Forest, witnessed starting from the Kubuqi desert and passing through Beijing and Tianjin, which overtook the Seoul sky. —Kwon Byung-hyun (Future Forest)

A drone view of the trees planted by Future Forest at Kubuqi Desert, Inner Mongolia, China. Photo: Suyeon Yun.

Entrance to *Air Bang*, Donuimun Museum Village. Photo: Kyungsub Shin Studio.

H₂O CO₂
H₂O CO₂

Sewoon Sangga. Photo: Kyungsub Shin Studio.

Retrospective Futures: Seoul Regeneration, exhibition (partner program organized by Urban Regeneration Headquarters, Seoul Metropolitan Government, 19 September–5 November 2017), Sewoon Sangga. Photo: Kyungsub Shin Studio.

"Pedestrial Deck," Third Level, Sewoon Sangga. Photo: Kyungsub Shin Studio.

PRODUCTION
CITY

PRODUCTION CITY

Yerin Kang
*Curator, Seoul Biennale 2017;
co-director, SoA*

Jie-Eun Hwang
*Curator, Seoul Biennale 2017;
associate professor, University of Seoul*

"Imminent commons" is an imperative in our era, and it is a process of understanding the complex correlation between production and consumption and of building new networks. Contemporary cities have developed into centers for mass consumption, giving rise to mass production systems. However, natural resources are being fast depleted, and many economies are experiencing limits to growth. Accordingly, international industrial production networks are being re-organized based on new value systems. Urban resource circulation cycles are changing so that the cities can be self-sustaining; technological advances are being continuously made in personalized production and small quantity batch production, while a new system of social values on creative industry is emerging.

Production City sheds light on the once robust inner-city manufacturing sites of Seoul and experiments with new possibilities for urban production. Amid efforts to either preserve them as historical sites or demolish them completely in massive redevelopment, the old inner-city neighborhoods in Seoul still remain a strong network of exchanging labor and technologies, with a variety of factories and resources spatially clustered by trade or industry. The Euljiro and Changsin-dong neighborhoods are a massive aggregate of small factories that form a unique urban landscape; their manufacturing ecology is undergoing rigorous changes. They are a special asset to Seoul, for it is there that we can look for positive solutions for urban production and urban regeneration.

In addressing these issues, *Production City* as an exhibition took the approach of becoming part of the neighborhoods. That is to say, the exhibition process became part of the production eco-system of the neighborhoods, in an attempt to have the Seoul Biennale contribute to the local environments. Thus, *Production City* is a collage of spectacles from Sewoon Sangga and the Euljiro area, and Changsin-dong. The former two neighborhoods remain the home base of urban manufacturing industries in Seoul, while Changsin-dong is an industrial-residential neighborhood with vivid colors of life and people from diverse backgrounds. *Production City* takes the Seoul Biennale as a platform for presenting sections of the past and present of the city and for creating practical mechanisms for predicting foreseeable futures.

The major exhibition and workshops for *Production City* take place at Sewoon Sangga, which is being reborn as "Again Sewoon" as part of the city government's urban regeneration program. The exhibition introduces the visitors to the fierce struggles of the printing, metal, machinery, and electronics industries in and around the area, as well as the local arts community which is now emerging. In the *Anatomy of Things* section of the exhibition, the visitors met a designer who explores the unique manufacturing and industrial norms and standards of the Euljiro area, read an affectionate humor of an architect, and an imagined industry of the future based on recycled resources, which is a global issue. The *Neo Manufacturing Workshop* section brought conventional architectural materials and technologies and applied robotics and 3D printing technologies. Through participatory manufacturing processes, the workshop demonstrated that Sewoon Sannga has an absolute advantage in continuing such collaborative experiments.

Project Seoul Apparel was held at a special gallery set up amidst the garment factories in the alleyways of Changsin-dong. It portrays, from the perspective of the manufacturers, the ecology of the clothing industry around the Dongdaemun area where the garment production–consumption network is internationally entwined. It proposes a new space for manufacturing in Changsing-dong. In addition to the exhibition, workshops, talk series, and field tours were organized where the participants experienced first-hand the various venues of production, had a chance to meet the artists, and explored the hidden neighborhoods of the city.

Production City portrays a city of co-production. In every step of the exhibition process, the local community, various stakeholders, artists and citizen-participants were involved; in fact the gallery still remains, and will continue to remain, as part of the Changsin-dong garment manufacturing ecology after the Seoul Biennale has

PRODUCTION CITY

closed. The garment producers became participating artists in the exhibition, while the visitors became the subjects of production, and bureaucratic red-tape was resolved with cultural activities.

Production City was first to show to the public the skywalk and the "makers cubes" at Sewoon Sangga. They are part of the Seoul municipal "Again Sewoon" urban regeneration program. Creative industry start-up companies and creators who are moving into the new space as tenants participated in the exhibition and introduced themselves as new neighbors to the public and to the existing tenants at Sewoon Sangga. Through the initiative of the Seoul Biennale, new facilities and resources were established at Sewoon Basement, which now serve as a laboratory for neo-manufacturing with active participation from the local manufacturers. It is hoped that the works by participating artists will become new consumer products available at Sewoon Sangga while the new garment factory initiated as part of the Seoul Biennale in Changsin-dong will act as a stepping stone for young designers and entrepreneurs who wish to enter the garment industry.

Anatomy of Things
Production City seeks an analytical and creative overview on the geography of resources of urban manufacturing. A closer look at the industries in the inner city of Seoul shows that it has sustained a set of their own legitimate local standards and recycling networks have intertwined with the global industrial issues of production. *Production City* discovers new kinds of values of production that are expected to reorganize the current framework of production and benefit the producer community.

Neo Manufacturing Workshop
New technology changes society. It offers innovative opportunities that challenge existing socio-economic systems. *Neo Manufacturing Workshop* proposes that new technologies can bring young labor and sustainable work back into the city. Rather than the logic that seeks to replace human work with machines, *Neo Manufacturing Workshop* envisions machines working with humans to create new modes of production and consumption. Scientists, engineers, artists, designers, and architects working in the field of artificial intelligence, robotics, 3D printing, and digital fabrication will be invited to explore hybrid approaches that can thrive in the inner city.

Project Seoul Apparel
Production City features a spinoff project that conveys dynamics in the garment industries. *Project Seoul Apparel* identifies the urgent issues facing the garment manufacturing business in Changsin-dong, a traditional textile quarter next to the ultra-modern Dongdaemun fashion retail district. The project proposes a better system that improves working environments and sustainable labor operations. Optimized by fast fashion of the Dongdaemun market, the production capacity of this area relies on individual small-sized factories. Global artist groups of architects, fashion designers, urban researchers, and filmmakers, from Korea and the United Kingdom, suggest provocative solutions through local networks of community governance.

ANATOMY OF THINGS

Sewoon-W303, Sewoon Museum. Photo: Kyungsub Shin Studio.

Looping City
BARE

Looping City is a research project on architecture and urbanism that sheds new light on the local recycling industry in the Sewoon Sangga-Euljiro area, the storied urban manufacturing center that has been suffering decades of decay. Rather than focusing on recycling products whose lifecycles have ended, the project focuses on recycling manufacturing byproducts, or materials discarded as part of manufacturing processes. Thus the project looks at the entire manufacturing cycle as a potential target for "neo-manufacturing" innovation, and for creating a new form of manufacturing cycle. In this vein, the project proposes to create a system of collecting manufacturing byproducts, which can be used as raw materials for 3D printing, a new technology that can help local manufacturing businesses and communities at Sewoon Sannga and the Euljiro area become self-sustaining by 2027.

More specifically, *Looping City* proposes a pneumatic tube system, a kind of circular transport system, to be installed at the manufacturing neighborhood in the Euljiro and Sewoon Sangga area. It features an unmanned collecting device called Tubo (an "urban robot") that roams around and collects materials discarded by the many manufacturing shops in the neighborhood. It also features a number of Tubo Stations where the robot would be charged and stored. The system also includes a Docking Station, a processing and redistribution center for the collected materials, at Sewoon Sangga. With the improvement of the pedestrian environment now under way in the Sewoon Sangga and Euljiro neighborhood, such a facility would mean an added infrastructure that could make Sewoon Sangga a hub of resource circulation.

Looping City is a project that rediscovers the virtues of Seoul as a production city, or the virtues of urban manufacturing. In doing so, it proposes to improve quality of life based on a new system of value circulation and local self-sustainability.

BARE—Bureau of Architecture Research & Environment is committed to research-based design approach and producing contextually sensitive proposals. Jinhong Jeon and Yuni Choi graduated from the Architectural Association School of Architecture and Cambridge University and they are currently teaching a design studio at Korea National University of Arts. BARE received the Arumjigi Heritage Tomorrow Prize (2015), Seoul Mayor's Prize (2015) and were the Young Architects Program finalists (2016).

Tubo, an "urban robot" prototype, for collecting recyclable manufacturing materials. Sewoon-W301. Photo: provided by artist.

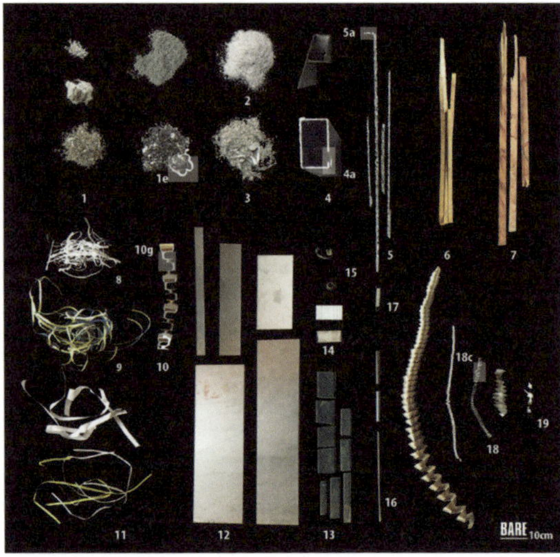

Recyclable manufacturing materials collected from Cheongyecheon and Euljiro areas. Photo: provided by artist.

Agbogbloshie Makerspace Platform
LOWDO + Panurban

Agbogbloshie Makerspace Platform (AMP) is a social design project built around the Agbogbloshie scrapyard and e-waste processing zone in Accra, Ghana. *AMP* triangulates an open-source makerspace kiosk with maker toolkits and a mobile app as a concept of "spacecraft"—empowering grassroots makers to gather resources and tools, learn peer-to-peer "by doing," produce more and better products, trade to generate improved income, and amplify their reputation as makers.

Makerspace refers to any open community lab or workshop where people can access tools and equipment for (digital) design and fabrication; typically, they are capital-intensive and housed in buildings that are fixed in place. Like other "crafts," e.g. hovercraft, watercraft, aircraft, and spacefaring vehicles, AMP spacecraft is an alternative architecture "for making" that affords maneuverability. Small-scale, incremental, and low-cost, spacecraft operate as a set of tools and equipment to "craft space" in different ways, enabling makers with limited means to navigate and terraform their environment.

DK Osseo-Asare is co-founder and principal of integrated design studio Low Design Office (LOWDO), based in Tema, Ghana and Austin, Texas and is Assistant Professor of Architecture and Engineering Design at Pennsylvania State University. He is co-founder of the Agbogbloshie Makerspace Platform (AMP).

The director of Panurban, Yasmine Abbas is a French architect and strategic designer who explores the intersection between people, technology, and space. Her work focuses on digital culture and contemporary mobility—neo-nomads, architecture, and (e) motion. She is the co-founder of the Agbogbloshie Makerspace Platform (AMP).

  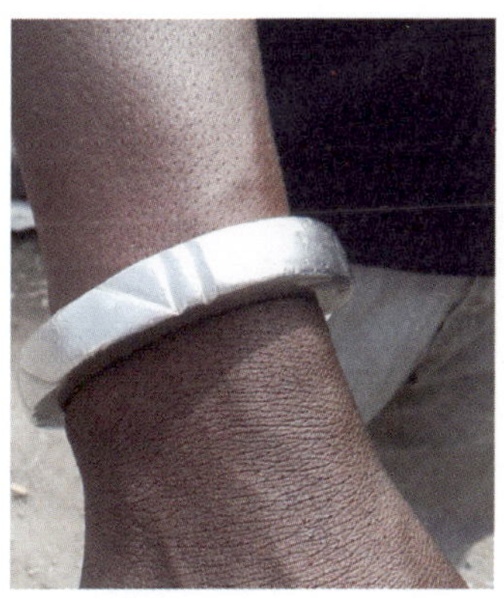

Pots and personal ornaments made with recycled metal. Photo: provided by participating artist(s).

PRODUCTION CITY

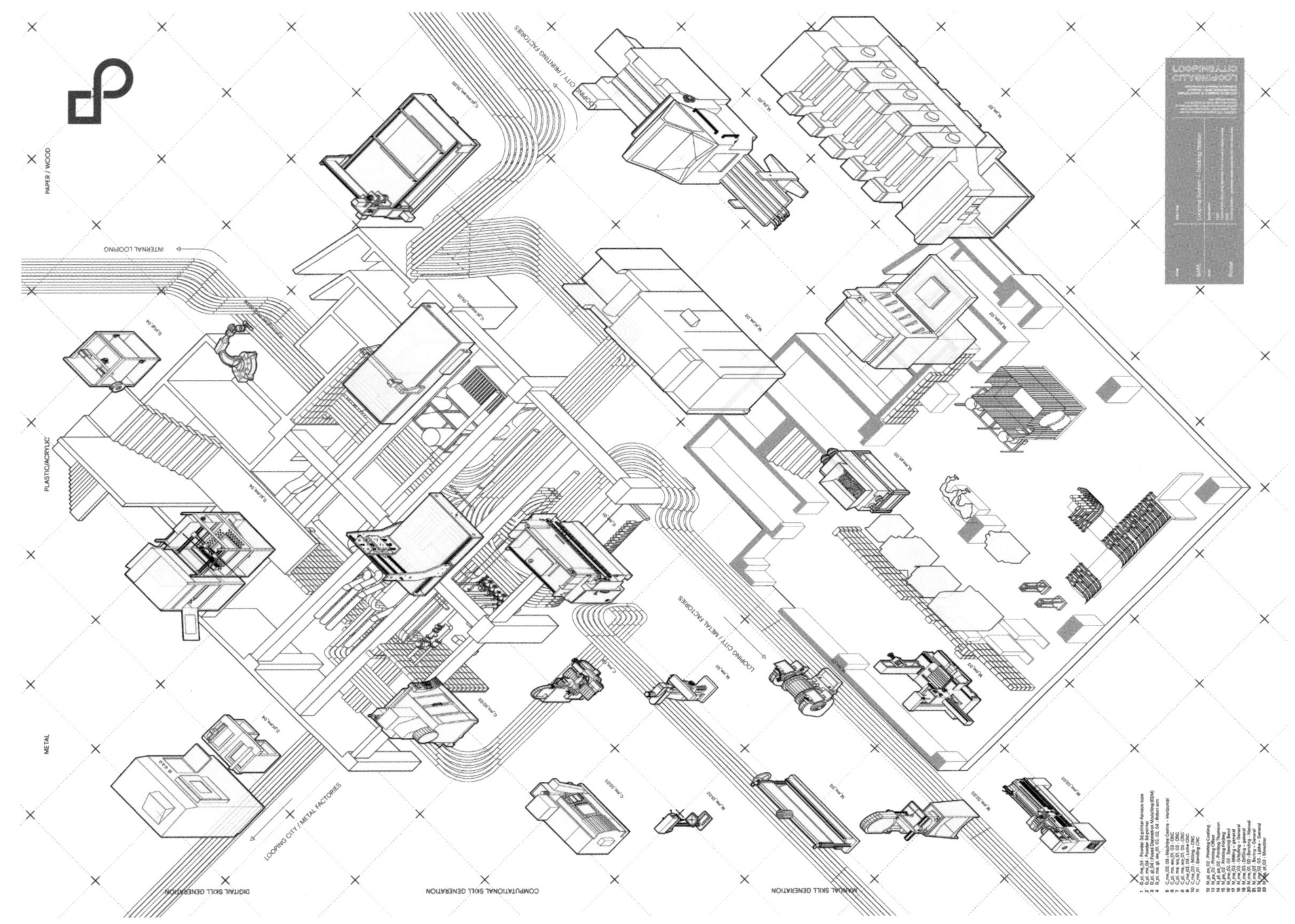

1   D_pl_me_04 : Powder 3d printer-furnace type
2   D_pl_me_04 : Powder 3d printer
3   D_pl_gl_04 : Fused Deposition Modelling (FDM)
4   D_pl_me_gl_wo_01, 02, 03, 04 : Robot arm

5   C_me_02, 03 : Machine Centre - Horizontal
6   C_pl_me_wo_01, 03 : CNC
7   C_pl_me_wo_01, 03 : CNC
8   C_pl_me_wo_01, 03 : CNC
9   C_me_02, 03 : Lathe CNC
10 C_me_03 : Milling - CNC
11 C_me_01 : Bending CNC

12 M_pl_pa_02 : Printing Coating
13 M_pa_02 : Printing Offset
14 M_pl_pa_02 : Printing Thomson
15 M_pa_02 : Printing Folding
16 M_me_02, 03 : Sawing Bend
17 M_me_03 : Milling - general
18 M_me_03 : Grinding - General
19 M_me_03 : Drilling - general
20 M_me_01, 02 : Bending - Manual
21 M_me_03 : Boring - General
22 M_me_02, 03 : Lathe - General
23 M_me_gl_03 : Shredder

Artist	Title / Year
BARE	Looping System – Docking Station
Poster	Docking Station : produces waste same as it's raw resources

Spacecraft

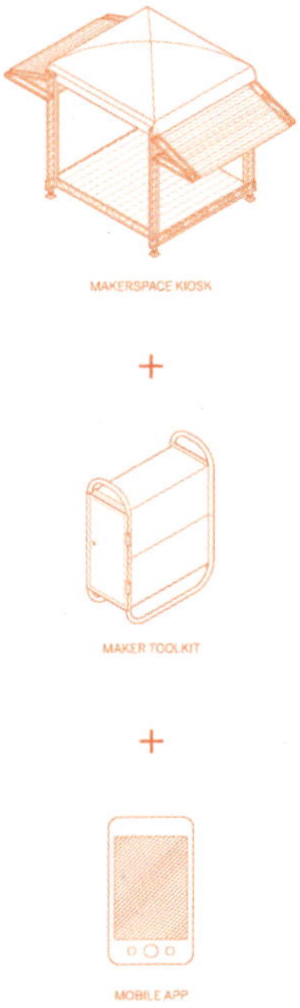

Agbogbloshie Makerspace Platform (AMP) has three components that function together as *spacecraft*: makerspace kiosk (modular construction system, mobile and expandable); maker toolkits (customizable per a given community's requirements); and mobile app (that amplifies grassroots makers' capacity for making and trading).

Like other "crafts", e.g. hovercraft, watercraft, aircraft and spacefaring vehicles, AMP spacecraft is an alternative architecture "for making" that affords maneuverability. Small-scale, incremental and low-cost, *spacecraft* operates as a set of tools and equipment to "craft space" in different ways, enabling makers to navigate and terraform their environment.

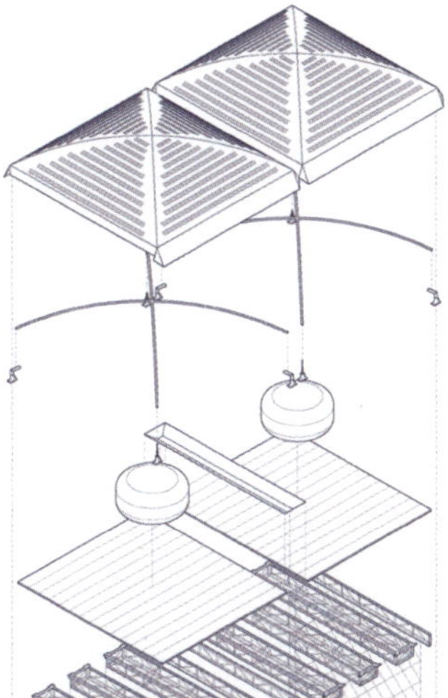

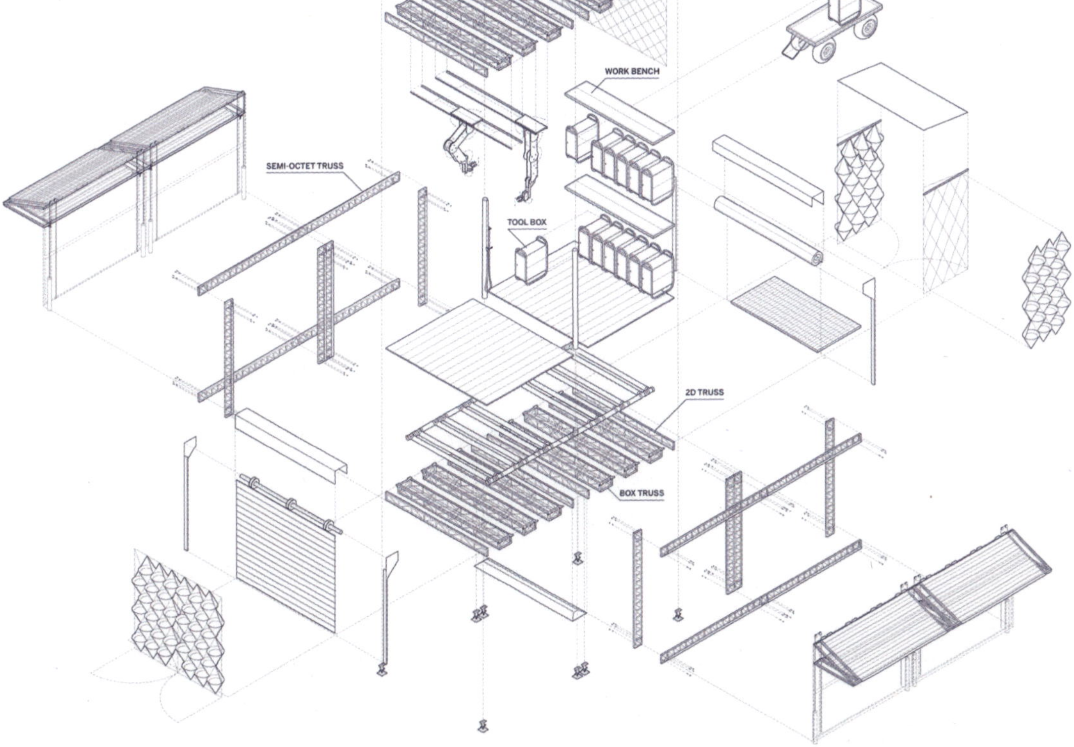

Diagram of Agbogbloshie Makerspace Platform. © Low Design Office (LOWDO) & Panurban (Yasmine Abbas).

BARE, *Looping City*, Sewoon-W301. Photo: Kyungsub Shin Studio.

Art and Disaster Project
Art and Disaster

Art and Disaster, a project team, was founded to send artists to disaster areas to help children overcome the hardships of the disasters and to recover their memories through art activities. Consisting of six Korean visual artists (Kang Jeauk, Shin Kiwoun, Ha Seok-Jun, Im Doone, Kim Kijong, and Kim Sungdae), the team visited San Fernando Central School in Tacloban, the Philippines. The area had been completely destroyed by the super typhoon Yolanda. The members brought a self-made 3D printer with them and held a workshop with the children to fix broken toys and to restore their memories destroyed by the typhoon. The current exhibition is an archive exhibition allowing the audience to have a look at the process of that project. It is also an international exchange exhibition; the team invited three artists from abroad during its last research trip to England.

As a collaborative exhibition *Art and Disaster Project* was organized independently from *Production City* and supported by the Arts Council Korea, 3D way, Hycore, Campus D, and Research Institute For City and Humanity.

Participating artists: Kang Jeauk, Shin Kiwoun, Ha Seok-Jun, Im Doone, Kim Kijong, Kim Sungdae.
Curators: Song Yovi, Kwak Hye Young
Invited artists: Alexis Milne, Eunju Hitchcock-Yoo, Arther Mamou-Mani

A child participating in the workshop shows a piece of work she created with the 3D printer. August 2015, Tacloban, the Philippines. Photo: provided by artist(s).

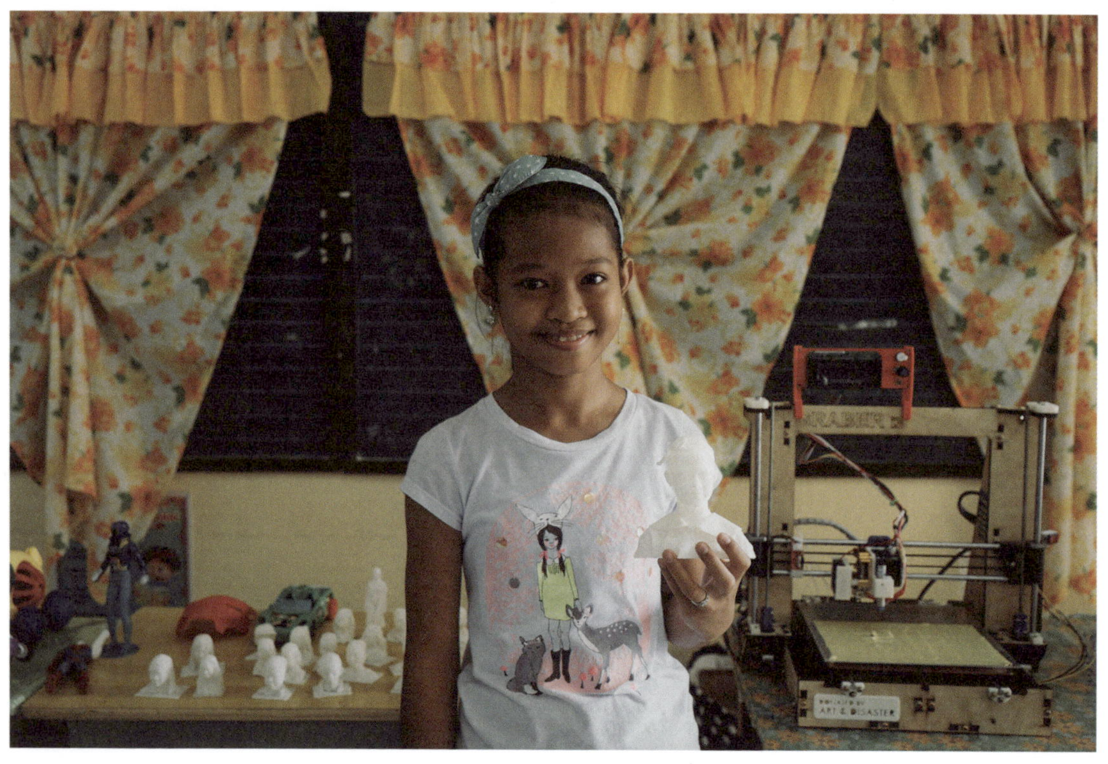

Overlapping City
Optical Race

Overlapping City traces people who make a living in the old sections of Seoul where small-scale manufacturing, wholesale and retail businesses are concentrated. Most of the small businesses in the neighborhood are run by baby boomers and members of the "X86" generation, or those who were born in the 1960s and went to college in the 80s. These two population groups also currently make up the core of the economically active population. The life cycles of the two population groups and the life cycle of Korean economic growth overlap. Once thriving and proud, the inner-city manufacturing neighborhoods have been declining for decades for at least two reasons. On one hand, the nation's industrial structure and distribution systems have changed. On the other hand, Seoul itself has now become a mega-city. Today, a new attitude and prospect for former inner-city neighborhoods are leading to increased real-estate values in the neighborhoods concerned. However, most of the baby boomers and the X86 generation members who make a living in the neighborhoods remain tenants. From tenants to the property owners and the city government officials, the stakes are high. Amidst the tension and complicated claims of rights and entitlements, the prospect for a better future and the current state of affairs in the neighborhood are likely to exist in parallel for some time. This gap in the tedious transition period provides an opportunity for artists and social activists to intervene. These are the children of the baby boomer and X86 generations, who grew up and were educated in the Korean economic boom years of the 1980s and 90s. They are highly-educated and are often cultural producers-cum-consumers. The city government hopes to revive the old manufacturing centers with the "cultural industry" activities and achieve a generation shift. Such a shift cannot be achieved without the help of the members of this post-baby boomer and post-X86 generation.

This project was realized as part of a join research project of Seoul Institute and Seoul Biennale.

Optical Race is a visual creation group formed by graphic designer Kim Hyungjae and data visualizer and researcher Bahk Jaehyun. They participated in the project A Tale of Three Cities in the Anyang Public Art Project in 2014. In the same year, they presented the project Chance Family in the group show Home Sweet Home in Arko Museum of Art, and published a book of the same name the following year. They also participated in the exhibitions *A Loner's Guide* (Common Center), *Subculture: Angry Youth* (Seoul Museum of Art) and *Experiments of Architopia* (National Museum of Modern and Contemporary Art, Korea) in 2015, and *Artspectrum 2016* (Leeum, Samsung Museum of Art) in 2016, and *Family Report* (Gyeonggi Museum of Art) in 2017.

Photo: Kyungsub Shin Studio.

Optical Race, *Overlapping City*, Sewoon-W302. Gallery façade. Photo: Kyungsub Shin Studio.

Format Variable
Na Kim

Format Variable examines how paper, which is the symbolic standard of the printing industry, changes into physical time and space through the printing and book-making process. And it presents the gap between the certified and non-certified standard of the paper size that is reflected in the process. Japanese paper specifications, which were known to have been influenced by Britain in the past, have been used till now in Korea through industrialization as two types of conventional paper size—Sarukgeonji and Kukgeonji. Dummy books of sixteen different formats will be made with this Kukgeonji (636 x 939 mm, mojoji 100 g/m^2), including standard and non-standard size. The sixteen formats are the sizes that divide the kukjeonji into 1, 2, 4, 8, 9, 12, 16, 18, 20, 24, 30, 36, 40, 64 and 128 without paper loss. Assuming that a book of 20 mm thickness is produced based on the format, shinkukpan (159 x 234 mm) which is the 16-division size of this plate, about 10 sheets of the paper are used. Based on this, if different formats are bound using the same amount of paper, books of various thicknesses are produced according to each format. These sixteen different dummies contain physical information of the specification in an organic relationship of paper, plate, and book.

The paper used in these dummy books does not contain any substantive information. However, it contains a graphic plane with color and position display for representing the visual information of the thickness and size of the books. On the other hand, these sixteen formats are expanded from *Format Variable* to be used as a booklet for the Production City exhibition in the Seoul Biennale of Architecture and Urbanism. The information on this exhibition is placed in different formats according to loose connections and suggests the function of printed matter. The visitors collect the prints and directly bind them to create a booklet containing the narrative of the individual.

Na Kim is a graphic designer. After studying product design and graphic design in Korea, Kim participated to Werkplaats Typografie in the Netherlands. Kim is currently based in Seoul, as a member of Table Union and was involved in an artist-run space, Common Center. Kim was selected as Next Generation Design Leaders in 2008, was awarded Doosan Artist Award in 2013, Today's Young Artist Award in 2014, presented by the Ministry of Culture in Korea. She was responsible for concept and design of *GRAPHIC* magazine from 2009 till 2011 and has been a curator for Brno Biennale, Chaumont Festival and Seoul International Typography Biennale. Kim's works been included in many international exhibitions at MMCA, V&A, MoMA, Milan Triennale Museum etc. www.ynkim.com

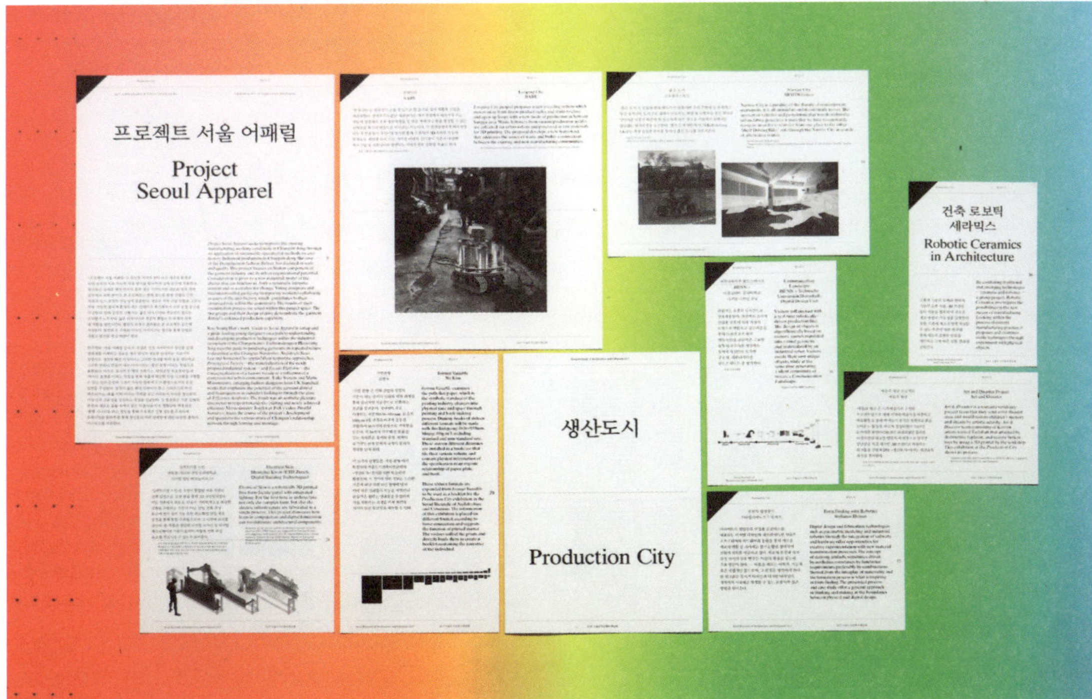

Leaflets for *Production City* in variable formats. Photo: provided by artist.

ANATOMY OF THINGS

Format Variable exhibition. Sewoon-W303, Sewoon Museum. Photo: Kyungsub Shin Studio.

Plus Cycling
Chanjoong Kim, Hyesun Lee

Recycling and up-cycling have emerged as a small part of the solution to the environmental problems engendered by mass production since the age of Industrial Revolution. The point of recycling is in the reuse of materials, as in the case where chairs are made out of used plastic bottles. Up-cycling is a way of finding new usability for discarded industrial products. The concept of plus cycling proposed in this exhibition is to create new values, by means of adding a minimum processing to products and parts that have been subject to standardizations in accordance with the mass production system. Containers, pallets, boxes, along with products loaded inside them are required to comply with the regulations of the international standards. One result of this is the dimensional similarities of industrially manufactured goods. Plus cycling plays with the fact that such similarities exist among industrial products across the board. The exhibition finds new usability for products that already have distinct usability, by combining and assembling them in accordance with their dimensional similarities. This is initiated with the idea that the sum of 1 plus 1 is greater than 2 and that what makes this possible is the standard.

Chanjoong Kim graduated in architectural engineering, Korea University and received a master's degree from Harvard University In architecture. Currently, he is the visiting professor at the Architecture Department of Kyung Hee University and serves as the Principal in charge of THE_SYSTEM LAB in Seoul, South Korea. Some of his works are Paul Smith Flagship Store, Hannam-Dong Hands Office, and Hyundai Museum of Kid's Books & Art in South Korea.

Hyesun Lee is a professor at Ewha Womans University of Seoul. Lee's area of expertise is design thinking and new product development. As a design practitioner, she produces hand-crafted lifestyle products for micro-customization, including Korean lacquer shoe care products, Yugi cutlery, Yugi candle holders, and Plus cycling products.

Small table for soju. Phtoto: provided by artist.

Small table for ramyeon. Photo: provided by artist.

Screw 001
Bongkyu Song (BKID)

Many shops lining the alleyways between Eujiro 3-ga and Sewoon Sangga are metal processing companies that cut, curve, weld, and bend metals. Nuts and bolts are used to fasten, or to control pressure between, two metal objects. As such, bolts and nuts are thought of as sidekicks or extras at best, and never considered important. Yet, bolts and nuts are subject to the strictest product standards, both national (KS) and international (ISO). *Screw 001* is an attempt to visualize the possibilities of new standards for these two metal products.

The project consists of three parts. First, it researched and archived the types, materials, usage, and production methods of the various screws manufactured in the Euljiro 3-ga and 4-ga area. Second, among the screws thus archived, a prototype was selected for "mass" production. Third, a thousand copies of the prototype were produced using only local resources available in the Euljiro area. The screw thus produced has the price and quality equivalent to a screw widely used in everyday life, while escaping at the same time the limitations of the KS and ISO regime. The exhibition shows nine applications of the new screw.

Bongkyu Song is an Industrial Designer, established the Industrial Design Studio BKID in 2009. He is carrying out projects in various fields from craft to new technology. His major works include the BMW i-series Charger, AUDI Smart acc and Siemens UltraSound. In 2009, KIDP selected him as the next generation design leader. He was selected as a young artist of the year by the Ministry of Culture in 2015 and selected as a young creative leader in Forbes Korea in 2013. Major works were introduced at Kumho Museum, MoA, SUN Contemporary. www.bkid.co

ANATOMY OF THINGS

A screw design. Image: provided by artist.

Screw 001 exhibition. Sewoon-W303, Sewoon Museum. Photo: Kyungsub Shin Studio.

MOTOElastico Studio. 4F, 215 Cheonggyecheon-ro. Photo: Kyungsub Shin Studio.

Narrow City
MOTOElastico

Narrow City is a product about the density of contemporary metropolis, it is all around us and it constantly moves. The amount of vehicles and pedestrians that travels within the urban fabric generates a mass that we have to navigate in order to transfer from one place to the other. The obstacles are always shifting in front of us: sometimes we move along, sometimes we cut through, sometimes we overtake.

Couriers experience daily the tight dimensions of the narrow city paths and creatively adapt to them. The characteristics of the goods they have to deliver push them to customize existing vehicles in search of optimum performance; the experience on the road helps them to choose the most effective route.

The Shelf Driving Bike is a new delivery vehicle designed around a red Benelli TNT125. It is a mobility experiment conceived to easily penetrate the tight corridors of the narrow city.

The main idea is to put flat, movable storage on wheels, maximising the horizontal loading capacity (220 cm) while retaining a very narrow width (only 42 cm). A new 20 mm tubular frame is attached to the side of the bike: it supports two modular triangular storage units assembled around the driving area.

The system can be easily adapted to different types of motorcycles.

This project was realized as part of a join research project of Seoul Institute and Seoul Biennale. Supported by Virginia Commonwealth University School of the Arts in Qatar and Benelli / Aprilia Korea.

MOTOElastico is a mobile Space Lab founded in Seoul by Simone Carena and Marco Bruno who currently work on architecture, interiors, exhibition and art projects. Born and educated in Italy, fine-tuned in California and rooted in South Korea since 2001, in all its projects MOTOElastico uses irony to critically challenge and playfully celebrate local customs and behaviors.

MOTOElastico, driving *Narrow City*. Photo: provided by artist.

Material prescription publication series *Garm*. Photo: provided by artist.

Material Prescription Garm

garmSSI (Jaeseon Yoon, Youngkyu Shim) +
URBANPLAY

Garm [the standard Romanization is *gam* —ed.] is
a Korean word meaning "material." It is also the
name of a series of books published by the artists
of this collaborative exhibition. The series is a
discussion on how to realize the creativity of the
individual. It starts with the "material,' the most
basic component of a house, or a space that
people inhabit. The series is intended to help
readers use good materials, by providing them
with information on material characteristics, how
to choose different materials based on their
characteristics, production methods, and even on
the names of manufacturing distribution brands.

As a collaborative exhibition, Material
Prescription Garm was organized independently from Production City.

garmSSI is the publication brand of
8apple. gammSSi is a creative action
group that archives and reorganizes
information on new materials and
construction methods based on
emerging culture.

URBANPLAY archives urban resources
through diverse convergence technology and conducts urban-related projects based on the archived data. In
particular, URBANPLAY continually
archives human-focused resources of
neighborhoods in Seoul in a digital
form and based on the outcome man-
ages URBANPOLY, an official online
media platform of urban content.
URBANPLAY constantly searches for
the sustainability of community-based
urban happenings through various
offline projects, including Familiar
Neighborhood, Local Curator, Walking
with Yeonhui, Yeonnam-week, and
Local-CT Project.

NEO MANUFACTURING WORKSHOP

B.A.T. and Lifethings, *ManuFaBrick* for *Wirye Residence*. Photo: Pil Joon Jeon.

Fabrication Agency in the City
TechCapsule

Fabrication Agency in the City addresses issues surrounding the gap between the architecture and manufacturing industries. It tells of what had to be given up and compromised in the course of constructing a building due to the limitations of ready-made products and the hard thinking that went into finding solutions in such situations. Apart from presenting the exhibition, *Wirye Residence ManuFaBrick*, it also presents a series of roundtable talks on materiality and process technologies. Architects and other experts are invited to share their experiences and stories.

With the opening of neo-manufacturing possibilities, new approaches to construction methods and securing construction materials and parts are becoming possible and economically feasible. The roundtable discussions provide opportunities to hear more about these issues from architects and other experts who have first-hand experience on these matters.

TechCapsule is a project group who mutually explore pragmatic potentials of technology such as robotic craft and digital fabrication applied to existing architectural industries. From the design process through the fabrication process to management and distribution, TechCapsule challenges technological advances and industrial applications in tectonic processes of architecture.

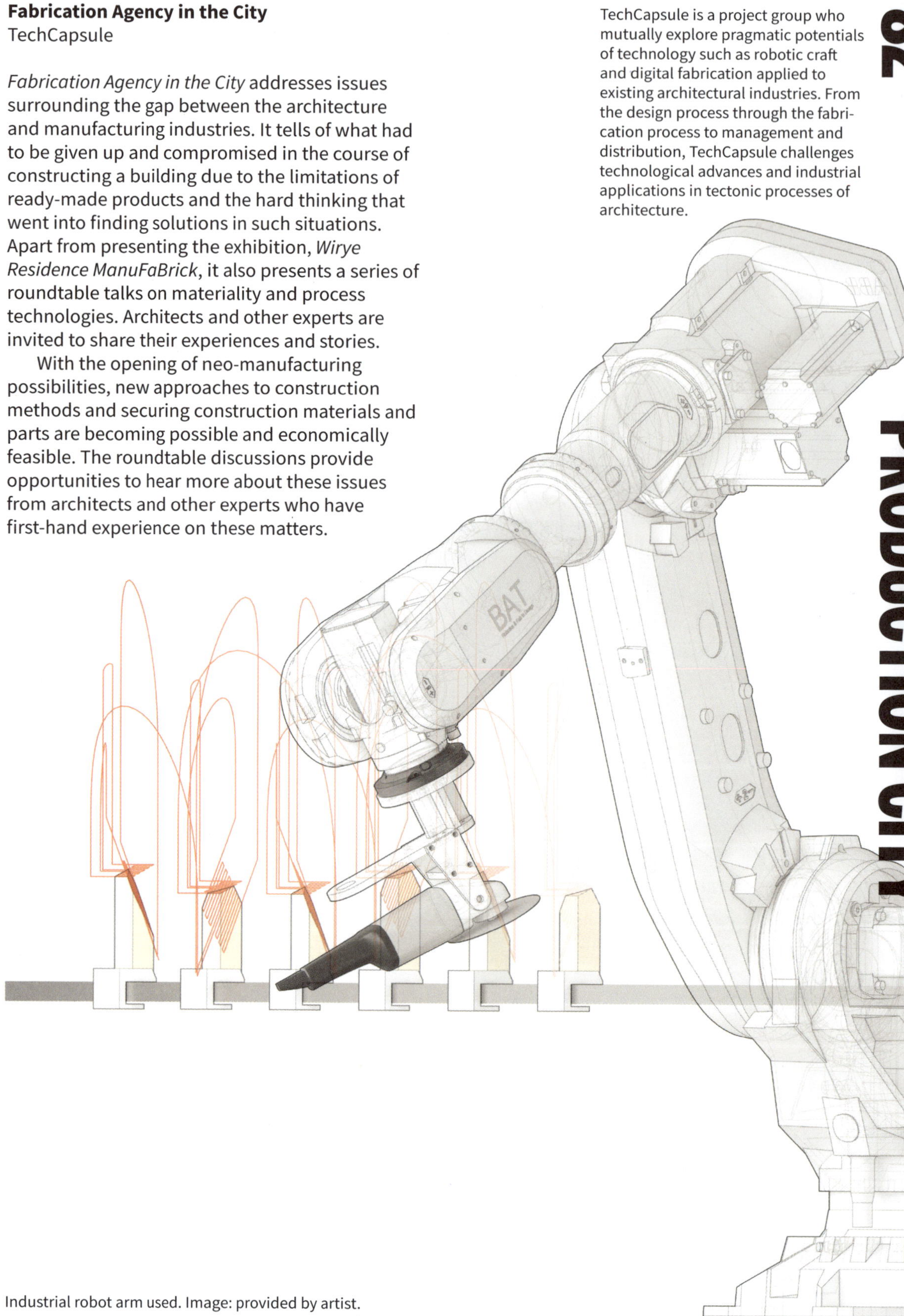

Industrial robot arm used. Image: provided by artist.

Wirye Residence + ManuFaBrick
Lifethings + B.A.T

Brick layering is a process of forming baseline corners and filling the space between them. The bottom of the brick wall in Wirye Residence starts parallel to the ground. However, the bricks would be piled up gradually along the roofline resembling a smiling mouth. About 600 bricks, each cut with a slightly different slope from the previous one, are needed to complete this design. An ordinary grinder will be connected to a robot arm to secure the necessary precision in cutting the bricks for this project—Lifethings (Soo-in Yang).

ManuFaBrick is a project that demonstrates how an industrial robot, as a piece of digital fabrication equipment, can intervene in the production process of irregular forms of bricks, and how this can bring new possibilities for brick as a construction material. Brick standardization and mass production systems have improved the price and quality of bricks. However, it has also led to the exclusion of architects from having a say on the shapes of the bricks they use. What would it take to produce bricks that deviate from the logic of "regular" shapes or standards? In reality, bricks are always and inevitably cut into various "irregular" shapes to meet the various and ever variable on-site requirements. This is done manually. However, as soon as the subject turns to designing irregular forms of bricks, the conversation suddenly becomes complicated with references to modules and connections. Does this mean that architects have to give up designing? Is a specialized robot developed exclusively for designing and producing bricks an answer to this problem? *ManuFaBrick* suggests 1) that it is possible for architects to intervene in designing bricks, 2) that a generic industrial robot can be utilized as a piece of digital processing equipment, and 3) that architects and other experts must make certain preparations in the face of changing times and technologies.

Soo-in Yang is an architect and public-art artist based in Seoul. His works range from architecture and participatory art to marketing campaigns in content and buildings to palm-sized devices. With the belief that the mixture of media can devise a more effective and inspiring solution to a particular problem, Yang aims to create "things" with stories that can touch "life" in a positive way. Yang earned a bachelor of architectural engineering degree from Yonsei University, Korea, and a master of architecture degree from Columbia University, where he was an Adjunct Assistant Professor and Founding Co-Director of the Living Architecture Lab. Since moving back to Seoul, Korea in 2011, he directs Lifethings/삶것, a multi-disciplinary design studio.

B.A.T (Be.A.Tek) is a group that conducts research along with field applications for utilizing digital fabrication machines ranging from 3D printers to 6-axis manipulators in various areas such as architecture, art, and design. In particular, B.A.T is capable of offering formal and informal shape fabrication solutions based on computation and using industrial 6-axis manipulators. The group works as a fabrication agency and provides services including design consulting, manufacturing, and in-situ installation of customized architectural frames.

B.A.T., *InFormed Ceramic*, Cheonggye-W304, Inside Tech Book Lounge. Photo: Kyungsub Shin Studio.

InFormed Ceramic
B.A.T

In construction, ceramic has been used only as a modular unit (bricks, tiles, or panels) with mass production taken as a given. The clay—the raw material—itself was never considered as a construction material, as ceramic was associated with standardized tile used to cover only flat surfaces. What would it take to use the clay itself as a new and independent module unit where the clay itself can be used?

Ceramic artists use ceramics in much wider applications than architects or builders do, who use them only as bricks or tiles. In any case, artists have to control for moisture and shrinkage rates as they work with various shapes and ceramic materials. They thus work with empirical data at their fingertips, which they acquire over the years. However, what they have acquired as empirical data is also limited to the particular material, form, size, and processing method that they work with. Architects and builders need their own set of empirical data that are relevant to the scales, materials, and components of architecture.

For *InFormed Ceramic*, B.A.T. developed a ceramic clay extruder. With this extruder, builders can use the ceramic clay itself as a construction element. Also, on a surface created by a complex application of robotic hot-wire cutting and milling, the artists layered the ceramic clay and generated a new module unit in an irregular form. The modules thus created were assembled to create a large pavilion.

B.A.T., *InFormed Ceramic*, an exhibition. Photo: Yi Taek-su.

B.A.T (Be.A.Tek) is a group that conducts research along with field applications for utilizing digital fabrication machines ranging from 3D printers to 6-axis manipulators in various areas such as architecture, art, and design. In particular, B.A.T is capable of offering formal and informal shape fabrication solutions based on computation and using industrial 6-axis manipulators. The group works as a fabrication agency and provides services including design consulting, manufacturing, and in-situ installation of customized architectural frames.

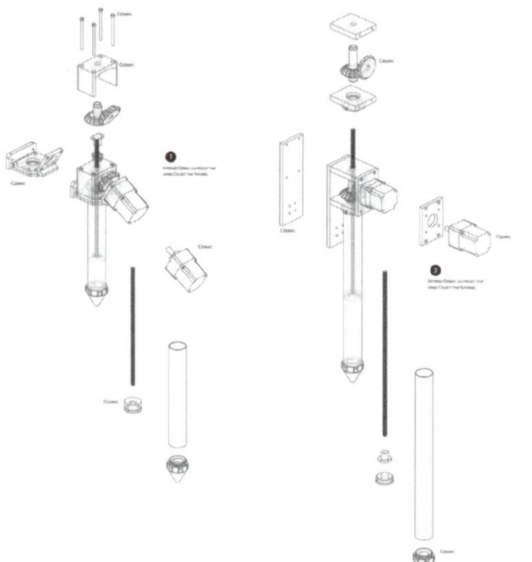

Ceramic clay extruder process. Image: provided by artist.

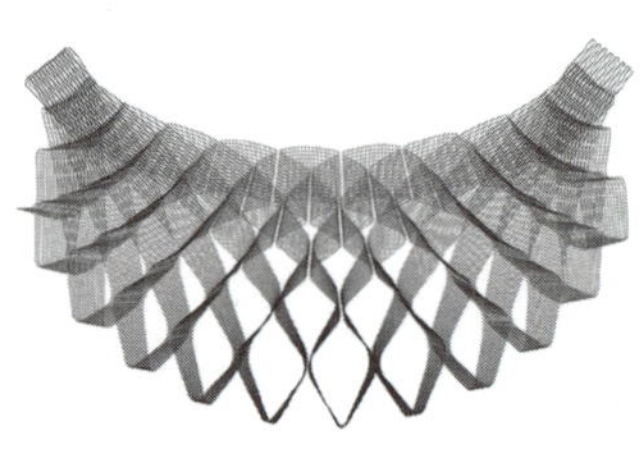

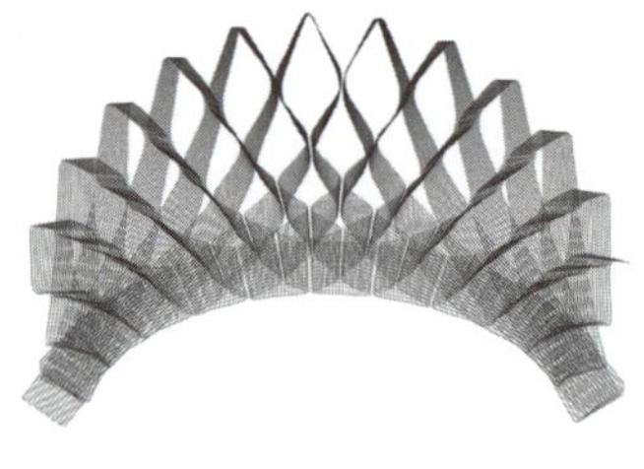

InFormed Ceramic tool paths. Image: provided by artist.

Digital Fossil—Deviant Object
Pil Joon Jeon

Before a technological leap is achieved, abnormal evolutions take place repeatedly to overcome problems—problems that can hardly be solved with limited technological competence. Such repetitions often result in monstrous but beautiful things that can never be obtained by normal processes. In order to produce such a "deviant object," this exhibition utilizes a technology used in constructing support structures of various patterns. The technology in question is expected to disappear gradually due to the development of the 3D printing technology. *Digital Fossil—Deviant Object* is a copy of the original but also an interesting by-product in itself. It is digital copy of the Sewoon Basement, which was once a boiler room for the floors above it, but is now reborn as a space for neo-manufacturing where support structures generating algorithms and robot technologies are available. As such, this exhibition is a spatial fossil, an archival record of the boiler room in the basement of Sewoon Sangga.

Supported by Stratasys Korea.
www.stratasys.co.kr.
In collaboration with Taewook Kang.

Pil Joon Jeon is a registered architect and co-founder of Studio LXJX. He has practiced at Llewelyn Davies Yeang, Foster and Partners and Now Architects in London and Seoul. His works range from architecture, product design, and film animation as well as computational design works in various media and scales. He received a bachelor of science in architecture degree from Hongik University, Korea and a diploma in architecture (RIBA Part II) degree from the Bartlett School of Architecture UCL in the U.K. He currently teaches a design studio at the University of Seoul and Sejong University.

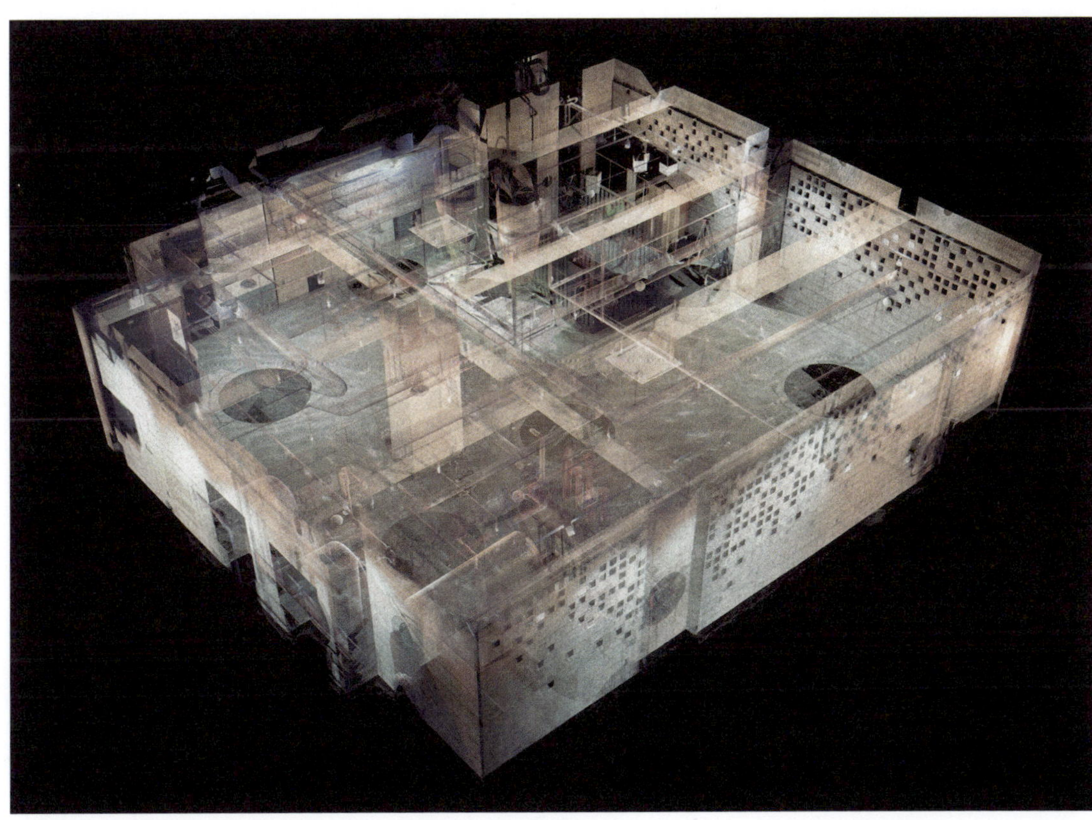

Sewoon Basement 3D Scanned Model. Image: provided by artist.

Reformable Mold
Hyun Parke

Casting is an effective way of generating multiple copies of a thing. However, the drawback is the initial high cost of constructing the mold. Furthermore, when it comes to making a mold, there is not much difference between past and present methods. 3D printers are effective at making highly customized items, but the types of usable materials are limited, and production speed is slow. Molding and casting are effective for making copies of multiple items and for using a variety of materials; but the form of the original mold or cast cannot be altered once it is decided. *Reformable Mold* fills the gap between these two manufacturing methods. It presents a new production method that has never been possible before. It also presents prototype products and suggests neo-manufacturing possibilities.

Technical Support: Byungjoon Kwon, Team Void.
In collaboration with YoungAh Sung.

Hyun Parke is a designer who loves to bring designs to tangible form, employing any type of process. His work focuses on designing and building contraptions to make things or to perform tasks.

Reformable Mold, exhibition. Photo: provided by artist.

(Un)Natural Ceramic Tiles
Dongwook Hwang

This exhibition will focus on two of the many aspects of ceramic printing. The first aspect is the physical property of the clay. In particular, it is important to observe the naturalness and flexibility of clay, as well as how its condition changes during the process of drying, and to reflect such observations in the work process. How the clay condition changes according to the temperature and humidity of the surrounding environment should also be taken into account in the work process. The second is to leave the traces of the robot arm and the extruder used in the project for this exhibition. One can often find chisel marks and other traces of the tools used on well-known statues or reliefs from the past. Such marks add character to the texture of the work; they sometimes decide whether the work is considered rough or refined. In the same vein, the main tools used in this work, that is, the robot arm and the extruder, leave their own marks. The question of how to use use the marks is the second important element.

(Un)natural Ceramic Tiles are square-shaped tiles made by the robot arm and the extruder. Natural cracks in the clay, together with the traces of the tools, are seen on the surface of the tiles. Each tile, based on observations of the clay, was expected to be cracked in a certain way and their current final aspect was created in combination with contingent and natural patterns caused by the surrounding environment, such as the temperature and humidity of the drying area. A total of 16 tile pieces were produced; while the artist had a large single image to present with these tiles, each piece was created individually.

Dongwook Hwang has worked for architectural offices in New York, Copenhagen, and Seoul. In 2016, he started Building Laboratory Architecture, the practice focusing on establishing naturalness using digital design approaches. Past projects include Incheon airport new terminal competition (in Heerim Architecture), Buljisunwon (TSP Architecture), Sewoon Sangga design competition (in Lokal Design), Nodeul Island design competition (with Urban Terrain Lab and Studio OL), Architecture Building Workshop in ACC (with Namho Cho).

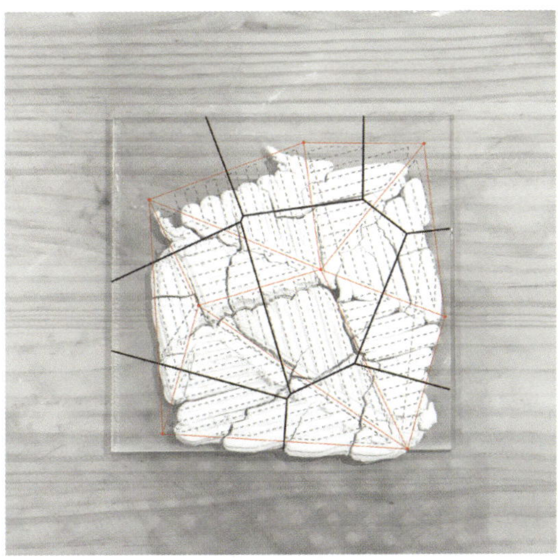

Unnatural ceramic tile pattern. Image: provided by artist.

Natural ceramic tile pattern. Image: provided by artist.

Two Hands
Sunshine Underground

Two Hands is an archiving project for the Neo Manufacturing Workshops where new technologies are demonstrated. As such the project focuses on capturing the images of the robot and human hands. It captures the elegant movement of the robot hand; the human hand must go through complex and difficult movements before the robot can work. The robot hand performs elaborate tasks according to CNC (computer numerical control) automation data; the human hands further refine what is already elaborated. *Two Hands* thus compares and contrasts the human and robotic input in the new manufacturing by means of comparing and contrasting two hands, one belonging to the robot and the other to the human. The work also shows the two hands forming a new relationship.

Sunshine Underground is a graphic design studio based in Seoul. Sunshine Underground produces work at the intersection of graphic design, user interface, moving image, and live performance. The studio has directed music videos of various K-pop artists including Younha and Lee Seung-hwan, and participated in the exhibition as a production team in media art installations displayed in Gwangju Design Biennale, Culture Station Seoul 284.

A robot hand and a human hand (top); robot making a 3D clay print (bottom). Photo: provided by artist.

Form Finding with Robotics

Stylianos Dritsas

Digital design and fabrication technologies such as parametric modeling and industrial robotics through the integration of software and hardware offer opportunities for creative experimentation with material transformation processes in ways which could not have been achieved in the past. Of particular interest to us is the realm of processes that no longer either attempt to map traditional human actions of design thinking and construction into the digital medium or the enforcement of design thought into materiality by powerful machinery such as the design complex forms machined or 3D printed in absence of material integration. Certainly those are valuable in automation of construction, manufacturing and general engineering but there are opportunities to discover new processes, some of which may become the new norm. The concept of deriving artifacts, sometimes driven by aesthetics, sometimes by functional requirements, preferably by combinations thereof, from the interplay of materiality and the formation process is what is inspiring in form-finding. The presented process and case study offer a general approach in thinking and making at the boundaries between physical and digital design.

Stylianos Dritsas is an assistant professor in the department of Architecture and Sustainable Design at the Singapore University of Technology and Design. His research, practice, and teaching work are in the area of digital design and fabrication. He is the director of Jeneratiff Pte Ltd and co-director of Robotics Innovation Laboratory at SUTD.

PET thermaforming plastic procedure by robot arm operation. Image: provided by artist.

PET thermaforming plastic procedure tiles. Image: provided by artist.

3D-printing electroconductive material, using a robot arm. Photo: Yu Seung-jun.

Electrical Skin
Hyunchul Kwon (ETH Zurich, Digital Building Technologies)

Electrical Skin is a robotically 3D printed free-form façade-panel with integrated lighting. For the first time in architecture, not only the complex form, but also the electric infrastructure are fabricated in a single process. This project showcases how leaps in computation and digital fabrication can revolutionize architectural components.

Research for the project and the workshop is carried out by the chair for DBT, ETH Zurich and supported by National Centre of Competence in Research (NCCR) Digital Fabrication. Research assistant: Thodoris Kyttas (master of advanced studies [MAS] student in Architecture and Digital Fabrication, ETH Zurich).

Architect Hyunchul Kwon is a doctoral researcher at Digital Building Technologies chair(DBT), D-ARCH, ETH Zurich, exploring new building technologies based on additive manufacturing strategies. His research focuses on multi-directional 3D printing of carbon fiber composites for architecture. He received a master of architecture (Dist) degree from The Bartlett School of Architecture UCL, where he taught and lectured thereafter. His work has been exhibited internationally in museums such as the Vitra Design Museum, the Zaha Hadid Design Gallery, the MAK Museum Vienna and the Design Exchange in Toronto.

The wave patterns of the participants' voices are formed with a robot cutter. Image: provided by artist.

Communication Landscape
HENN + Technische Universität Darmstadt Digital Design Unit

Visitors will interact with a real-time robotical-ly-driven production line. The design of objects is algorithmically based on visitors' sounds translated into virtual geometry and materialized by an industrial robot. Prosumers create their own unique objects, while at the same time generating a silent community of voices, a *Communication Landscape*.

Supported by ABB Germany.

HENN is an international architecture office with offices in Munich, Berlin, and Beijing and has expertise in the fields of culture and office buildings, teaching and research as well as development, production, and masterplanning. Continuity, coupled with progressive design approaches and methods and interdisciplinary research projects, forms the basis for a continual examination of current issues and for a consistent design philosophy. Forms and spaces are no mere objective, they are developed from the processes, demands, and cultural contexts of each project.

Technische Universität Darmstadt Digital Design Unit (DDU) develops computational design techniques and processes that improve collaboration, simulation, and materialization within the field of architecture to contribute to a versatile living environment.

Seoyeon Cho, *Facade Platform*, Changsin-dong Spinoff Gallery, exterior. Photo: Kyungsub Shin Studio.

Changsin-dong, a Platform for a New Industrial Ecosystem

Seungmin Kim + Isak Chung

Changsin-dong is a neighborhood in Seoul where low-rise residential buildings and small garment factories are concentrated. Located in the vicinity of the Dongdaemun fashion complex, it produces and supplies low-end fashion clothing lines to the complex. In the heyday of the garment industry in Korea, much larger garment factories filled what is now Dongdaemun Fashion Complex and the upper floors of the adjacent Pyeonghwa Market. Today, owing to the changes in the character and size of the garment industry, they have been replaced by small factories with no more than an average of three employees. These small factories have penetrated deep into the alleyways of Changsin-dong, formerly a residential neighborhood. The neighborhood once faced the threat of being erased. However, the "New Town" plan for the neighborhood was cancelled and it was instead designated by the city government as a leader in urban regeneration. The official designation ends this year. In the meantime the neighborhood received much media and public attention. *Project Seoul Apparel* begins with an examination of positive and negative impacts brought on by such attention in both public and private spheres.

The Changsin-dong garment industry is losing its force. Young people in the nation's garment industry do not want to work here. What is needed is not an urban environmental regeneration but an industrial boost along with qualitative improvement of the environment. *Project Seoul Apparel* delves into issues that small factory owners and workers in the neighborhood cannot, for they have more immediate issues of survival to deal with. The project proposes new sources of work and formation of new networks, as well as improvements in the environment and its systems. The proposal reflects many possibilities that are rooted in local reality and understood by the local population. The project intends to make sure that system streamlining does not stop environmental repair. It also aims to raise the functional goal and design qualities; owners and workers believe they are producing at their highest level, but, in fact, they feel function and design could be improved. Changshin-dong is used to working at a fast pace, mostly producing design copies. Could they change? The freelance "guest workers" are mostly used to doing only repetitive work. Could small factories relying on such a workforce change the quality of their output? Is there a new role they can play? How is it possible to improve the production system of mid-sized factories for both internally and externally sourced production? Architects, urban researchers, fashion designers, and film directors are some of the participants in this project. They are fully aware of the issues elaborated above. What we would like to see take place are advanced forms of networking and work environments in which the various local factory owners and guest workers, young fashion designers and producers, workers, sellers, and relevant city administrators and officials can come together, meet each other and work in solidarity. The question is, what would it take to create such a network and environment? And how diverse would they be?

Project Seoul Apparel was a joint project of *UK/Korea 2017–18 Connected City*. It was organized in collaboration with the Seoul Design Foundation Garment Industry Team and advised by Dr. Chun Soonok who is an eminent labor rights advocate in Korean garment industry and currently a member Korea's National Assembly, and by the associates of the Fashion Programmes of the Royal College of Art, London.

Stephanie Seungmin Kim is the director of Iskai Contemporary Art, a curatorial research center specializing in large-scale, international exhibitions. She holds a BA from Sotheby's Institute and an MA in the history of art from UCL, University of London and is currently pursuing a PhD in Curating Contemporary Art at the Royal College of Art. Kim has directed more than eighty exhibitions in fifteen cities, including Liverpool Biennial City States (2010, 2012), UK–Korea Friendship Year Exhibitions (2013), UNESCO Paris HQ Exhibition (2014), Venice Biennale Parallel Exhibition and Singapore Open Media Festival (2015), Jikji Korea International Festival (2016), and many others. She received the Minister of Culture, Sports and Tourism Award in 2009.

Isak Chung is a director of a.co.lab and an assistant professor at Dongyang University. Chung has conducted public research projects and social architecture works including the Master Plan of DMZ Peace Park, Artist Residence at Propaganda Village, Yeonpyeong Library, Hello Museum, and Dongducheon Community Rehabilitation Center. He was co-curator of the urban art project 2015 Seoul Seoul Seoul and served as the associate curator of the Korean Pavilion for the 15th Venice Architecture Biennale in 2016. Chung is credited as an honorary professor of culture and art and was awarded the Excellence Prize of the Korea Public Design Award in 2015 by the Ministry of Culture, Sports & Tourism.

Changsin-dong Spinoff Gallery. Photo: Kyungsub Shin Studio.

Guide to Seoul Apparel
Koo Young Han (Urban Hybrid)

The Dongdaemun area in Seoul is the optimal place to start a fashion business. A variety of raw materials can be purchased at the Dongdaemun Market and skilled fashion makers in the residential areas of Changsin-dong and Sindang-dong offer specialized services. *Guide to Seoul Apparel* places resources of the fashion industry and a series of production processes of the Dongdaemun area on the map, by means of which it sheds new light on Seoul as a garment production city. Data collected through local studies concerning the current status and resources of the Dongdaemun Market, Jongno 5-ga and 6-ga, Changsin-dong, and Sindang-dong are visualized on maps and printed materials.

Guidebook 1: Super A3 Map is an archive map for creative people. It will be distributed free of charge at the 630-1 Changsin-dong Exhibition Hall. All processes including designing, purchasing raw materials, producing, and selling can be recorded on the map. Together with ready-made items such post-its or memo pads, a more three-dimensional archiving is possible.

Guidebook 2: Double A1 Map is an ultra-large, three-dimensional map of the heart of Seoul. The 8-kilometer distance from the Seoul Station to Wangsimni is depicted on a single page, allowing the viewer to see at a glance many interesting places in Seoul. It has been exhibited at 630-1 Changsin-dong, at the Design Studio space, together with *Changsin Wardrobes*.

Seoul was not planned as a city for production. Seoul's manufacturing neighborhoods were created spontaneously as part of a manufacturing ecosystem. A map expressing a production city such as this should reflects the traces of those who actually use the space. It is hoped that this small archive for a better production city will lead to a meaningful discussion to improve *Project Seoul Apparel* businesses.

Koo Young Han is an urban researcher who tries to combine big data and spatial data to analyse the complex city system. He continues to work with maps hosting MySpecialMap.net and SmallSeoulAtlas.com. Recently, he received a PhD in urban planning. His research is about analysing and describing local fashion industry networks in the Dongdaemun fashion cluster. He studied in Shared City Lab at GSES, SNU, and is a co-founder of Urban Hybrid.

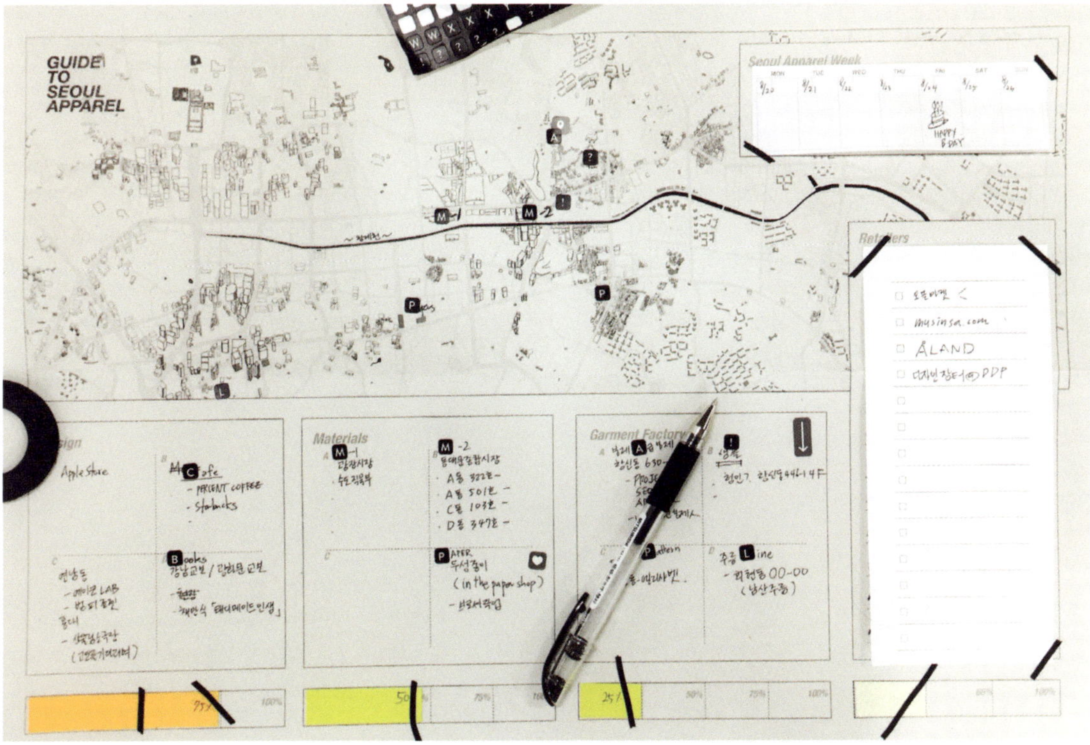

Guide to Seoul Apparel package. Image: provided by artist.

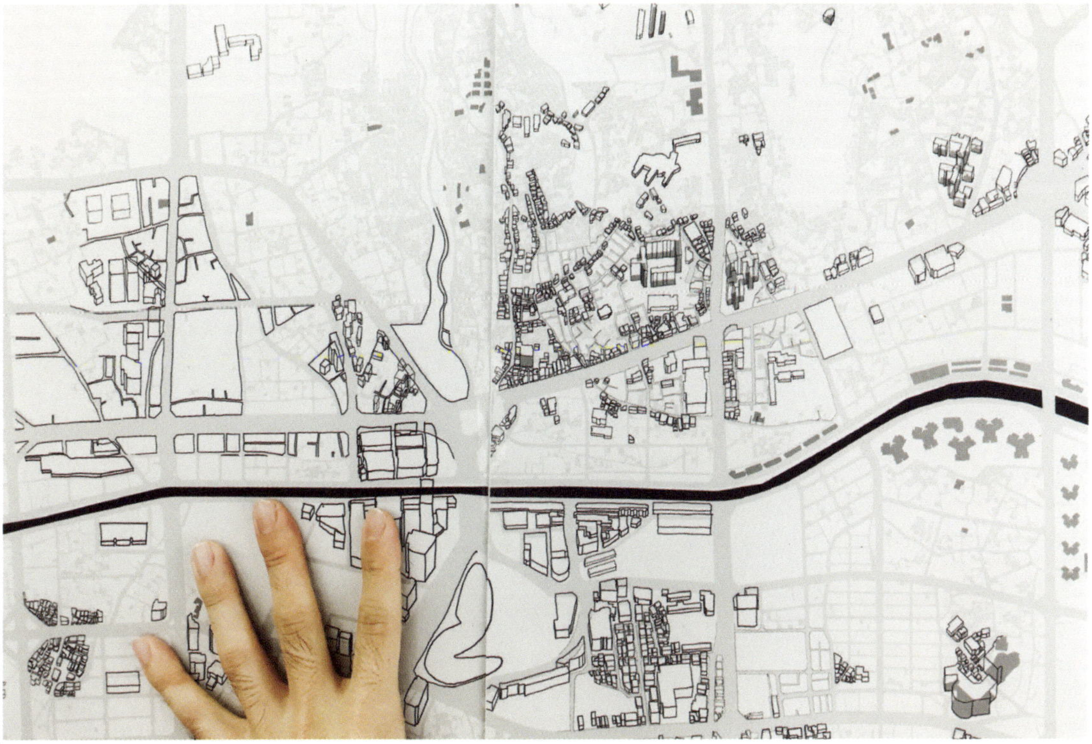

Map of Changsin-dong, *Guide to Seoul Apparel*. Image: provided by artist.

Changsin Wardrobes
Heeyoung Jung

Changsin Wardrobes presents designs focusing on fabrics, processing methods, sewing forms, and subsidiary materials used in the Changsin-dong area garment factories. Completed costumes are displayed in the archiving bag for the audience's perusal, along with information on the fabric, the raw material sources, production processes, and production partners.

Through repeat business *Project Seoul Apparel* seeks to accumulate data concerning clothing and clothing manufacturing processes, while *Changsin Wardrobes*, in sharing the data, endeavors to build up a substantial and useful archive for collaborations between designers looking for production partners and the sewing factories in Changsin-dong .

Heeyoung Jung runs her own brand, BUMPY GEORGETTE, which designs scenes for each concept, then manufactures and sells components of the space. Jung engages in production activities regardless of the space, craft or design area. She has participated as a mentor for Craft Design Star-product Development Project at the Korea Crafts & Design Foundation (KCDF) since 2016 and is a DDP 2016 Design & Cultural Product Development Business selected company.

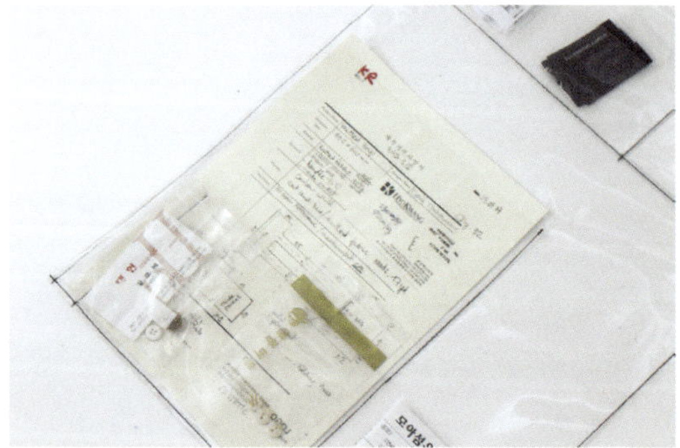

Order sheet. Image: provided by artist.

Archiving bag. Image: provided by artist.

Prototypical Factory
Jieun Lee

The main cause of the decline of the Changsin-dong garment industry is its exclusive reliance on Dongdaemun Market for sourcing its work. The factories typically have short production times, the workers work long hours and receive low wages, and factory conditions are usually sub-standard. Workers can hardly make a living working under such conditions, and their sense of self-worth decreases. Ultimately the younger generation of garment industry professionals, designers and workers alike, would become completely indifferent to the neighborhood.

With these thoughts in mind, *Prototypical Factory* proposes a unit factory prototype which, as a precedent, can vitalize the sewing industry in Chansin-dong. What this project has in mind is the improvement of the physical environment of the factories. At the same time, it hopes to also bring about a change in the production system and space in such a way that direct collaborations between new designers and the temporary workers would be possible. It would be "a place of collaboration" and a "multi-purpose storage drawer." What is expected is that such a setup would bring about client diversification, co-existence through collaboration, and improvement of workers' technical skills and their sense of self-worth, and that the improvements with such a macroscopic approach would ultimately lead to revitalization of the Changsin-dong garment district.

Jieun Lee (BSc, AA Dipl, ARB/RIBA) is an architect with experience in Korea and the UK. Lee is a principal of SSWA and an adjunct professor at Korea National University of Arts. Emphasizing qualities of "attitude/principles/sensitivity," she has contributed to various public projects including House of YeeSang, Haedo Elderly Welfare Center, Gasan Community Center, and Gumcheon Folly Park.

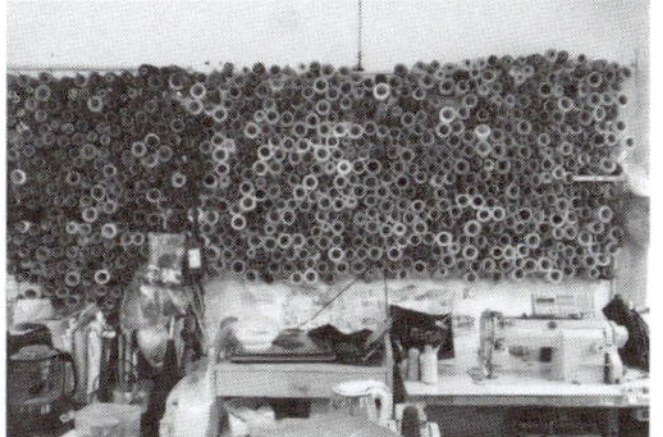

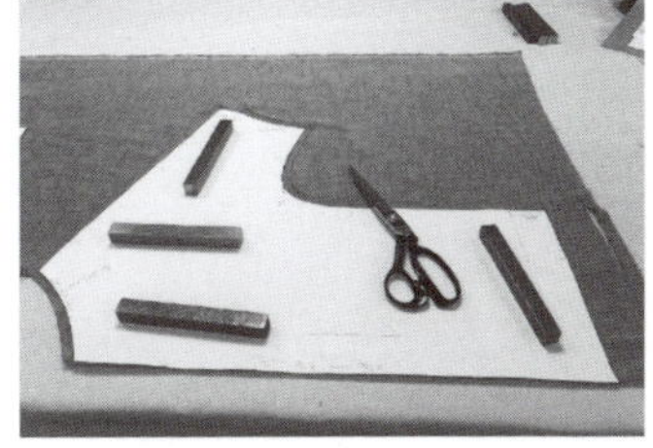

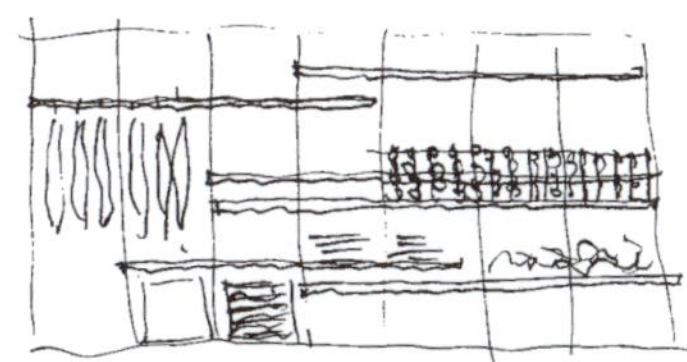

Conceptual drawing for *Prototypical Factory*. Image: provided by artist.

Façade Platform
Seoyeon Cho

Façade Platform proposes a general-purpose elevation system for Changsin-dong garment factories. The project starts with an observation that the garment factories densely clustered in Changsin-dong share a number of common architectural characteristics. First of all, they are generally located at street level. Second, the front of the building (the façade) is relatively narrow compared to the depth of the building. The elevation, or the façade, is where the building and the city meet. It is a window through which various levels of communication take place. It is through here that not only people but fabrics, sewing materials, semi-completed garments slated for delivery to the next processing post come and go; it is also where the garbage from the factory, fresh air, scattering dust, steam and condensation from irons, refrigerants for air conditioners, and so on, go in and out. The façade is also the "face" of the factory; the signboard hanging on the façade of the building literally identifies the place as a factory. The face of a factory is also the face of the people working in the factory as well. The current faces, or the façades, as represented by the letters, materials, and a wide array of information displayed by them, seem somewhat disorganized. *Façade Platform* recognizes such diversity and provides a framework, a platform, for a practical reorganization of the diversity. The project provides solutions to the individual problems the factories face. Ultimately, the project intends to reconstruct the collective impression of the Changsin-dong area.

Seoyeon Cho graduated with a BSC from the Department of Architectural Engineering at Korea University and an MSC from the Swiss Federal Institute of Technology at Zürich, Switzerland. Since then, he has worked as an assistant professor in the Department of Architecture at Dankook University. He considers architecture that reflects the current time and space most rationally from the perspective of being a product of accumulated times and places.

Study of façades. Photo: Seoyeon Cho.

A scene from the film *Parallel Scenarios*. Image: provided by artist.

Parallel Scenarios
Jongkwan Paik

Parallel Scenarios shows the progress of *Project Seoul Apparel* through video works. The scenes are composed of the two-dimensional images of the works created by participating architects, urban researchers, and fashion designers. For example, a scene in the video is a computer monitor screen; it is the scene of one of the participants operating a computer to do the drawing to effectively reorganize a vacant lot at 630-1 Changsin-dong. Another scene is an infographic map showing the current status of the Changsin-dong garment factories. Yet another scene is a shot of a designer marking and cutting the fabric according to a pattern. The screen alternately shows the marked fabric and the scissors cutting the fabric. Experts from different fields had ideas built upon their own areas of work; the ideas that stood on different levels outside of the project coalesced, sometimes by accident, with the physical space of Changsin-dong as an adhesive agent. *Parallel Scenarios* presents a three-dimensional view of the "narrative" of the scenario called *Project Seoul Apparel* by overlapping the process of completing the space at 630-1 Changsin-dong with the process of completing a piece garment (a piece of work) from the design stage to the final completion stage.

Jongkwan Paik completed a BA in psychology and an MFA in film. He continues to produce experimental films based on research with in-depth study of images. His film *Cyclical Night* (2016) received the Director's Prize from Jeonju International Film Festival and the Jury Prize from Seoul Independent Film Festival. His documentary *Unfold the Theater* (2014) was screened at Seoul International Architecture Film Festival.

Efficiency Aesthetics
Luke Stevens, Marie Maisonneuve

Presented through the graphic codes of factory ephemera, *Efficiency Aesthetic 1* features observations on themes of hybridity and the complex multiplicities of re-appropriation at work within the global fashion industry. These observations are transformed through a process of repeated translation, revealing the poetics present within this breakdown of brand logos and consumer slogans. Through an extensive residency and working with specialists in Changsin-dong, *EA1* includes Seoul within a global debate about the speed and retranslation of fashion where the "original" or origins of a design are now impossible to trace or track. The language of fashion, its translation and the reappropriation of luxury branding/signifiers is represented to suggest Seoul is repositioning itself as a very knowing and reflexive community of makers with a burgeoning young designer led fashion culture.

EA2 reflects the importance of the human network within Changsin-dong, enabling a complex yet efficient industry. The knitted harness produced in the UK creates an emotional container for the worker. Locally mass-produced knitted bags introduce the notion of time, care and sustainability. The content of the bags compare the components used within the two locations.

EA3 is a series of hand-customized *tosi*, or the garments widely worn by workers within the manufacturing industry. Mass-produced by local factories, the *tosi* become a platform to gather comments on the future of the manufacturing industry in Changsin-dong. Testimonies are collected from a wide range of sources—from the factory floor to government—offering a place for both celebration and critique.

Graphics for *Efficiency Aesthetics* envelopes. Image: provided by artist.

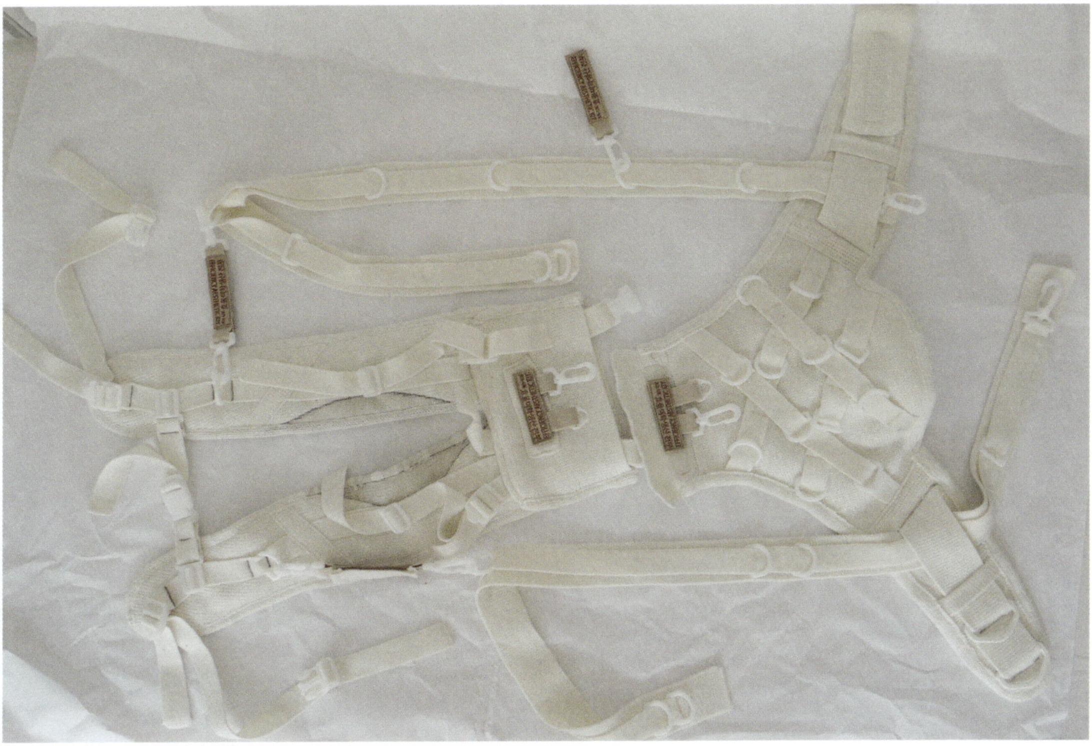

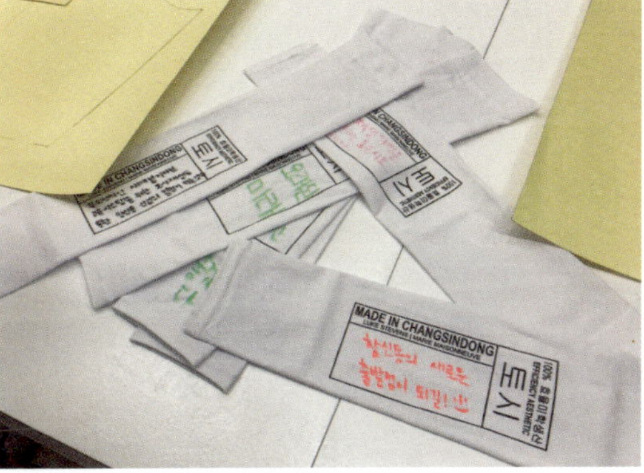

The structure of knitted harness. Image: provided by artist.

Participatory *tosi* ("arm glove") project.
Image: provided by artist.

Efficiency Aesthetic 2 was supported by Zegna Baruffa Italia.

Luke Stevens is a designer living and working in London. Luke graduated from the Menswear Programme at the Royal College of Art in 2016. Recent exhibitions include Toilet Break, London Design Festival (2016); Modebelofte, Dutch Design Week, Eindhoven (2016); FABRICLIVE, Averard Hotel, London (2016).

Marie Maisonneuve is a French designer living and working in London. She graduated with a master's degree in menswear knitwear at the Royal College of Art in 2016, and continues her practice freelancing for London Fashion Week. She has also taken part in exhibitions including, Modebelofte: Adaptive Traveler, Dutch Design Week (2016); Nomadic Fluidity, Performance show, Averard Hotel London (2016). Marie recently became involved with an exciting collaborative fashion label named CONGREGATION design.

Participatory Workshops

Recycling Network Workshop
22–23 August 2017
AMP + BARE+ Art and Disaster + Fining
E-Waster + PRAG

The ultimate goal of recycling includes a wide range of issues faced by the manufacturing industry, such as resource depletion and production ethics. The organizers of this workshop would like to consider recycling not simply as a step in the production process but as part of it. Recycling issues must be examined from the perspective of the entire production system. The workshop has practical definitions of recycling issues that fully reflect local concerns and conditions. The goal of the program is to innovate the recycling system itself. It reconstructs new values of productivity within the existing system, and it suggests real benefits and possibilities that can be returned to the manufacturers.

Participatory workshop:
Reformable Mold

Participatory workshop:
Robotic Craft Education

Reformable Mold
23–24 September 2017
Hyun Parke

Casting is an effective way in generating multiple copies of a thing. However, the drawback is the initial high cost of constructing the mold. Furthermore, when it comes to making a mold, there is not much difference between past and present methods. Workshop participants experienced casting a form of their own design through *Reformable Mold* which enabled the participants to express various forms using the computer.

Robotic Ceramic Workshop
13–14 October 2017
Pil Joon Jeon + B.A.T + Sena Gu

If the latest manufacturing techniques are combined with traditional crafts, what would the results look like? *Robotics Ceramic Workshop* is a place where pottery, one of the oldest crafts, and the latest robotics technology meet. It allows the participants to be familiarized with various cutting-edge techniques and skills used in clay 3D printing, 3D modeling, robotic control via visual scripting, and basic operating methods of a robot arm. The workshop was planned to give participants an opportunity to make first-hand products of their own design.

Robotic Craft Education
20–22 October 2017
Stylianos Dritsas + Dongwook Hwang

Digital design and fabrication technologies such as parametric modeling and industrial robotics through the integration of software and hardware offer opportunities for creative experimentation with material transformation processes in ways that could not have been achieved in the past. The workshop investigates the domain in between physical and digital design and fabrication in the context of architectural robotics. The objective of the workshop is to overcome the conceptual hiatus between physical and digital form-finding and explore a new perspective that fuses materiality with its formation process.

Production Talks: Network Series

Recycling Network
8 September 2017, 7–9 pm
AMP, BARE, Finding E-Waste, Art and Disaster, PRAG

The ultimate goal of recycling includes a wide range of issues faced by the manufacturing industry, such as resource depletion and production ethics. In this sense, the idea of recycling simply as an extra step in waste management is inadequate. Furthermore, recycling is a global issue. Participants listened to architects and artists from Ghana, the Philippines, India, and Korea (Euljiro), who talked about the status of industrial waste, activities of their groups in promoting recycling, and their thoughts and suggestions. They shared their thoughts on the need to renew the definition of the value of productivity and on how such a broad change could bring real benefits to those who are producers in such a system.

System Understanding and Suggestion
21 September 2017, 7–9 pm
Presentation: MOTOElastico

This talk provides the audience with an opportunity for getting to know the research and the work process of MOTOElastico, a participating artist in the Seoul Biennale, while examining the environment in which products are manufactured and delivered in the Euljiro and Dongdaemun areas. The participants then had a discussion on the possible ways in which the Euljiro and Dongdaemun areas could change in the future.

New Movement at Sewoon Sangga
19 October 2017, 5–8 pm
Presentation: Tenants of Again Sewoon

There are old and new tenants at Sewoon Sangga. Their blueprints for Sewoon Sangga and the Euljiro area sometimes differ and sometimes overlap. Participants toured Sewoon Sangga with the city officials as well as other stakeholders involved in the new developments at Sewoon Sangga where the past and future coexist.

Euljiro Collaboration: By Euljiro
31 October 2017, 7–9 pm
Hyesun Lee, Jeong Gi-won, By Euljiro designers and manufacturers

By Euljiro was a component of the larger project that was *Euljiro: Lightway 2017* (1–5 November 2017), which was a series of projects, exhibitions, and public events organized by Jung-gu Office (Seoul) and Seoul Design Foundation, independent of the Seoul Biennale 2017. For the By Euljiro project, artists and designers were matched with local lighting manufacturers in the Euljiro area to produce, exhibit, and sell new products. *Production City*, a component of the Seoul Biennale, invited the By Euljiro team as an example of the collaboration that is possible between designers/artists and local manufacturers, and to give a public talk. Topics of the talk and of the following discussion included new approaches to and possibilities for design, production, distribution, and consumption of lighting fixtures, as well as a potential for a comprehensive approach to local industry and neighborhood regeneration.

Production Talk: Recycling Network

Production Talk: Euljiro Collaboration

Production Talks: Fabrication Agency Round Table

Robotics: Materiality in Robotic Fabrication
4 September 2017, 7–9 pm
Saqib Aziz (HENN Berlin), Hyunchul Kwon (ETH Zurich)

Industrial robots are machines that were originally designed for repetitive automation work. In more recent years, they have been utilized for creative production. It has been shown that they can be utilized for customized work. The round table was organized to hear from some the Seoul Biennale participants who used a robot to create new works.

Brick: Niche of Universality
13 September 2017, 7–9 pm
B.A.T., Soo-in Yang, Kim Yang-gil, Han Sang-gon

Brick has been the most familiar and universal building material in human history. Any new method of brick manufacturing and brick construction would be hard to come by. However, big and small attempts have been made continuously. Architects/designers, manufacturers, and contractors are all affected by this building material. This round table was prepared to hear about how they select what bricks to use, and what their roles are.

Metal: Lucid Touch of Craftsmanship
11 October 2017, 7–9 pm
Joyeong Industry Co., Ltd., Kuk Hyeong-geol, SoA, Nameless Architecture

Joyeong Industry is a local metal works company based in the city of Daejeon. The company has been working with a number of different architects whose projects required idiosyncratic forms of metal processing. This roundtable focuses on the form and process of collaboration between the manufacturer and the architects.

Ultra High Performance Concrete (UHPC): A Struggle for Introducing a New Material
25 October 2017, 7–9 pm
Lee Jeong-hoon, Chanjoong Kim

Concrete is the most cost-effective building material of our time. It is a product that can fully benefit from economies of scale. There are many efforts to improve its performance and to thus expand its market. In 2016, architect Chanjoong Kim used UHPC in a building project for the first time in Korea. In the process his team went through a battery of hurdles with the authorities to prove the new material's performance and safety standards. Since then, a new ecosystem of relations has developed among researchers, architects, and contractors around the usage of the new material. In the last of the round table talk series, two architects gave their first-hand experience of using UHPC and of the new relations that developed.

Production Talk: A New Wave at Sewoon Sangga

MOTOElastico, *Narrow City*. Daerim-W305. Photo: Kyungsub Shin Studio.

Toru Hasegawa and Mark Collins, *Brainwave Flaneur*.
Photo: provided by artist.

WALKING THE COMMONS

WALKING THE COMMONS: ENVIRONMENT, USER, CREATOR

Kyung Jae Kim
*Curator, Seoul Biennale 2017;
co-director, Common Practice*

Soo-in Yang
*Curator, Seoul Biennale 2017;
director, Lifethings*

Traditionally, pedestrian environments were built with the purpose of moving people from one point to another in space. The relationship between the two, that is between the environment and the user (pedestrian), was also uni-directional. An institution or an individual provided the physical infrastructure, and it was the role of the public to accept and use it. Today, we witness the development of smart mobility, and in particular, rapid technological advances in driverless cars and other personal mobility vehicles or devices. It is conceivable that, at some point in the future, it would no longer be necessary for humans to walk even a short distance. Walking will no longer be a utilitarian activity, of moving oneself from point A to B, but an activity for leisure. The four projects of *Walking the Commons* (see the diagram in the next page), experiment with how the creator, an intervener—such as a designer, for example—may intervene in the relationship between the environment and the user and add values worthy of pedestrian experience. Ultimately, the projects ask if creators could intervene in the relationship, redefine it, and reorient its direction.

In *Musicity*, the creator (C) is inspired by the environment (E), and the output is delivered to the users (U) at certain points in space, or coordinates. Here the relationship is somewhat unidirectional, where each music created by a composer is dependent on the physical coordinate/environment only to become part of the environment again. The user, in order to access the creator's music, must come to the same coordinate where the creator was initially inspired. In this sense, *Musicity* is coordinate-dependent. In terms of this coordinate-depenency, the environment to creator direction in *Playable City* is the same. However, in this case, the experience of the user can affect the output and the environment surrounding it. Thus the user-environment relationship here is bi-directional. *Brainwave Flaneur* brings a radically different approach to the conventional relationship in regard to the environment and how it is perceived. First of all, by participating in the project the user delivers data to the creator as to how she or he perceives and responds to the environment. The creator then interprets the data, which then can be used in future space designs. Such a project has much to suggest to design processes in public facilities in that data based on experience can be very important in designing new environments. Lastly, *Soundlines*, a project in which the relationships are most advanced, is where each of the three relationships operate on an interactive basis. Here the pedestrian experience takes place between the virtual environment (E') created by the creator and the physical environment (E). In turn, the user experience effects change in the virtual environemnt(E') where the real and the virtual are combined to give birth to a new ecology. In this regard, it is more innovative than other similar projects.

When smart mobility becomes a reality in the near future, the purpose of walking will change from mobility to leisure. The physical aspect of walking will not change, but people will now walk to play. Accordingly, enhancing the value obtained through walking will become increasingly more important.

Here, the party responsible for designing the pedestrian environment must be able create cultural and social values of walking beyond the scope of designing the physical environment or providing pedestrian amenities. The creator, that is, an intervener, must play the role of a choreographer in that she must design the pedestrian experience and coordinate various experiences in order to give new meaning to the act of walking.

Walking the Commons, Information Container, DDP. Photo: Kyungsub Shin Studio.

E
U
C
뇌파산책
B
E
U
C
플레이어블 시티
P
E'
E
U
C
소리숲길
S
이용
범위
E
U
C
뮤직시티
M
이용
범위

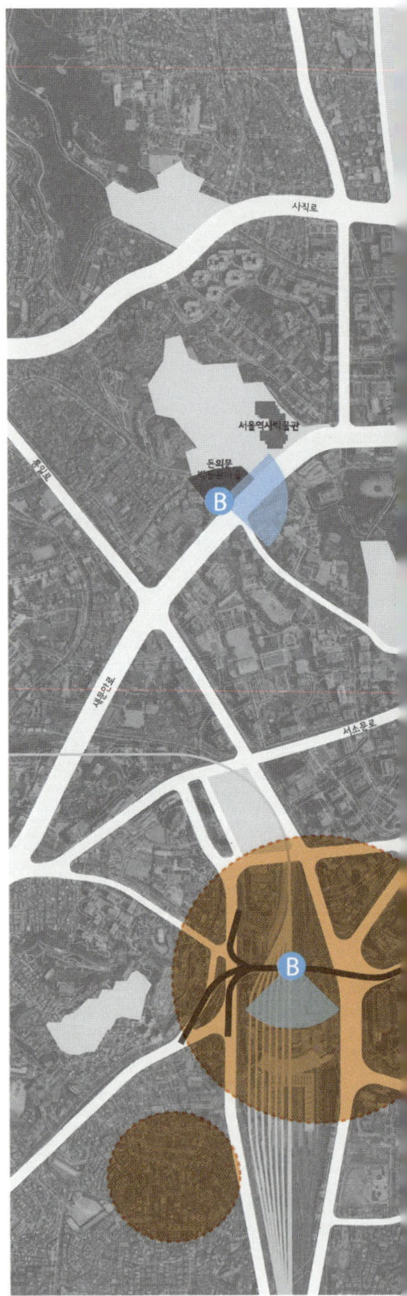
사직로
서울역사박물관
돈의문
박물관마을
통일로
새문안로
서소문로
B
B

율곡로
종묘
S
종로
세운상가
오토엘라스티코
청계천로
을지로
퇴계로
남산
한양도성
B
창신동
DDP

BRAINWAVE FLANEUR

Toru Hasegawa and Mark Collins

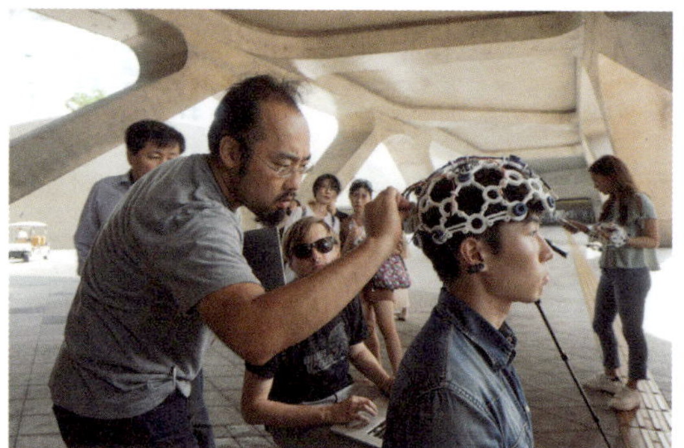

Utilizing low-cost EEG (electroencephalography) and geo-spatial tracking, the *Brainwave Flaneur* project correlates measured brain responses to curated environments situated throughout the city of Seoul. The use of EEG in-situ, or "in the wild," is a new frontier in neuroscience abetted by advances in mobile computing, increased robustness in sensors and new data processing capabilities. By measuring the evoked neural responses of multiple participants to prototypical and specific urban conditions we can visualize a hidden cognitive impact of the built environment.

The project focuses on visualizing neural signals that speak to a fundamental aspect of living in cities: stress. Participants of the workshop performed biofeedback exercises meant to augment specific EEG power bands—alpha, beta, theta and low gamma. These "brainwaves" are linked to the ability to downshift the brain into a more relaxed state of mind and even expand cognitive capabilities. The workshop produced a multitude of impressions to a diverse set of sites, coalescing in a shared dataset of neural recordings.

The equipment used in the project is the creation of OpenBCI, a NYC-based technology startup that it democratizing access to biosensing technology. The OpenBCI system, named for its open-source approach to development, is a 3d-printed headset coupled with a powerful bio-signal processor. Workshops began with an educational introduction to the technology and a hands-on experience with this BCI (brain computer interface) and brainwave visualization. Workshop participants did a simple biofeedback exercise in a comfortable setting and then traveled to a nearby site for a period of in-situ observation.

Zones of observation were located throughout the city, mirroring the Biennale's citywide siting. Each zone featured a unique urban landscape of stimulation ranging from elevated and underground pedestrian thoroughfares, areas of intense commerce, and the Dongdaemun Design Plaza, a dynamic arts complex in the center of Seoul. All participants contributed to a shared visualization of their experiences, staging a citywide image of neural activity. In this neural cartography project, accumulations of sensed experience highlight sites that provide feelings of safety and even sanctuary from urban overstimulation.

Analysis
Strong caveats should be noted; noise and electrical interference, some by surrounding power lines and other "in the wild" elements, means a low signal to noise ratio. Workshop participants contributed data to a shared visualization that reflected their sensed brain waves, and attempts were made to minimize unwanted noise. That said, analyzing the data as a group offers some intriguing ideas on how urban analysis via EEG recording could be realized. We focused on the "big three" power bands—alpha, beta/theta and gamma. Each is linked to a specific neural state, from meditative, drowsiness and active cognition (respectively). This EEG band analysis allows us to re-organize the exhibition sites according to the brain states they evoke.

Perhaps unsurprisingly, the ultra-contemporary "hybrid" landscapes of the Dongdaemun Design Plaza and the Seoullo 7017 Skygarden correlated strongly in our dataset. These active sites read as the extreme high and low in the beta/theta topological map. Participants showed more indicators of relaxation and cognition in these sites. The more conventional urban forms were almost indistinguishable from each other in our data, despite being strongly differentiated physically (ranging from underground walkways to parks). Participants showed similar alertness, or cognitive engagement, in these conventional sites, signified by a strong low-gamma activation.

Contemporary architecture, and the trend towards creatively mixing the indoors and outdoors, is epitomized in these two sites by Zaha Hadid Architects and MVRDV. Their forms minimize the inherent visual noise of urbanism and nature while offering long concourses of simplified circulation for our Flâneurs. This dataset suggests they might also offer a mental respite to visitors as well.

Bio-Sensing in Planning
Bio-sensing metrics will be one among many data points that can impact planning, design, programming, and administration of public spaces. We propose that this is the natural extension of the city's progressive planning mandate—to support their occupants' well-being in a safe and accessible city. "In the Wild" brainwave sensing gives a unique window into what are fundamentally subjective human experiences of their environment. The resulting visualizations, from neuro-topographic maps to neural space plots can help us to understand if our most daring architecture will act as an urban stressor or therapy.

Toru Hasegawa has been teaching and practicing in New York City and Tokyo since 2006. Toru is currently a Co-director of Columbia GSAPP's Cloud Lab and an adjunct assistant faculty member at the Columbia University GSAPP where he teaches advanced design studios and seminars on building construction technology and spatial computing. He is also the co-creator of Morpholio's apps, developing new ways in which the proliferation of device culture, the development of the cloud, and the ubiquity of social networking, are collectively shaping the creative process. He is also the co-founder of Proxy Design Studio which explores potentials within the computational paradigm for a range of clients and institutions, providing expertise in both design and realization.

Mark Collins is a teacher, designer, and programmer investigating the culture of technology in architecture. At Columbia University's Graduate School of Architecture, Planning and Preservation, Mark co-directs the Cloud Lab, an experimental laboratory that explores the design of our environment through emerging platforms in device culture. Mark is an adjunct assistant professor at the GSAPP where he has led studios, seminars, and workshops on design computing and digital fabrication. Mark is also a co-founder of Morpholio, a suite of mobile tools empowering creative individuals. Morpholio's apps have been featured everywhere from Wired to Fast Company and its creative community boasts more than a million users.

The observation task, which included recording of eye blinks and other artifacts for 15 second intervals prior to observation, is visible in this time plot of filtered EEG data.

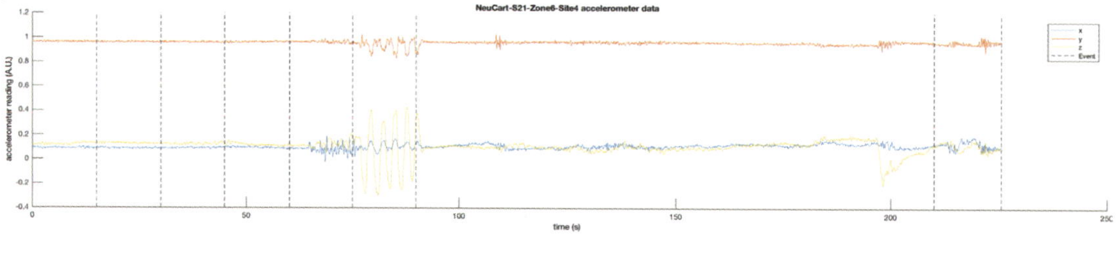

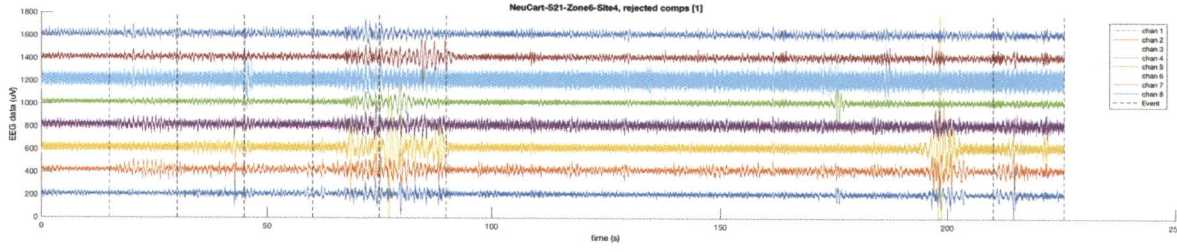

Neurally-similar locations cluster together in this Neural Frequency Space diagram. Position in each dimension represents a "big 3" band power.

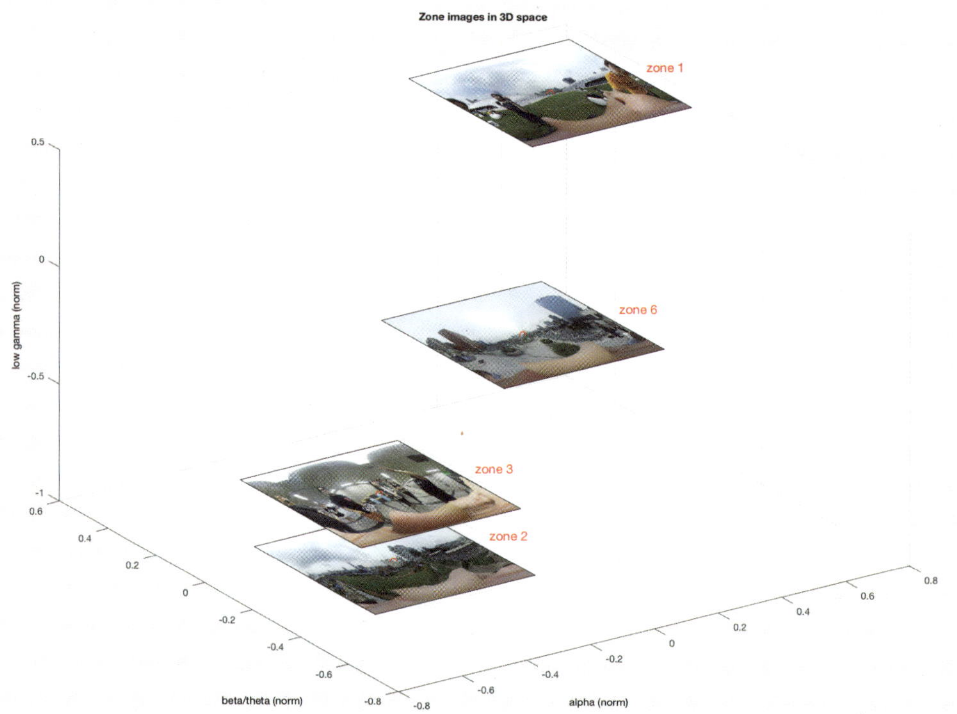

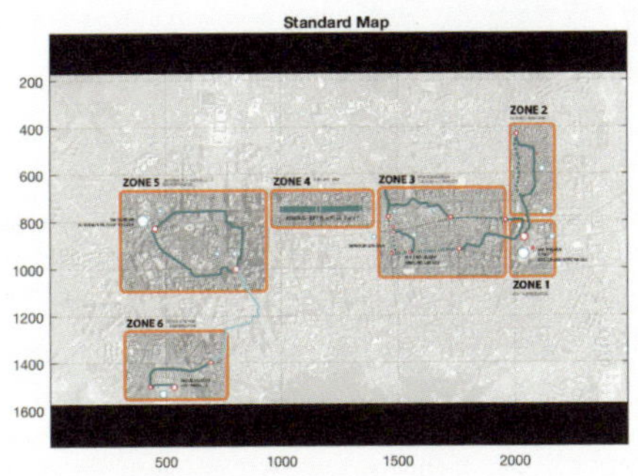

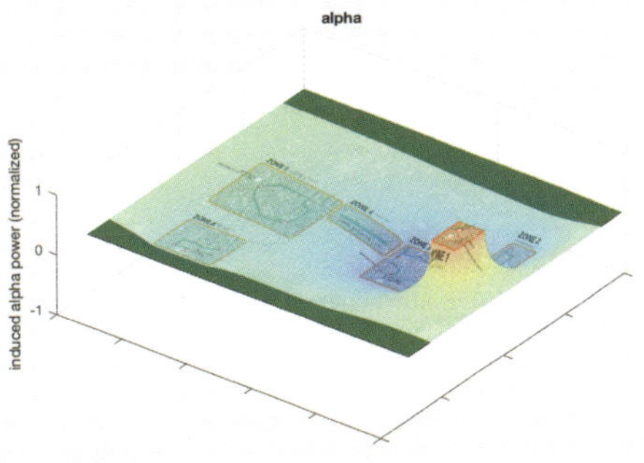

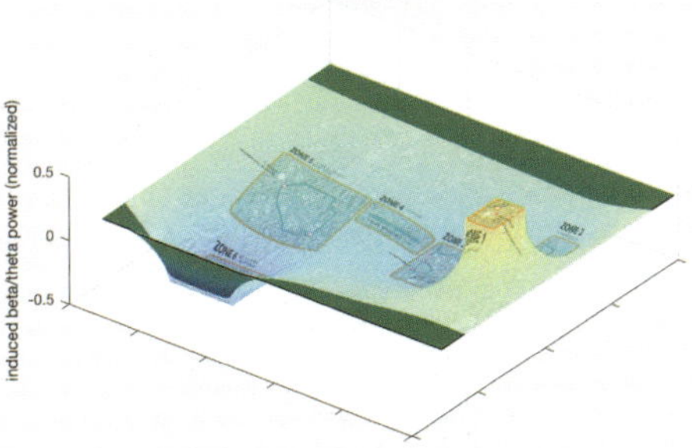

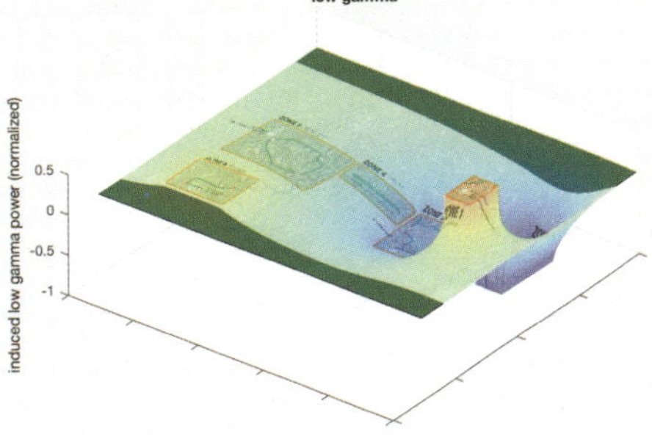

Neuro-topographical Maps. Elevation
and color of zone indicates power in a
"big 3" frequency band.

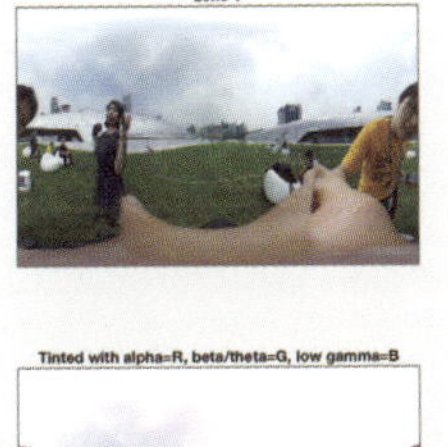

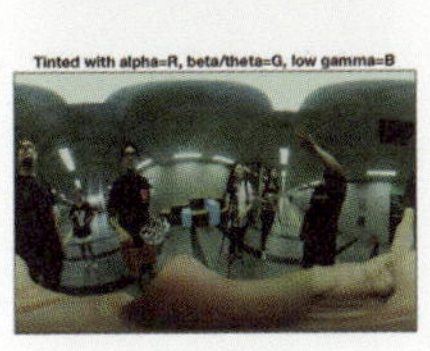

Normalized power in each "big 3"
band added to R/G/B channel. Red
represents alpha's relaxation, green
represents beta's drowsiness, blue
represents gamma's cognition.

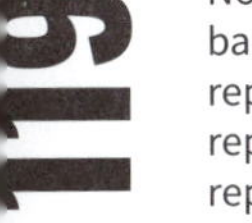

SOUNDLINES

Kayip, Gangil Yi

A city is a super-organism, the result of an emergent phenomenon in which the intimate interactions of the sub-structures lead to new features of the superstructure. Even the micro-act of people who move to another region leads to macro-structural development of the city. However, it is extremely difficult to observe this evolution which takes place over a very long period of time from a human point of view. The *Soundlines* project seeks to expose the essential attributes of these cities—the macroscopic structure that grows through bottom-up processes— through urban environmental data. This data maps the interaction between virtual ecosystems and human beings. By exploring the sound forest through a mobile app, pedestrians will be able to experience the urban mechanism that exists beneath the daily space. The sound forest grows from multi-layered data which constitutes the urban environment. In multi-zoned sites, data that quantifies the urban environment provides growth for virtual botanical communities. The plant species that constitute each community produce sounds of different textures. While walking through the sound forests, visitors will experience the various sound combinations generated by the plants. Visits to each area will then again become important data which will determine the advancement of the forest ecosystem. The constructed sound forest ecosystem is the result of the interaction between urban space and human beings as well as an auditory reflection of the bottom-up processes of the urban mechanism. While experiencing the urban space in a synesthetic way, the visitor's footprints are left behind in the forest and are converted into sound form through an emergent process which repeats the life cycle.

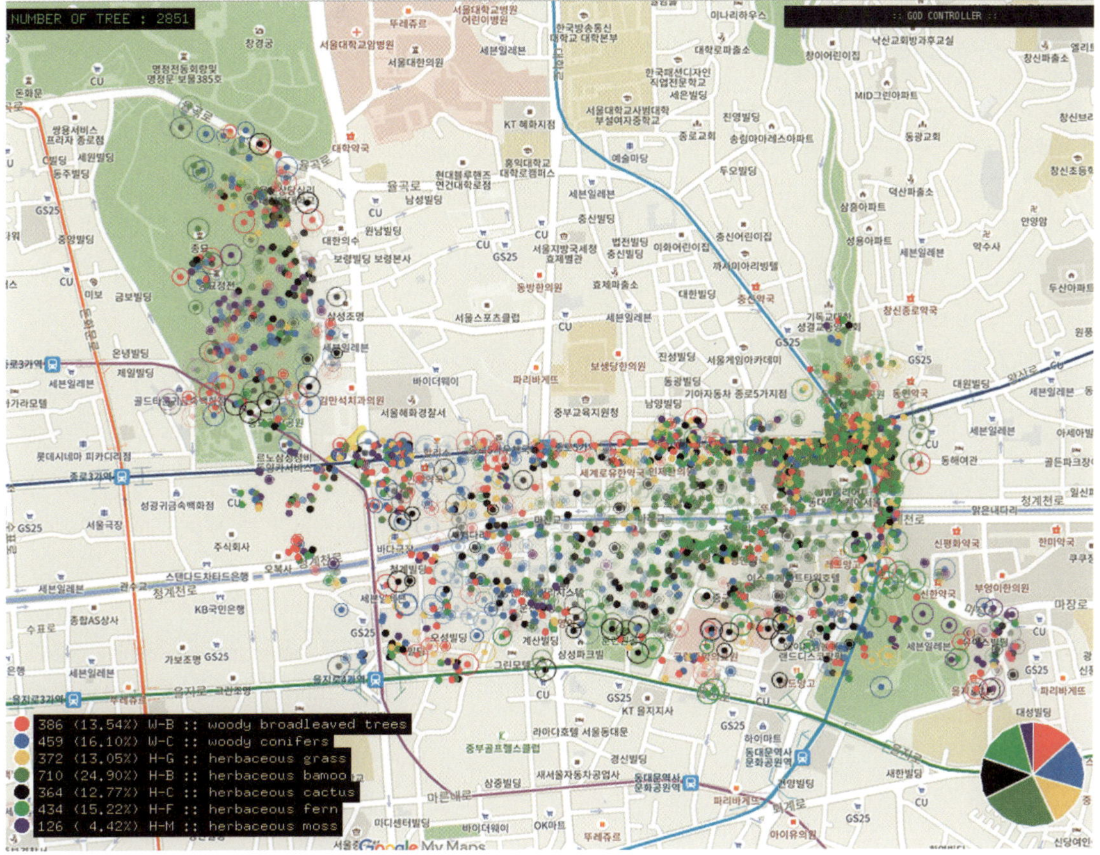

The control center application shows the dispersion of "sound plants" by species.

Kayip is a composer who is interested in capturing spaces which do not actually exist through sound, and has been working on music that focuses on the texture and tone of sound itself rather than melody. Recently, he has worked as a programmer and media artist, and has been working on reinterpreting existing spaces through sound and its visualizations. He majored in contemporary music at the Birmingham National Conservatory and the Royal Conservatory. He was selected by Brian Eno to take charge of arranging and editing the 40th anniversary performance of the Apollo Moon landing at the London Science Museum in 2009. He won the Aberdeen Music Prize for writing a new orchestral song for the BBC Scottish Symphony. From 2007 to 2010, he was selected as a composer for the UK's contemporary music support organization, "Sound and Music." djkayip.tumblr.com

Gangil Yi received an MA in music technology from Korea National University of Arts (KNUA) and has been presenting mixed media exhibition and performance works. In his composition he actively embraces electronic circuitry and computer programming technologies. *Coincidental Noise, Coincidental Scape* (YOGIGA Gallery, 2011) was his solo exhibition. Group exhibitions include *Sora Kim—Abstract Walking* (Art Sonje Center, 2012); and *Sounding Sounder* (Seoul Art Space Mullae Studio M30, 2014). Since 2011, he has been collaborating with contemporary dance choreographers Hyunjoon Jang, EunJin Choi, and Jeong Ah Yoon. Yi was the sound collaborator for an experimental dance work choreographed by Jeong Ah Yoon that was selected for Archive Platform 2016, an annual invitational performance program sponsored and organized by Korea National Contemporary Dance Company. The title of the performance was *Classification and analysis of contemporary dance performance experiences that are shaped by the distance between the dance stage and the audience, and the verification of the impact of its actual reenactment on the dry persimmons degree of the art audience of the subject that accommodates turtles.* Since 2016, Yi is the co-presenter, with sound artist Jiyeon Kim, of an artist-run radio project *Weather Report* (Jeju, 2015–current). He is also a contributor to Remote Streaming Technology, a project initiated and developed by a UK sound art collective Soundcamp. Currently, as a member of media art collective "Upcycleroundup," he is working on preparing for an upcoming sound performance workshop Twees-Up, to be held in March 2018.

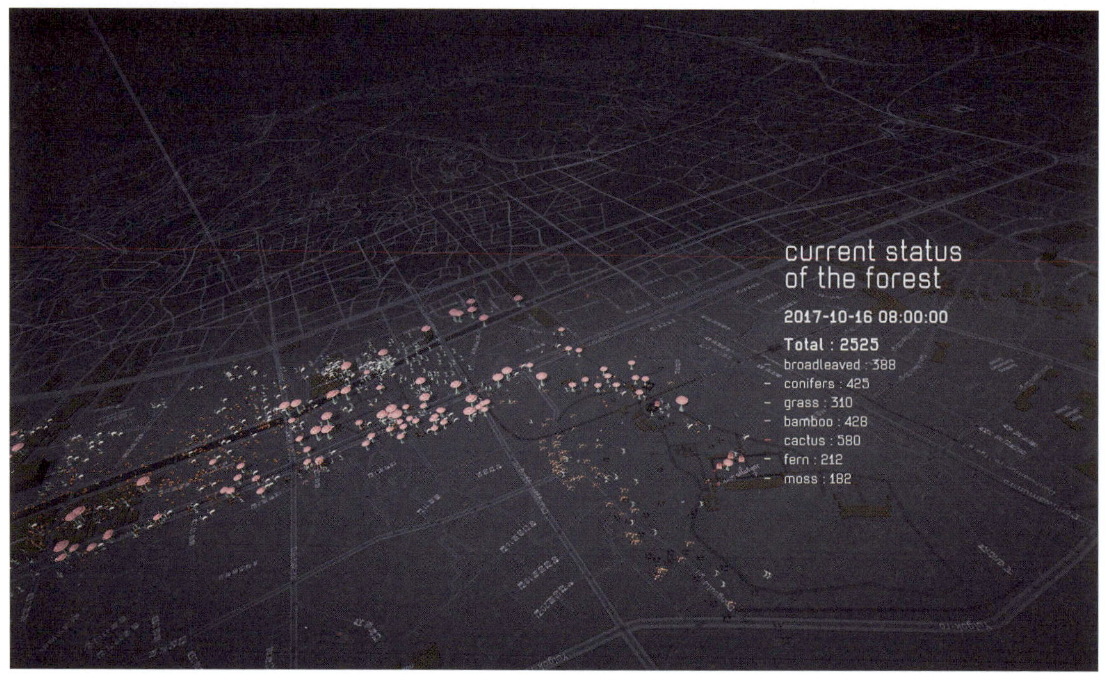

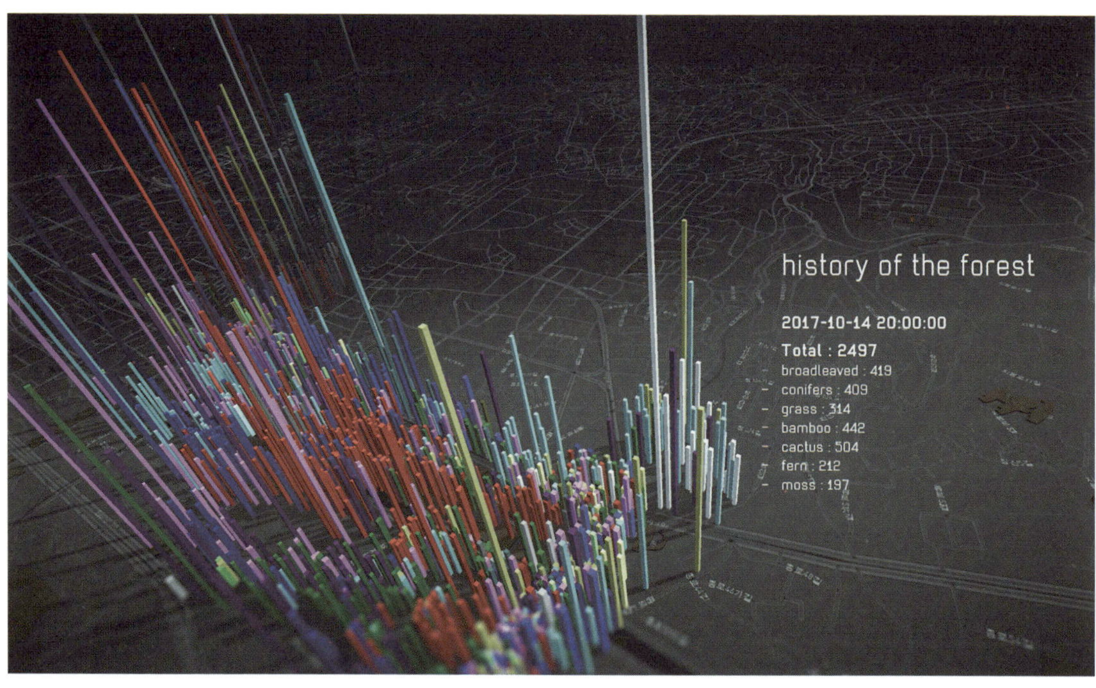

Overview of sound forests through data visualization.

Time lapse showing the forest growing.

MUSICITY

Musicity is a component program of *Connected City*. It commissioned artists to compose original music in response to particular aspects of the city that inspired them and to set up sound installations. The purpose was for the music and the city to meet. Seven musicians from the UK and Korea composed music for seven locations. These exclusive tracks were geo-tagged, each to the relevant location. When a user arrived at the tagged site, the music played automatically by responding to the positioning service.

Musicity tour. Photo: Kyungsub Shin Studio.

Hoehyeon Citizens Apartment. Photo: Kyungsub Shin Studio.

Sound Systems
Steve Guy Hellier

Based on the idea of opposing "sound systems" in a space with the audience watching from the side-lines, each "sound system" generates treated sounds from two distinct categories creating an aural tension between the "making" and modern "consuming" of Seoul. The space between the opposing "sound systems" is mediated by dancers, trying to move/exist between the tensions present in the piece caught in the allegorical audio crossfire.

Hoehyeon Citizen Apartment: Two 10-floor apartment buildings were built in 1970, where one of the two was demolished and the other is still in use. This building symbolizes economic development in the 1960s and 70s. This is the last publicly funded apartment building in Seoul. It is planned to be remodelled as an arts space and housing for young people.

Steve Hellier attended Goldsmiths in the late 80's where he studied fine art. After leaving, he formed Death in Vegas with Richard Fearless writing and recording their first album "Dead Elvis" which gained commercial and critical success. Steve has spent the last few years making audio related pieces for *Musicity* at Tallinn Music Week 2016, Museum of London "Deed and Prosper" and more recently was a resident at WORM in Rotterdam and did sound installation work at Resonant Edge festival 2017 (Edge Hill University). Steve has also been involved in Mark Leckey's (Turner Prize winner 2008) recent film "Dream English Kid" which is currently on display at Tate Britain. www.steveguy-hellier.com

Follow the Flow (Ambient Electronic Classical)
Hannah Peel

From the flow of the river that used to be, I found an area immersed in rolling change, politics, and mass crowd inundations. Zaha Hadid's architecture follows this historical culture of Seoul and each unique curve and individual metal panel, in the heat of the day, allows a cool breeze to drift around the building. I felt calm and at peace. Sounds of the surrounding city distantly echoing through the smooth and graceful spaces, allowing the mind to wander and the imagination to soar. Allowing enough space for your ears and mind to wander through the curved white corridors and escape to the grassy roof and beyond, the mix of electronic and classical music echoes the metal, concrete and natural areas. With 40,000 individual panels making up the exterior of the building, I used the number 4 throughout—a tempo of 40bpm, 4 layers of audio, 4 vocals cues, 4 piano strikes from the grounds of DDP and 4 hits of a traditional gong I bought when leaving Seoul.

Dongdaemun Design Plaza (DDP): DDP is a multi-cultural complex located at Dongdaemun History & Culture Park Station in Seoul, Korea. Since its foundation on 21 March 2014, DDP has staged diverse cultural events including exhibitions, fashion shows, product launch shows, forums, conferences, and various cultural events. DDP is where new design trends begin and cultures are exchanged. It is a venue that introduces new products and fashion trends, that shares knowledge through exhibitions, and that offers diverse programming to share new design. www.ddp.or.kr

Based in London, UK, the Northern Irish artist, singer, and electronic composer Hannah Peel released her new solo album Awake But Always Dreaming to great acclaim at the end of 2016. Drawing on personal experiences with her grandmother "awakening" from dementia with music, Peel has described this album as "a dive into the rabbit hole of the brain" and was awarded "No.1 Electronic Album of the Year" by *Electronic Sound Magazine*. A collaborator with the likes of John Foxx (Ultravox), The Magnetic North and OMD, Peel's next instrumental "odyssey" album for September 2017 takes a traditional Colliery brass band and synths to escape reality on a journey into space… titled "Mary Casio: Journey to Cassiopeia." www.hannahpeel.com.

Dongdaemun Design Plaza (DDP). Photo: Kyungsub Shin Studio.

Seoullo
Gabriel Prokofiev

In this composition I wanted to create a musical accompaniment to Seoullo. Responding to the special sense of journey we experience walking on the bridge, the music moves through three stages:

i) Starting with the sense of mystery and the gradual feeling of escape from the busy city,

ii) Then moving into a warmer mood, observing the different people we pass, and also the different plants, trees, and city-scape beyond;

iii) Finally arriving at a feeling of elation and reflection as we start to relax and really appreciate the magic of Seoullo.

Seoullo 7017: The Seoul Station overpass was constructed in the 1970s as a response to the growing traffic congestion in Seoul. For decades, the highway connected the eastern and western halves of the city. It is transformed into an elevated pedestrian walkway/linear park which opened on 20th May, 2017. Seoullo 7017 has gardens, terraces, and exhibitions and features 24,085 plants representing 228 species of trees, shrubs, and flowers.

Gabriel Prokofiev is a London-based composer, producer, DJ, and founder of the Nonclassicalrecord label & night club. Composing music that both embraces and challenges western classical traditions, Gabriel has emerged at the forefront of a new approach to classical music in the UK at the beginning of the 21st century. gabrielprokofiev.com

Seoullo 7017 (Seoul Skypark). Photo: Kyungsub Shin Studio.

In Numerous Rooms
Jang Young-gyu

This work archives Sewoon Sangga, a commercial/industrial neighborhood steeped in the modern and contemporary history of Seoul, through sound. It collects, edits, and reconstructs sounds made in a motif of space, such as the sounds heard from there in the past or from movies set in and around the complex. The mixture of the sounds that existed in that place and the imaginary sounds generated by the buildings of Sewoon Shopping Complex creates a layer of reality and illusion.

You can hear the sounds while walking around the central square of the building. The sounds heard while walking along the corridors of the spaces in which many people reside collide with the history of this particular place from 1968 to the present.

Sewoon Sangga: Sewoon Sangga is designed by Korean architect, Kim Swoo Geun. It is known as one of the first modern buildings in Korea from the 1960s, as well as the first residential-commercial complex and a center for home appliances. This complex enjoyed the economic boom of the 1970s before going into decline as the government underwent massive development projects in other areas such as Gangnam and Yongsan. In 2009, it was decided to demolish this building but in 2014 it was newly decided to keep it due to concerns of further recession of the local economy and disruption of the industrial ecosystem.

Jang Young-gyu, a musician, composer, and member of Uhuhboo Project, Ssing Ssing, and Be-Being, has been involved in numerous projects in the fields of film, theater, dance, and visual art since the late 90s. He has shown experimental musical tendencies through textures of sound and segments of rhythm. Recently, he has been exploring the areas of traditional instruments, sounds, and performances and working toward realizing new structures of tradition by connecting them with contemporary music.

Sewoon Sangga. Photo: Kyungsub Shin Studio.

Cheongpa Hill: A Memory Brought by a Wind
Kayip

During the colonial era, the Yongsan district in Seoul served as the military base of the Japanese Government-General of Korea. The hilly Cheongpa-dong area, adjacent to Seoul Station, was built up as an up-scale neighborhood of the Japanese officers and officials. In the decades since then, Cheongpa-dong has turned into a collage of landscapes created by numerous events as various architectural styles of different eras have appeared. The emotions created by the scenery of Cheongpa-dong with such a background are well captured by the poet Seungja Choi's "Do You Remember Cheongpa-dong." Walking along an alleyway stretching along a hill leads to the illusion that her poetic words have been fully realized and laid open. As I walked through the alleys of the town, I thought it would be more interesting to make a sound in response to the landscape reminiscent of the text rather than to make a sound directly in response to the scenery here, and to add it back to the actual scenery.

The music is accompanied by fragments of the poetic words constituting "Do You Remember Cheongpa-dong," and a wind generating spot was installed for a windchime. The windscreen installed around Cheongpa Hill visualizes the text and generates the sound of the wind through the windchime. The poem transformed into sound evokes old memories of Cheongpa-dong and the music created as a reminder of the space where the story of the poem happened is added to the sound of the landscape and the audience hears the combination of these two pieces of audio, walking along the alleys of Cheongpa Hill overlaid with the image of the poem. The memories that have disappeared seem to be like the wind that stays for a while before leaving again, evoking many stories that have passed through here in the form of sounds. There is nothing that exists forever, but there is nothing that disappears forever either.

Cheongpa Hill: Located near Seoul Station, it was a settlement for the Japanese in the past and some of these houses still remain in this area. In the 1980s, due to urban environmental maintenance projects, many of the *hanoks* (Korean traditional houses) were converted into villas and small sewing factories were gathered into the village, creating a unique feature. The panoramic view of Seogyeo-dong can be viewed from Cheopa Hill.

Kayip is a composer who is interested in capturing spaces which do not actually exist through sound, and has been working on music that focuses on the texture and tone of sound itself rather than melody. Recently, he has worked as a programmer and media artist, and has been working on reinterpreting existing spaces through sound and its visualizations. He majored in contemporary music at the Birmingham National Conservatory and the Royal Conservatory. He was selected by Brian Eno to take charge of arranging and editing the 40th anniversary performance of the Apollo Moon landing at the London Science Museum in 2009. He won the Aberdeen Music Prize for writing a new orchestral song for the BBC Scottish Symphony. From 2007 to 2010, he was selected as a composer for the UK's contemporary music support organization, "Sound and Music." djkayip.tumblr.com

Cheongpa-dong. Photo: Kyungsub Shin Studio.

Hanyang Nanbong-ga
Music Group NaMu

There is a new view of Seoul from Baekbeom Plaza which is located between Hoehyeon-dong and the foot of Mt. Namsan. Trees are arranged in a nice layout surrounding the square which is quite spacious. High along the horizon, beyond a forest of high-rise buildings, apartment buildings together with a village of houses, where the hands of urban development have been slow, can be viewed at a glance. Looking out at all of this, together with the Seoul City Wall which is just beside the plaza, it is surprising and delightful to discover the diversity that is mixed into the big pot known as "Seoul."

From the early Joseon Dynasty to the present day, the walls of Seoul have been preserved for hundreds of years. "Hanyang Nanbong-ga" is a song about the flaneur of the past and the flaneur of the present, who strolls here and there, telling the story of the world from person to person while enjoying the flavor of that world. Music Group Tree composed a song with a new interpretation, containing motifs from the melody and lyrics of "Long Nanbong-ga" and "Sasul Nanbong-ga" which were sung in Hwanghae Province.

Namsan Park (Baekbeom Square): Namsan Park is the largest park in Seoul and is home to many species of trees and plants. Baekbeom Square was created in 1968 to commemorate Korean independence activist Kim Koo. It is located between Children's Square and Central Square in Namsan Park. Seoul City Wall was restored in 2013 in this section and this wall is connected to Sungnyemun.

Music Group NaMu is a group that deeply embodies the artistry and spirit of Korean traditional music, accepts various genres of music, and makes music that contemporary people can play together. Their music is characterized by improvisation through interaction, which has the great strength of gathering art forms from various genres and audiences together in one spot. Music Group NaMu has been working with artists from diverse fields such as dance, documentary, classical, and jazz since 2013, showing audiences the creative ability and outstanding performance of the three musicians. For several years, they have been invited to various festivals, proudly performing both traditional and contemporary orchestral music and have been encouraged by the Korean music industry.

Namsan Baek Beom Plaza. Photo: Kyungsub Shin Studio.

Naksan Park, Seoul. Photo: Kyungsub Shin Studio.

Neon Bunny is active at home and abroad, having received the Best Pop Recording award for Korean popular music when she debuted. She has been featured in local and international media such as Pitchfork and FADER in particular, and was recommended as "better K-pop" on John Oliver's Last Week Tonight.

That Hill
Neon Bunny

A meeting of traditional Korean trot melody and modern arrangements. What characterises this work are reminiscences about the artist's joy and sorrow for her childhood memories, the artist's parents and their generation, and the chronological arrangement of changes over time at Naksan Park.

Trying to escape poverty,
I came to Seoul empty-handed.

There is that boy still in my father's eyes.

At least, I wanted my children
to have a better life than mine.
Not a ring shined on my mother's fingers.

He goes up the hill again today and
reminisces about the days gone by.
When all the allies in the rolling neighborhood
were aglow in the light of the setting sun,
the years gone by made him cry.

Out of breath on the staircase of a steep hill,
I smell the cooking of rice
over the wall of a low-rise house.

A big moon, as gorgeous as a gourd,
rises over a white stone wall,
but the rattling sound of the sewing machine
never ends.

Naksan Park: Naksan Park gets its name from its camel hump-like appearance. In Korean *nakta* means camel and *san* means mountain. So people refer to the park as Nakta Park or Naksan Park. The mountain is solid granite bedrock. The Joseon royal family enjoyed the natural beauty of the granite mountain, but during the Japanese Colonial Period, a hasty manner of urban planning resulted in the demolition of most parts of the mountain. In an effort to save the remaining green belts, Naksan was designated as a park on 10 June 2002. Located in the center of Seoul, this historical and beautiful park allows its visitors to view the magnificence of the entire city.

PLAYABLE CITY

The *Playable City* concept has captured the imagination of cities across the globe, offering a new way of connecting people and thinking about the city. Started in Bristol by Watershed (www.watershed.co.uk), a cultural venue and producer, *Playable City* has expanded to places such as Lagos, Recife, and Tokyo, exploring the future city with a team of local artists and other creators, and generating new ideas rooted in the specific city environment. Over three days in Seoul, *Playable City* hosted a mini festival of participatory games and exhibitions that invited the public to explore and re-imagine public space along the Cheonggye stream.

Fishy City: City Eats Fish as It Grows, a Game, Cheonggyecheon
Borahm Kim

Cheonggyecheon is a recovered public stream in downtown Seoul. Has anyone ever looked into Cheonggyecheon to examine the fish? Why are they living there? Every element in the city has its own reason for existence. Things of no use are disposed of, or they disappear eventually. In 2006, after two years of massive renewal construction, the city reported 19 species of fish in Cheonggyecheon. Four years later there was another report; the number of species had reduced to 16, but the population as a whole had increased up to seven times. How is this possible in a stream in the middle of downtown? Why is this happening? What are they for? The participants in this game were asked to come up with their thoughts and examine the fish.

Borahm Kim divides the space by the imaginary and real. The imaginary space is the space of the imagination shown in exhibition space or video, and the real space is the everyday space. The place of our daily lives spawns a multitude of events but most get buried and hidden. By creating a situation in which these two spaces (imaginary and real) overlap, she hopes to discover the invisible things in space, the things that happen in space, and the possibility of space. Borahm has mainly produced experimental performances and installations using media such as video, surround sound, installation, performance, and a mobile app (APP). She has produced site-specific performances in which the audience moves through the space. They include *57.2 Degree Tilted Terrain* (2015); *Untitled Mountain* (2015); *Untitled Train* (2016); *Para-Structures* (2017); and *Plug-in City* (2017). vimeo.com/borahm

Media Graffiti, a Participatory Game, Cheonggyecheon

Sun Kim

Like graffiti on the long, open Cheonggyecheon wall, people will enjoy drawing or doodling with their fingers instead of using spray paint or pen on the screen. It does not lead to natural decomposition because it is expressed in virtual space rather than directly on the wall. Many people can be accommodated and enjoy a place to freely express their feelings. The artistic value of graffiti may be questioned, but it will play an important role in giving freedom of expression to participants. Also,I hope the work will become an artistic wall for the citizens in conjunction with the urban beauty of Cheonggye stream.

Sun Kim is an artist, designer, and visual director in a wide range of media including drawing, installation art, design planning, and public projects by collaborating with people from various fields. After graduating from Korean National University of Arts in Seoul, she went on to study at the Chelsea College of Art and Design in London. Above all, she has been to 40 countries all over the world. Her experiences of having encountered these various worlds have most definitely increased her skills and powers of perception as a visual director.

Photo: Kyungsub Shin Studio.

A Walk with My DIY PET in Cheonggyecheon, a Participatory Exhibition, Cheonggyecheon
Yang Sookhyun

I am interested in the way that industry-standard technology is embraced within the digital platform and how it is embodied through digital fabrication. For this purpose, I'm working on hacking and transforming mass-produced products. This project is a work that induces behaviors such as collaboration, walking, and playing as well as defining specific space.

The surrounding area of Cheonggyecheon is mostly an industrial district made up of factories and warehouses. It is hard to find people taking walks with pets because it is not a residential area. It is also not easy to take a walk with animals because the trail along the Cheonggyecheon is narrow. I propose a playful activity that transforms the balloon of mass production into a fish shape, called Blimp, to make my own pet. Because the promenade of Cheonggyecheon is narrow, this fish-shaped pet will swim across the Cheonggyecheon.

Yang Sookyun (1982) defines contemporary media as "everything produced by technology" and believes that the media experience accumulated in the technology-human-environment is embodied, becomes a new imagination, and transforms into another energy. She is interested in the experience created by the physical space filled with "technical objects" and expresses them in various ways by combining this embodied media experience with technical imagination. She has performed numerous media projects with members of the media artist group Jonpasang such as Hyper-Matrix (2012), Brilliant cube (2013–14) and P-city media 2.0 (2016) and has exhibited at Intel & Vice the Creators Projects (2011), Da Vinci Creative (2014), Asia Culture Complex (2015), KOFAC GAS 2017, and Cheong ju Craft Biennale (2017). She is currently working on Project Team A-Maker at the MMCA Chang-dong Residency. www.maumchine.net

Photo: Kyungsub Shin Studio.

Dance with Me, a Participatory Exhibition, Cheonggyecheon

Eunkyoung Lee, Minji Kim

An interactive installation using motion recognition technology, *Dance With Me* is a playful activity under Gwanggyo bridge where the audience dances with the animals living in Cheonggyecheon.

In 2005, the Cheonggye stream was restored, and the number of habitats increased as the green tracts were regenerated. Now in its 12th year, Cheonggyecheon, has become popular with the citizens and many animals. *Dance With Me* was born from the idea of people playing with those animals together. People walking on foot will meet animal representatives who now live there. When people move their body, the animals will dance and move with them. They will hear various sounds, even making music.

Eunkyoung Lee and Minji Kim are an artist and designer duo based in Seoul. Eunkyoung worked as a content designer at d'strict. She was involved in multiple projects including holographic performances and new media exhibitions. Currently, she is working as an artist after obtaining her MFA in Computational Arts at Goldsmiths. Her main area of interest is dramatic changes in life brought about by technology.

Minji Kim majored in computer engineering and worked as a software engineer for 7 years in broadcasting and media. She has been working as an interaction designer after receiving her MA in interaction design at Goldsmiths. She is enthusiastic about designing new, more enjoyable experiences between people and technology to improve quality of life.

Photo: Kyungsub Shin Studio.

BAHN, a game, Sewoon Sangga
Strangers at Honja Factory

The game starts with a text message. The sender is a seventeen-year-old girl named Bahn. She sends a request for help that she be found. The game participant exchanges text messages with this teenage girl. The player explores the nooks and crannies of the city as he or she follows the footsteps of the girl. The signposts and places the player encounters as he follows Bahn's instruction are relevant to what Bahn experienced after her arrival in Seoul and to her personal memories. For each mission completed and place found in the game, Bahn's age decreases by a year. By the time the player arrives at the final stop in the game, Bahn's age is ten. A ten-year-old child is lost in a city that is new to her. Who is she? Where is she from? Is she actually lost?

Strangers at Honja Factory is a project team consisting of two artists. They are IM Do One (Honja Factory) and Eunju HITCHCOCK-YOO (Strangers). Im designs art products and devices based on her research on digital technologies and their mechanisms. Hitchcock-Yoo and the Strangers are a street performance group engaged in pushing the boundaries of street performance. The group is particularly interested in communicating intimately with the audience during the performance and in intervening actively in the process.

Photo: Kyungsub Shin Studio.

International Street Games
Rosie Poebright

JUMP! | 1+ players. Jump onto the target and enjoy your reward—best style wins!

GIANT FISH | 1+ players. Build a giant fish to decorate the square using fish-scales

LEMON JOUSTING | 2–10 players. Two spoons each, one spoon for the lemon, the other to knock your opponent's fruit down. If your fruit is knocked down you're out of the game. Lemons must be balanced not held down. Last player with balanced lemon wins.

ESCAPE THE NET | 2–10 players. Two teams—put on the protective clothing. To win you must cross to the opposite side of the net first. Each player takes a turn to take one step into a new section of net; they can then launch one water balloon at the other team. Under-arm throwing only, the higher the better. The other team must prepare their umbrellas to protect them from the rain. The bravest will get to the other side first and win!

LAZER BALL | 6–10 players. Two teams. Positions are a laser pointer, reflector or blocker. Get past the blockers to hit the target with your reflected laser light. Winning team has highest score when time is over.

Rosie Poebright is a digital artist, storyteller and real-world game designer. She works with a powerful mix of ingredients to design her experiences—most importantly audience agency, interactivity and embodiment. As creative director of Splash & Ripple, "Architects of Extraordinary Adventures," she makes experiences that transport people from their normal everyday lives to an extraordinary space where they can play with new ways of thinking, feeling and being. She works across live events (multi-location theatrical street games) and long-term installed adventures in museums and heritage sites. An academic grounding in psychology and anthropology informs Rosie's people-centric focus.

Connected City
Kyu Choi

Urbanization of human population is the most distinct characteristic of the 21st century and its most pressing issue. Once, economic growth was considered the most central urban issue. Today, cities around the world are making great efforts to become more liveable and to make their economies more sustainable. Seoul is not an exception. While Seoul has changed dramatically in the past seventy years since 1945, particularly in regards to how the nation's rapid economic growth has affected the city, it is grappling with many of the vexing problems of a megacity. They include social and economic inequalities and the cultural issues of urban homogenization. Towards the goal of making itself more livable and sustainable, Seoul changed the core axis of its urban policies from one that relied on growth and development to one that gives priority to sharing, co-existing, and co-governing.

Notwithstanding the shift in the policy direction, Seoul is still a rapidly changing city, in terms of its architecture, environment, space, and economic structure. For the citizens experiencing the rapid changes as a matter of daily life, what role should art and culture play? *Connected City* is a festival where city, art, technology, architecture, regeneration, and collaboration are key operative words. Artists from Korea and the UK are commissioned to create music, urban games, stories, exhibitions, and performances and to share them with the public in Seoul.

The goal of *Connected City* is first to provide the public an opportunity to re-experience and re-imagine the city through creative projects centered around public spaces. The second is to expand urban art experiences by combining state-of-the-art technologies with site-specific works around public spaces. The third is to deliver projects that are based on local and community life and culture, so as to expand people's appreciation of local communities and to expand local community participation in art activities.

The cultural and artistic creativity of a city depends on the active interaction between the city's local communities and artists. The *Connected City* program, as it pertains to the Seoul Biennale, includes *Musicity* and *Playable City*. *Musicity* enables Biennale visitors to re-experience the urban space of Seoul through music, while *Playable City* presents games and exhibitions in which members of the public can participate, where art, technology, and playing are combined.

Connected City is co-hosted by UK/Korea 2017–18 Creative Futures, the Urban Regeneration Bureau of Seoul Metropolitan Government, and the Seoul Biennale of Architecture and Urbanism 2017. It is co-organized by Producer Group DOT (www.producergroupdot.kr), the Urban Regeneration Bureau of Seoul Metropolitan Government, Seoul Walk (https://seoulwalk.org), Seoul Biennale of Architecture and Urbanism 2017, and the British Council Korea.

Currently working as creative director of UK/Korea Season Festival 2017–18 at British Council, Seoul, Korea, Kyu Choi's professional career started with festival management and artistic direction, first at the Chuncheon International Mime Festival and then at the Ansan Street Arts Festival. In 2005 he founded AsiaNow Productions where he developed, produced and presented innovative Asian contemporary physical theater, dance, and interdisciplinary arts. In addition, Choi has been a curator and facilitator of three artist-residence and workshop projects. For emerging and mid-career producers in Asia, Choi has developed the Asian Producers' Platform and APP Camp 2014–2017 with the aim of creating a stronger network of Asian producers where they can work more effectively across the region.

Walking the Commons Information Container. DDP. Photo: Kyungsub Shin Studio.

City of Explorers, Workshop #3. 16–17 September. Nanum Hall, DDP. Photo: Haneul Kim

City of Explorers, Workshop #3.
16–17 September. Academy Hall, DDP.
Photo: Jooeun Sung

PUBLIC PROGRAMS

SEOUL BIENNALE, SEOUL GOVERNANCE

Soik Jung
Director, Division of the Seoul Biennale of Architecture and Urbanism, Seoul Design Foundation

Today the city is no longer understood as a mere aggregate of physical spaces and facilities. It is a system of operations in which the physical environment, non-physical assets, and the people interact with each other. It is also the main culprit responsible for environmental degradation and a host of social problems. At the same time, the city is also an effective system that could put future solutions in operation. With half of today's entire world population living in cities, such an understanding serves as the foundation for a variety of urban policies and governance systems around the world.

In the case of Seoul, it is all the more necessary to recognize the city as a system. It is a 2,000-year-old city with ten million people living in an area of more than six-hundred square kilometers featuring major natural systems represented by the Han River and Bukhan Mountain. Seoul is also the political, economic, social, and cultural center of the nation and a megacity where twenty million people live and work everyday. Accordingly, what the city needs today, perhaps more than ever, are flexible and organic urban policies and governance systems. In pursuing improvements for sustainable life and habitat for its citizens, Seoul should take into account the need for flexible social, cultural, economic, welfare, environmental, and spatial policies. In particular, an organic governance system is much in need. In other words, it is important for Seoul to ask how and with whom it will design and implement urban policies, and how it would communicate them to the public, or its ten million citizens.

One answer is the Seoul Biennale of Architecture and Urbanism (hereafter "Seoul Biennale"). Consisting largely of the *Thematic Exhibition*, *Cities Exhibition*, and *Live Projects*, the Seoul Biennale 2017 was an experiment, one that champions the causes of flexible and innovative urban policies and of breaking away from many of the conventions and practices of urban bureaucracy. The experiments and discussions thus generated by the Seoul Biennale 2017 were shared with the public through a series of programs that the division organized. Where the citizens are the true stakeholders and principal owners of the city and its built environment, the Seoul Biennale had to first and foremost celebrate and engage its citizens, along with artists, architects, academics, and other professionals and experts. Thus *Public Programs* was a mechanism by which the Seoul Biennale proactively reached out to the public, or a means by which the Seoul Biennale became truer to itself as a biennale of architecture and urbanism. They were organized with the goal of communicating with the public in

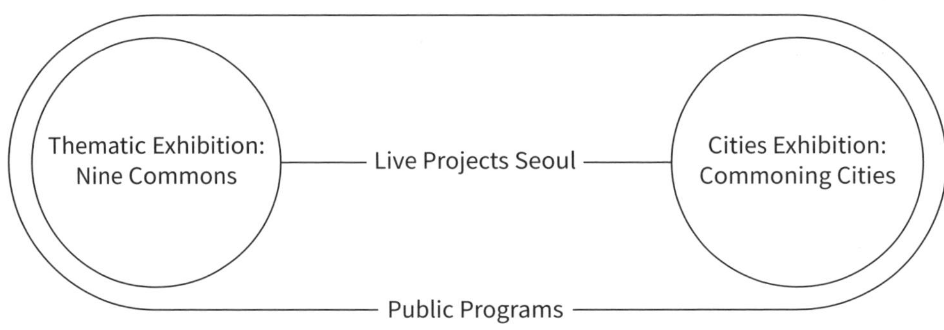

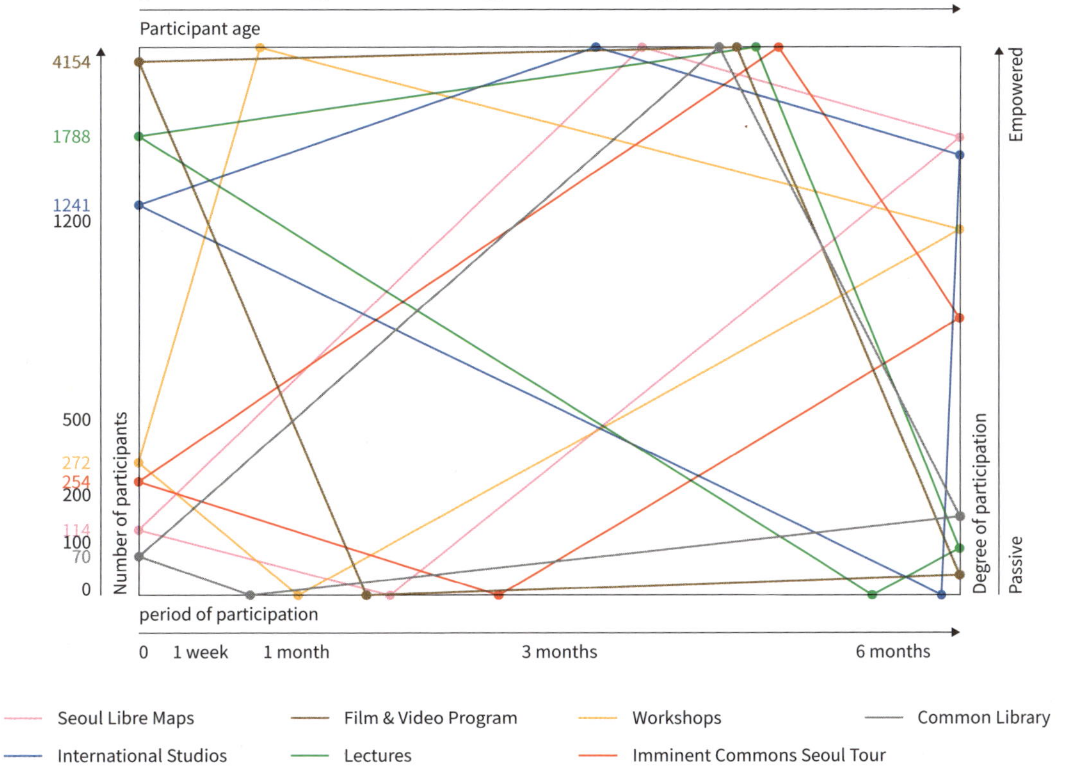

a language accessible to them, employing a variety of media and methodologies to reach a wider public, and engaging the public in more events where they could have first-hand experience with the Seoul Biennale urban policy experiment and the related contemporary discourse. At the same time, they were intended to provide a platform where exchanges among architecture professionals, experts from various fields, artists, and members of the general public could take place, or where they could become partners in action beyond the scope of the Biennale.

Seoul Libre Maps, International Studios, the Film & Video Program, Common Library, the *Lectures Program*, the *Workshop Program*, and *Imminent Commons Seoul Tour* were the seven projects that comprised the *Public Programs*, engaging approximately 20,000 citizens in the process. In addition, about sixty institutions, universities, organizations, and artist groups from Korea and aboard also collaborated in the various programs. Each program had its own target population and a medium of engaging the participants in conversations about, or actions for, "imminent commons," the theme of the Biennale. The *Film & Video Program, Common Library*, the

Lectures Program and the *Seoul Tour* were programs that were open to the general public. These programs approached the issues of "imminent commons" from a broad perspective. Film, for example, is one of the most popular mediums today. By adding forums and guest talks to a series of film screenings at various venues throughout Seoul, the *Film & Video Program* provided the audience a tool for better reading urban spatial features through discussions of film images and narratives. *Common Library* offered books and publications on imminent commons in the form of a book shop within one of the main Biennale venues. The purpose of *Common Library* was to allow members of the public to familiarize themselves with issues of the contemporary discourse on urbanism at their own chosen time and speed. The *Lectures Program* presented thirty-two speakers in four different talk series, starting from months before and ending well after the opening of the Biennale. The program began with a series giving an overview of imminent commons from the broad perspectives of the humanities and social sciences and moved on to lectures on the curatorial directions of the two major Biennale exhibitions and the *Live Projects*.

The two series were followed by a series on more specific Biennale content and narratives, gradually closing in on specific aspects of the Biennale itself. The *Public Programs* series also took the participants to the places of "imminent commons." *Imminent Commons Seoul Tour* also took the participants to such places as Haengchon, Sewoon Sangga, Seoul Upcycling Plaza, and the Seongbuk Art Village, which are neighborhoods in Seoul that are not necessarily widely known but are illuminating as venues of imminent commons.

Seoul Libre Maps, *International Studios*, and the two educational programs (the *Lectures Program* and the *Workshops Program*) targeted more specific populations. The programs were designed to empower participants to be the owners of the discourse on imminent commons and to take action, not simply to provide them with a better understanding of the Biennale theme. In this vein, *Seoul Libre Maps* was a program designed to identify the significance and domain of maps as commons, and to create a new kind of map. On a series of two-day weekends, the program participants held workshops, conducted field surveys and interviews, and collected and shared resources and created maps together based on their newly acquired insights on, as well as their newly acquired tools of understanding, the city. The International Studios program was joined by students from thirty universities from Korea and abroad. From fall semester 2016 to spring semester in 2017, different groups of students ran architecture studios in a number of Seoul downtown areas, namely the vicinities of Seoul Railway Station, Euljiro, and Dongdaemun. From their studios, they carried out joint research projects on the theme of "imminent commons" and proposed thoughtful designs. Their output, together with the discussions shared at workshops and symposiums, were compiled in the exhibition *Active Archive*. Educational workshops were held for participants as young as infants and children, as well as for middle and high school students and college students on seven different occasions. Age-specific activities were organized for space awareness and for enjoying and expressing the city with planning and exhibitions. Infants acquired a sense of space through play, while children walked through old downtown neighborhoods of Seoul to feel, discover, and express the city viscerally. Middle school students understood the power of the earth and made earthquake-resistant structures during the workshop. High school and college students visited Sewoon Sangga, discovering for the first time the many spaces and occupants there. They designed and made architectural models that reflected their feelings during the visit.

Thus for the past two years, the Seoul Biennale employed a variety of languages, in live venues, and continuously expanded points of contact with the public in an effort to make the discourses on the present and future of the city accessible and to engage with the public. This is not to say that the public is a passive recipient of education or edification. Rather, it is to say that what Seoul needs today is no longer a government led by experts and bureaucrats but a governance based on cooperation with its citizens. *Public Programs* was designed to operate as a platform for such governance.

The 20,000 citizens who participated in the *Public Programs* are but a small fraction of the 10-million population of Seoul. However, within the two-year period that the *Public Programs* were held, increasingly more participants came through word of mouth, that is, through the recommendation of previous participants, indicating that the influence of the programs was not confined to its 20,000 "graduates." Some of the graduates are being reborn as proactive citizens who think and express their thoughts and take action when necessary. Such changes can be seen in their wish for more such programs, their curiosity about the intention and outcome of the Seoul Biennale, and specific demands for topics and venues they want to see included in future Seoul Biennales. The changes in the participants are a testimony to the possibility that the Seoul Biennale, and more specifically, the *public programs*, can function as a mechanism for strengthening municipal governance through stronger engagement with citizens.

SEOUL LIBRE MAPS

E Roon Kang
*Curator, Seoul Biennale 2017;
director, Math Practice*

Wonyoung So
*Curator, Seoul Biennale 2017; data visualization
specialist, MIT Senseable City Lab*

Logo of *Seoul Libre Maps*

1. Full articles are available at: https://
medium.com/seoul-libre-maps

Maps shape our understanding of the world by mediating space; at the same time, they are a field of complex interaction among capital-, state-, and civil control and decision making. *Seoul Libre Maps* proposes ways to overcome the social, technological, and political restrictions related to online map-making. Using open data and open-source mapping tools, the project aims to reexamine the role of maps as commons. In doing so, it poses ironic questions on the notions of information and efficacy; takes a critical look at a dependency on a global infrastructure and imagines a decentralizing local agency; and visualizes symbolic and literal disasters in order to narrate alternative urban histories.

Geographic information has traditionally been considered a national asset and key element of national security; the general public did not have easy access to it. For instance, the Soviet Union possessed and managed sophisticated maps of countries around the world including the U.S. but the general Russian public only had access to crude maps. However, accessibility to geographic information has undergone radical improvement thanks to the public release of satellite imagery and the public use of GPS; Google Maps (2005-) and smartphones have quickly and further dismantled the geopolitical authority held by maps during the Cold War. Accordingly, the medium by which we consume geographic information has also drastically shifted into the current online maps. Still, as one can imagine from Google's scale of operation, creating and maintaining online maps requires a large amount of resources. As Hanbyul Jo points out, what to show or not to show on a map is the decision of a few companies that provide such services, and can involve intense conflicts of interest. While access to geographic information has greatly increased in the transition from Cold War maps to Google Maps, the flow of information is still very much unilateral—only following capitalist logic, instead of that of national security.

On the other hand, collaborative open mapping platforms such as OpenStreetMap (2004-) have coexisted with commercial maps, fostering an alternative track of history guided by the goal of open, collaborative, and extensive geographic information. While Google Maps and smartphones mediated the change in people's consumption and conception of maps, open data and open source mapping tools enable a more accessible and low-cost map-making. As online maps become more entangled with everyday contemporary life, people's capability to actively create and freely utilize maps—and not be limited to the role of passive readers—also becomes more important. Open data, as well as the diverse projects spun off of it, which involve tasks such as improving the accessibility of data sets, rendering data, and building control interfaces, saw the formation of a community consisting of individuals and organizations that create, use and improve such tools. This type of ecosystem balances the excessive control by states and companies over geographic information; such resources improve people's agency to spread individual stories and to reproduce their knowledge and skills.

Meanwhile, in South Korea, big IT companies are main providers of maps, such as Daum Maps (currently Kakao Map), Naver Map, Kimgisa (currently Kakao Navi), and SK's T Map—the latter two specializing in GPS navigation. One thing to note is that the government maintains a closed attitude with regards to geographic information, a position heavily guided by a national security rationale. A direct example was observed in 2016, when the government blocked Google from exporting map data from the country's physical territory into the company's servers. Moreover, the public seems to generally agree that such control is justified. This exclusive attitude towards geographic information, combined with the Korean internet's notable underdevelopment of open source and collaborative platforms, greatly undermines openness and its potential benefits. While the country's online map services are up to speed with global trends when one thinks of them as commodities, the notion of maps as common goods, easily accessible and contributable by individuals and civil society alike, is mostly under-discussed in Korea.

Seoul Libre Maps proposes "libre mapping," one that makes use of open tools such as OpenStreetMap, as an activity seeking to improve such an alienating situation. Libre maps, created by local participants in workshops facilitated by artists, designers, and engineers, exist in diverse forms. In *Uninformation Mapping and Video*, distorted maps drawn by the people of Seoul are edited so that they contain "correct" spatial information, and a music video is created as a result. *Read/Write Offline Mapping* imagines open-source mapping in a situation where a global internet and data centers are unavailable. *Cheonggyecheon, Dongdaemun Gentrification*

questions how one can map what has disappeared, through mental mapping activities about street vendors in Cheonggyecheon and Dongdaemun areas, and engages in mapping Cheonggyecheon's dangerous flood gates. These libre maps make extensive use of open source mapping tools, and the results are contributed back into open source communities—providing demo cases of open mapping. Through this process we hope to encourage an independent mapping culture, as well as progressive discussions around maps as public resources.

Uninformation Mapping & Video
Minkee Bae

Minkee Bae's *Uninformation Mapping & Video* is an example of "un-informational design activity," and it is an attempt to deliver an answer to the question of how to renew information design as a discourse within the current state of graphic design, through "un-informational design," paradoxically. "'Un-informational design activity,' aimed at the delivery of obscured information for its laid-back consumption" as written in the workshop description is an extension of such a distorted approach.

On the top of the approach, Bae and workshop participants collected poor-quality maps produced in Seoul. Despite their imperfections, they often achieved their goals. In the workshop, participants "took images that were distorted, effectively, for some goal—and corrected them, ineffectively, for no goal whatsoever," which implied "un-informational perversity." A combination of pre-collected images and additional ones were collected by themselves onto a single screen-based map using OpenStreetMap, and the final result is on view as a non-interactive, single-channel video. Key points in the images were mapped to their actual geographic location. In order words, the distorted images were corrected via yet another distortion.

Minkee Bae graduated from the Department of Design, Seoul National University in 2008 and earned a master's degree and a Ph.D. from the same university in 2011 and 2015 respectively. From 2011 to 2016, he worked as an editor of the magazine DOMINO and participated as an early member of the collective Optical Race. His design practice is relatively equally distributed between teaching—at the University of Seoul, Ewha Women's University, Seoul Women's University and Kookmin University—and collaboration with publishers, architects, and fashion companies. He participated in the solo exhibition Put Up & Remove (2016, Platform Place) and the group exhibition XS: Young Studio Collection (2015, Ujeongguk).

Minkee Bae, *Uninformation Mapping & Video*, a mapping workshop. 24–25 June 2017, Korea. Image: provided by artist.

Single channel video (2017), 20 min., color, sound. Commissioned by Seoul Biennale. Images: provided by artist.

Workshop outcome, print-ready (2017). Commissioned by Seoul Biennale. Images: provided by artist.

Read/Write Offline Mapping

Dan Phiffer

In *Read/Write Offline Mapping*, the artist Dan Phiffer introduces a new version of offline-friendly map software for occupy.here (http://occupy.here), a web-based message board system that could be accessed from physical proximity and which he first developed for the Occupy Wall Street movement. Using this system, he organized a workshop where participants could imagine situated social networks which could help decentralization. The maps produced by workshop participants only existed on an offline server where we could only have access to Dongdaemun Design Plaza in which the server was installed.

Workshop participants produced maps such as "My Vegan Experiences," or "Connecting Dots: Triangles of Each Life" from an individual perspective, as Phiffer encourages them to "think about which aspects of our lived urban experience might not be reflected in the familiar utilitarian smartphone maps designed to move us efficiently through the city." Thus, it emphasizes the role of users not only as consumers of maps but also as producers who participate in the creating/editing process of maps. Moreover, in situated, offline social networks, they experienced that "digital interactions can create familiarity with one's fellow embodied humans through gestures that are too abstract for IRL conversation."

Dan Phiffer is an artist, programmer, and researcher based in Brooklyn. He helps build open source mapping tools at Mapzen and is an Impact Resident at Eyebeam Art + Tech. Dan is interested in how computers shape our ways of thinking, and how our values are reflected in the systems we build. His projects have been exhibited at the Museum of Modern Art, MoMA PS1, SFMOMA, Ars Electronica, and Transmediale. His work has been written about in the *New York Times*, *New York Magazine*, *Rhizome.org*, and *Hyperallergic*.

Dan Phiffer, *Read/Write Offline Mapping*, a mapping workshop, 1–2 July 2017, Seoul. Image: provided by artist.

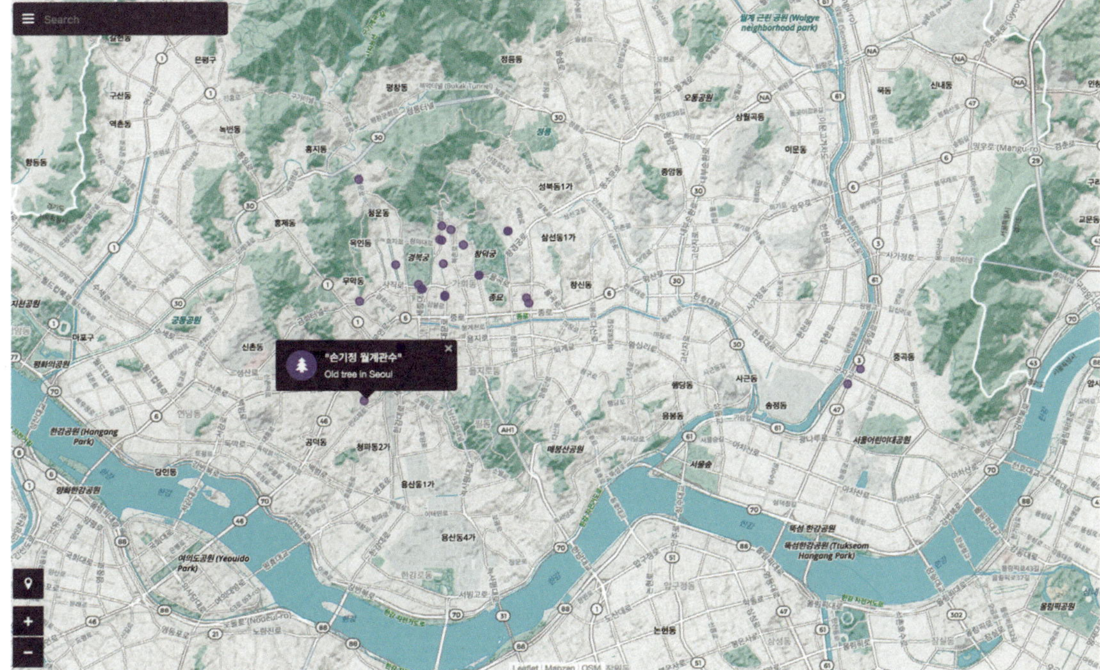

A computer server with a wifi router.
Booklet, 420 x 297 mm. 2017.
Commissioned by Seoul Biennale.
Images: provided by artist.

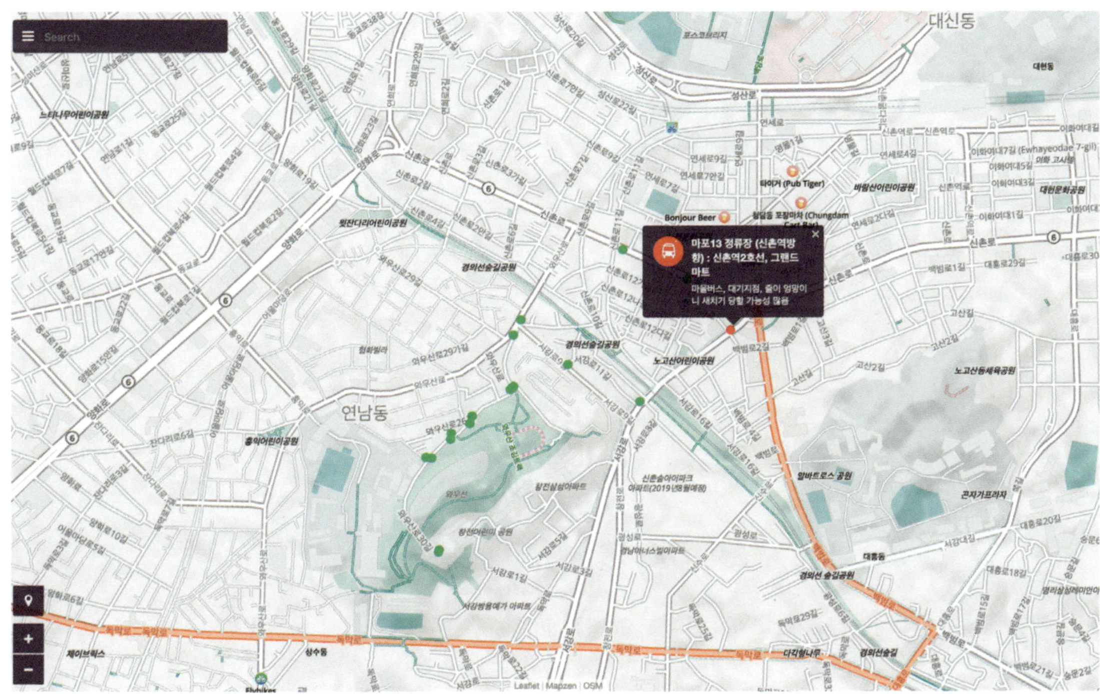

Listen to the City, *Cheonggyecheon, Dongdaemun Gentrification*, a mapping workshop. 8–9 July 2017, Seoul. Image: provided by artists.

Cheonggyecheon, Dongdaemun Gentrification
Listen to the City

Listen to the City deals with literal and symbolic disasters, Cheonggyecheon and Dongdaemun gentrification, to narrate alternative urban histories. On the first day of the workshop, participants mapped the stories of poverty activist Inki Choi who has spent his childhood in Cheonggyechon, Soon-gwan So who has done business in Cheonggyecheon for a long time, and Jongsook Woo, who has operated mainly around Dongdaemun. On the second day, they produced a Cheonggyecheon disaster mitigation map in which they marked sewer gates, which would open when rainfall is over 3 mm per hour, and emergency ladders on OpenStreetMap.

Through these activities, Listen to the City uses a different context to question the gentrification and documentation of urban histories: Were the planning of Cheonggyecheon and Dongdaemun Design Plaza sustainable? What other things have been neglected in the development's decision-making? From whom do the history of the city narrate? They have rediscovered and documented the long-neglected history of ordinary people and reconsidered the diverse urban cultures that have been erased by developmentalism. Meanwhile, stories that have disappeared about the cities raise awareness and demonstrate the necessity of archiving geospatial information that does not exist anymore, which is considered to be a challenge in open mapping.

Listen to the City is an art, design, and urbanism collective consisting of artists, urban researchers, and designers. Started in 2009, they have collaborated with many designers and researchers and visualized undocumented histories and entities in urban space. Listen to the City have been interested in the relationship of power that owns space and the commons, through research and activism projects about Naeseongcheon, Okbaraji Alley, and Dongdaemun Design Plaza. In 2014, they published Hidden History of Dongdaemun Design Park and the Star Architect, which is a history and criticism of building Dongdaemun Design Plaza.

Three pieces of peddler memory map, each 1189 x 841 mm. Interview with three peddlers, single channel video, color, sound. Three peddlers interview booklet. Cheonggyecheon disaster prevention map, 590 x 2020 mm. Cheonggyecheon sluice gate video, 2017, single channel, color, sound. Commissioned by Seoul Biennale. Images: provided by artist.

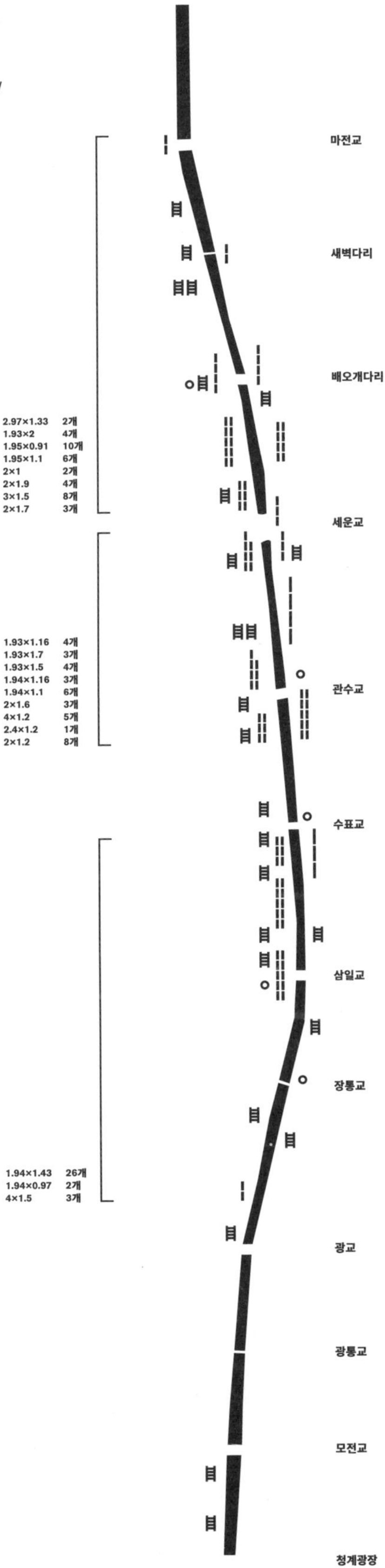

Views on Digital Maps and Open Data
Hanbyul Jo

Hanbyul Jo's Views on Digital Maps and Open Data is an essay that deals with international politics and industries, Augmented Reality games and open source communities, and data servers and borders. It discusses the commerce and commodity of map data and looks at the reality of South Korea. The article is published in the *Seoul Libre Maps* leaflet, and the website Medium published two interactive maps, *Make a Map of Your Interests* and *Exporting Seoul Map Data by Voice and Hand*, respectively.

Notably, in *Exporting Seoul Map Data by Voice and Hand*, Jo did an experiment in which she, who lives in New York, drew data on behalf of her friend in Korea who was describing what the data looked like, in order to export Seoul map data overseas, which is prohibited, in a legal manner. Through this process, the national geospatial data is lossy-encoded—but meaningful enough—by humans and could be duplicated over borders. She took indirect strategies for dealing with the questionable circumstances around exporting geospatial data of Korea, thereby rebutting the contradiction around which the government tried to regulate immaterial data into the physical space.

Hanbyul Jo is a New York-based software engineer. She works at the open source mapping company Mapzen, where she develops tools to make web mapping more accessible. Hanbyul's personal work reveals narratives in datasets by combining them on maps, such as in her recent projects Mapping the Candles and Seoul Building Explorer.

Hanbyul Jo, hyperlinked text including interactive contents from *Views on Digital Maps and Open Data*, a research project, 2017. Commissioned by Seoul Biennale. Images: provided by artist.

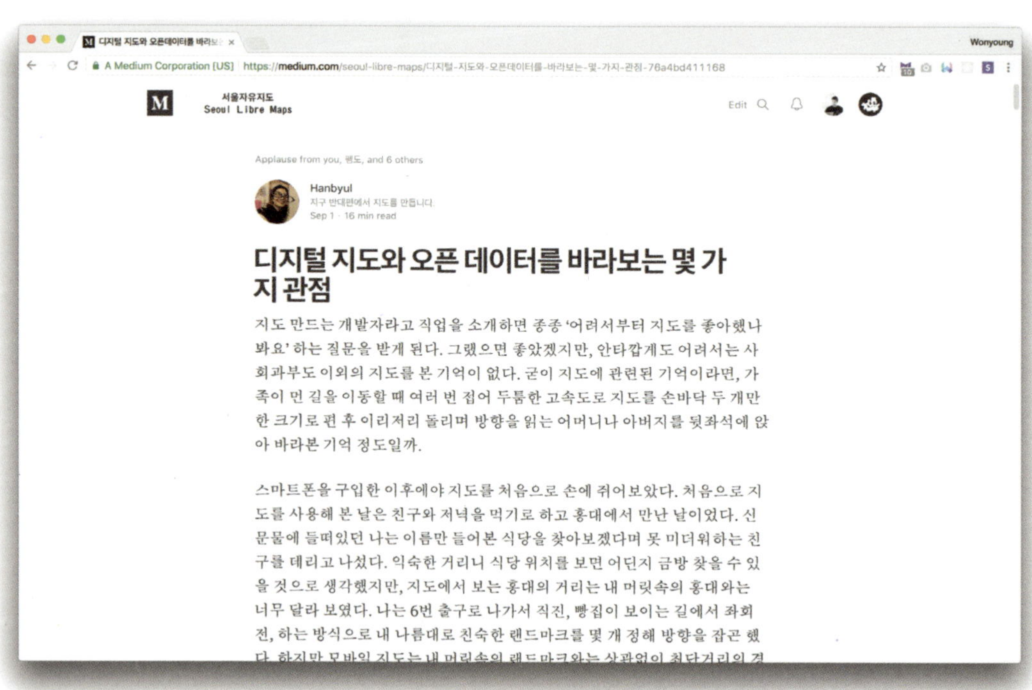

디지털 지도와 오픈 데이터를 바라보는 몇 가지 관점

지도 만드는 개발자라고 직업을 소개하면 종종 '어려서부터 지도를 좋아했나 봐요' 하는 질문을 받게 된다. 그랬으면 좋았겠지만, 안타깝게도 어려서는 사회과부도 이외의 지도를 본 기억이 없다. 굳이 지도에 관련된 기억이라면, 가족이 먼 길을 이동할 때 여러 번 접어 두툼한 고속도로 지도를 손바닥 두 개만한 크기로 편 후 이리저리 돌리며 방향을 읽는 어머니나 아버지를 뒷좌석에 앉아 바라본 기억 정도일까.

스마트폰을 구입한 이후에야 지도를 처음으로 손에 쥐어보았다. 처음으로 지도를 사용해 본 날은 친구와 저녁을 먹기로 하고 홍대에서 만난 날이었다. 신문물에 들떠있던 나는 이름만 들어본 식당을 찾아보겠다며 못 미더워하는 친구를 데리고 나섰다. 익숙한 거리니 식당 위치를 보면 어딘지 금방 찾을 수 있을 것으로 생각했지만, 지도에서 보는 홍대의 거리는 내 머릿속의 홍대와는 너무 달라 보였다. 나는 6번 출구로 나가서 직진, 빵집이 보이는 길에서 좌회전, 하는 방식으로 내 나름대로 친숙한 랜드마크를 몇 개 정해 방향을 잡곤 했

자가 어느 지역을, 어느 정도 확대해서 보고있는지를 바탕으로 사용자가 필요
한 데이터를 유추하여 사용자에게 전송한다. 이렇게 변환된 데이터는, 데이터
의 속성과 중요도를 잘 나타낼 수 있는 기호를 통해 표현되어 사용자가 이해할
수 있는 형태로 보여진다.

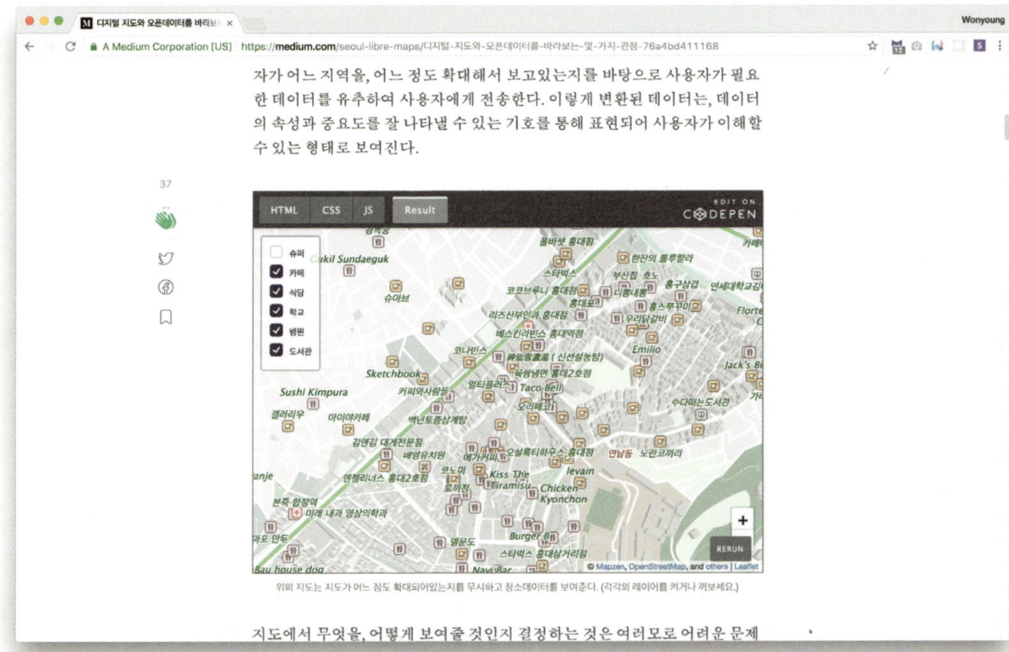

위의 지도는 지도가 어느 정도 확대되어있는지를 무시하고 장소데이터를 보여준다. (각각의 레이어를 켜거나 꺼보세요.)

지도에서 무엇을, 어떻게 보여줄 것인지 결정하는 것은 여러모로 어려운 문제

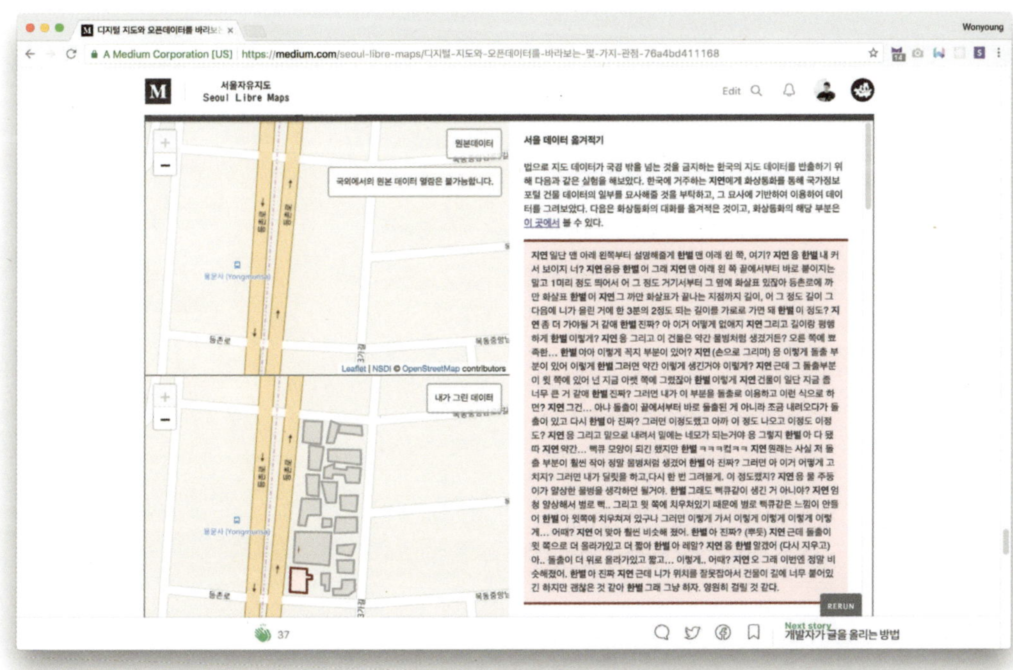

Exhibition of *Seoul Libre Maps*, DDP. Photo: Kyungsub Shin Studio.

ACTIVE ARCHIVE: SEOUL BIENNALE INTERNATIONAL STUDIOS

John Hong
Curator, Seoul Biennale 2017; professor, Seoul National University

The Role of the Archive

An archive is by definition an urban common. Through its Greek origins, it is a record of a city's culture and activities, housed within government institutions. Urban historian Spiro Kostof in his nine points that constitute urbanity goes so far as to insist a city cannot exist without its archive. If one thinks through the logic, it makes obvious sense: property lines are drawn, financial records registered, original ideas claimed, and relationships between individuals and companies legally defined. In the democratic context, these documents become part of the public domain. It is our right to access them and this right (theoretically) allows us to engage in our systems of governance and transformation.

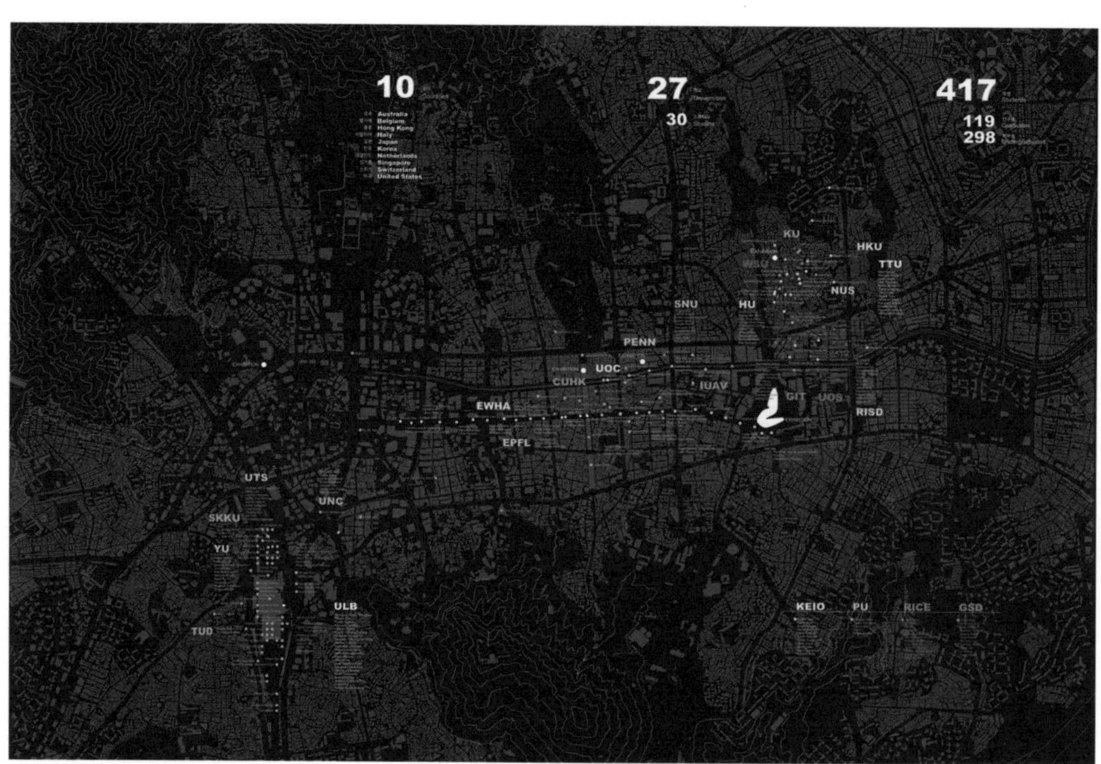

Map of student projects: Three major areas of research included the work of 417 students from 27 universities from 10 different countries.

City as Process exhibition container at DDP: Featuring University of Seoul, Washington University in St. Louis, Hong Kong University, Korea University, Georgia Tech, and Università Iuav di Venezia.

A 30-meter-long model of the Euljiro Underground at the DDP by the partner studios of Dominique Perrault (EPFL) and Yoonhie Lee (EWHA).

At the same time, the connotation of what constitutes the physical space of the archive is, to put it simply, completely mind-numbing. Where the spirit of the archive is to represent the common good, its body is the basement repository of endless shelves containing similar documents indiscriminately mixed. The extraordinary lumped together amongst the overwhelmingly ordinary is only navigable with the help of grumpy experts. And since the archive is part of the lasting systems of the city, there is no urgency to visit it today because it will be there tomorrow.

From the conception of the Seoul Biennale title "Imminent Commons" I argued (and failed) for archiving to be added as the exhibition's tenth common. Why? The answer is context specific. In terms of architecture and urbanism, Seoul is a city that reinvents itself, not just spatially (which it does with reckless abandon), but also through its conceptual stratums. As an example, the idea of fragmentation and radical juxtaposition was once used as a point of criticism for Seoul's urban fabric. Just as the word "bad" now means good in street lingo, fragmentation in Seoul is the new "bad." We have renamed and politicized "discontinuity" as "diversity" and therefore it has become cool and full of potential.

Therefore, Seoul's physical and conceptual shifts put the city in constant flux. Its spatial timeline advances not through decades, but in a matter of months and weeks. The case in point is the research areas selected for the International Studios that roughly trace the exhibition sites of the Seoul Biennale. They span the vibrant garment factories of the Changsin-dong region just outside of the east gate, the Euljiro region with its swarm of micro-businesses amongst the megastructure of the Sewoon Sangga, to the Seoul Station region where the newly opened 7017 Seoullo highway-turned-park is catalyzing new connections.

Even as this swath spans the old city core, it is also the center of a myriad of new policies manifesting in construction projects leveraging the existing city as a new resource—a marked shift from the recent past where these parts of Seoul may have been erased. To these means, the exciting yet ultimately empty buzzword, "urban regeneration" has been tried on by universities and governments alike with inconclusive results. The diverse assets and complexities of these sites resist any overarching conceptual approach. This is where the research of the International Studios is so important in defining a way forward.

Visitor as Curator

The creation of an *Active Archive* necessarily devolves the role of a single curator in the effort to pluralize the term. The core challenge of the *International Studios*, to actively engage audiences while still functioning as a repository, was compounded by the conflict between the quantity of documents and the size of the exhibition space. Across the 27 participating institutions, there were 1700 drawings to be displayed within a diminutive 110 m2.

A subset of this challenge was to also open the academy. Let's face it: Most of the general public does not know what goes on within the confines of architecture schools—the incredible body of knowledge is created amidst the pointed criticism of peers and professors through the span of grueling all-nighters. After a review where only a few dozen are present, the work is removed from the walls and relegated to the realm of ephemeral dreams. And yet the design research within our schools is the imminent weather vane for the future of the profession and our cities.

In this context, the *International Studios* view Korea through the eyes of 417 students and professors, with institutions spread over 10 different nations. This important work is literally a global network, registering urban thinking at the

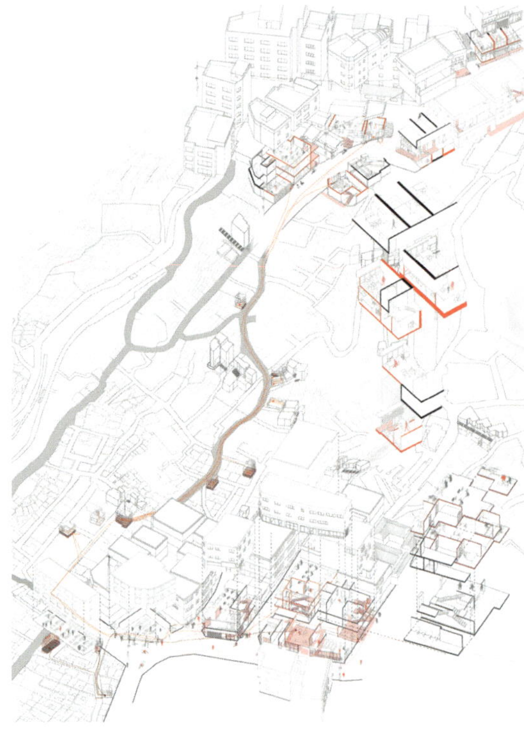

"Delivery" and live-work networks in Changsin-dong by Connie Yeung Man Ki, Canossa Chan Yuet Sum, and Justin Kong Sze Wai, Eunice Seng and Koon Wee Studio, HKU.

Data Room of *Active Archive* at the main exhibition venue in the Donuimun Museum Village.

scale of continental drifts while also demonstrating the surprising convergence of ideas despite the aforementioned isolation of the universities. In the main venue at the Donuimun Museum Village, the medium of the exhibit took on three different forms that demonstrate the compelling depth of thinking: A *Data Room* documents the abundant research of all the studios, pixelating the myriad of factoids so audiences can reassemble them for their own conclusions. A *Panoramic Archive* then brings these pieces back together within a synthetic and comprehensive record of all the work. Finally, a *Micro-Auditorium* replays the key public events and symposiums that shaped the outcome of the *International Studios*, inviting audiences to re-engage in the salient questions of the Biennale.

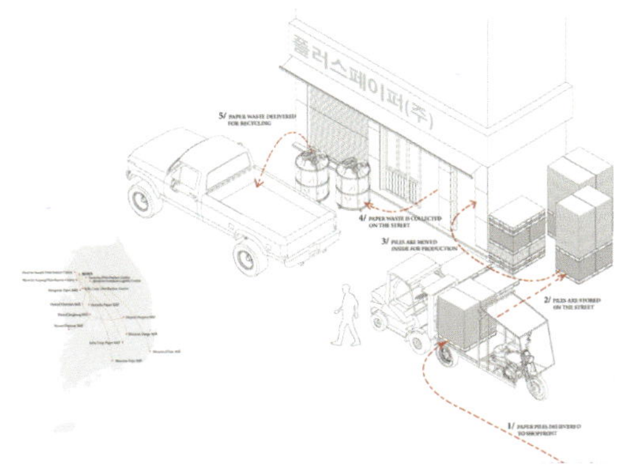

Delivery logistics in Euljiro by Chan Wai Sum Sam, Peter Ferretto Studio, HKU.

Data Room

As if reading a book backward from its bibliographical references, a *Data Room* of background research conducted by all the studios works as the entry point of the *Active Archive*. Formatted as 200 individual postcards, each captures some compelling information about the three Seoul-based sites. We can pick through the complex delivery networks that are integral to the livelihood of Changsin-dong and Dongdaemun. We can also track the life of the urban poor and their segregation within the public realm. In the Seoul Station region, we can begin to apprehend the area's complex underground to over-ground section and how numerous historical sites are hidden with this fabric.

In architecture schools, we have sat through the tedium of presentations where seemingly unending data justifies and "rationalizes" a design approach. However, disaggregated from a specific proposal, these fragments of research become more potent in the way they isolate and reveal a fascinating and sometimes absurd factoid about Seoul. Their flashcard-like format allows visitors to become their own curators in assembling an evidence-based conclusion. The postcard is also admittedly the lowest and slowest format of information exchange, pre-dating the easy immediacy of the internet. The back of each card even has a place for stamps and a note so you can disseminate the information across oceans and nations. Not that anyone would, but the potential itself changes the very way one reads the data: as something that travels, has agency, and which is ultimately meant to be shared.

Physical and metaphorical window from *Data Room* to *Panoramic Archive*.

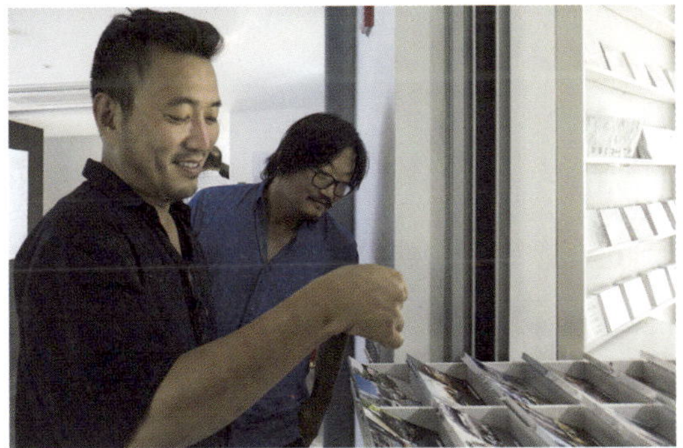

Separated from their projects, the fragments of data sometimes reveal absurd details about Seoul.

Panoramic Archive displaying Simon Kim's Upenn studio.

Panoramic Archive

Linked to the _Data Room_ through a literal and metaphorical window, the _Panoramic Archive_ is at the opposite end of the spectrum of the postcard. As an all-digital interface spanning the width of the room, instead of separating it asks users to synthesize, unfolding a horizon of drawings, photographs, and text. Even as it archives the breadth of all the _International Studio_ contents, it can be curated in a fine grain manner by participating universities, the nine Biennale themes, or the designated research sites. This allows visitors to engage the archive through both its ephemerality and through its depth. The speed at which one can peruse the contents allows an overview of the global arc of all the school's work, where the large-scale screen allows immersion into the detailed space of the drawings.

Even as the diversity of the work is dramatic, for the purposes of this writing, it is more useful highlighting what is common. When comparing across schools, for example, the most striking aspect is how analysis and design have converged to a point where we can barely distinguish between them. Instead of idealized ambitions, projects tweak the everyday and re-systemize it.

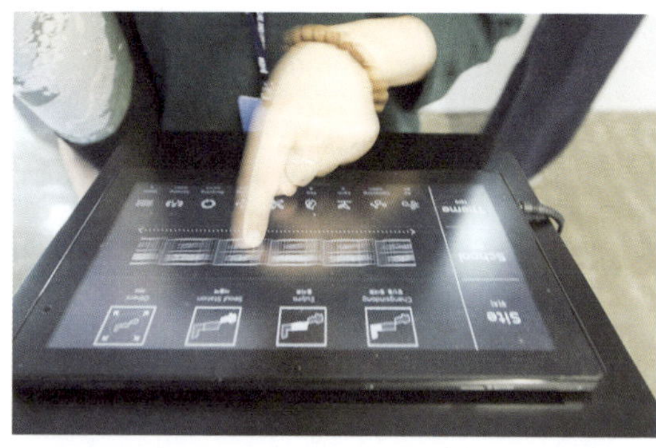

The _Panoramic Archive_ can be interactively curated by each visitor.

Perhaps this is related to the "hacker" movement where inherited logics become a playground to be used and misused. Rice University's "Standard of Democracy" studio under Professors Urtzi Grau and Guillermo Fernandez-Abascal best express this tendency through a brief that critiques the "futility of extravagant ambitions" in a design for a multi-regional parliament. In particular, their studio's *Back of House* drawing by June Deng, JP Jackson, and Sai Mai hacks the common, but necessary, elements of meeting rooms, hallways, bathrooms, and mechanical systems into new configurations for heightened communication.

When curating by site, imminent futures are inextricably linked to Seoul's complex past. History is made visceral and tangible as if the body of the site through its very labor needs to go through a difficult transition of rebirth. Unlike the ease of urban renewal, there seems to be an inherent pleasure and pain in the palimpsest. In Alejandro Zaera-Polo's "Imminent Commons" studio for Princeton University, Ying Qi Chen creates a series of immersive sections documenting the history of Sewoon Sangga. In particular, its brief but notorious status in the 1980s as an epicenter of pornography and illicit skin-trade seems to be a reminder that an innocent urban regeneration is impossible—that the futures of our sites will always be marked through guilt by association.

In terms of a thematic curation of the work, all studios were tasked with embedding the master concepts of the Biennale: the Resource Commons of earth, air, water, and fire and the Technology Commons of making, recycling, moving, connecting, and sensing. Perhaps the aforementioned difficulty of each site was a looming factor: Rather than mining the poetics of the terms within distilled research, the sheer complexity of each project's contingencies intertwined with the themes.

For example, "Air" became central to the studios of professors Dominique Perrault of EPFL and Yoonhie Lee of Ewha University in taking on the underutilized underground of the 1.5km Euljiro underpass. Attempting to alleviate a stubbornly compromised but key urban site, projects such as *Crossing Boxes*, by Jyungryun Shim act as ventilating respirators—connecting, coordinating, and untangling the difficult intersections of above-ground streets with the underground infrastructure. Likewise, with the

Back of House for a new parliament by June Deng, JP Jackson, Sai Ma, Urtzi Grau and Guillermo Fernandez-Abascal studio, Rice University.

Technology Commons, creative urban making in the Euljiro region was central to the partner studios of Peter Ferretto of the Chinese University of Hong Kong and Hangman Zo of Seoul National University. Their students grappled with the difficulty of existing residual zones, transforming them into fabrication and educational programs as if to prove the rarified conditions of the site can act as a generator of programs.

The three modes of curation ultimately allow for vastly different ways to deliver the information to diverse audiences. During the opening week, the Australian Embassy hosted an event where the University of Technology Sydney commandeered the *Panoramic Archive* so that the exhibit (at least during the 2-hour event) was wholly dedicated to their school. In other instances, joint classes between universities were held where old rivalries were rekindled through the critique of the "ahhs" and jeers of student participants. The archive also served as a critical tool for an in-depth meeting between high-level Seoul City officials in discussing the real potential of the projects, as well as for locating future sites for a new generation of architecture and urban design competitions.

Micro-Auditorium

Sharing ideas within the institution is one thing, but place people into the midst of a public forum and a new heightened anxiety to clearly define those ideas emerges. Even if no one was nervous, the public events of the *International Studios* formed a kind of nervous system for the program, a connection of real-time synapses not possible through email or conference calls. With a stage in the room, the jetlag of our international guests was quickly displaced by the jolt of decorum required to present before an audience. As a cornerstone of the *Active Archive*, the *Micro-Auditorium* documents the year of intensive public meetings leading up to the opening. In particular, the videos highlight the fascinating discourse from the three major symposiums that focused on the studio sites.

The first event, *Imminent Dongdaemun*, held at the University of Seoul in the Fall of 2016, presaged the many challenges professors and students would face. Participating institutions included the University of Seoul, Chinese University of Hong Kong, Seoul National University, Hongik University, Ewha University, Rhode Island School of Design, Sungkyunkwan

Sewoon Sangga in 1980 by Ying Qi Chen, Alejandro Zaera-Polo's studio, Princeton University.

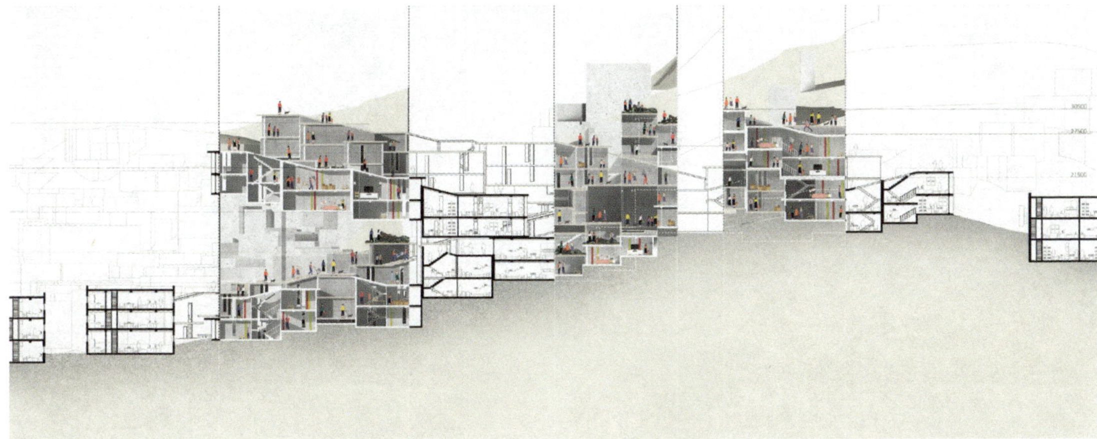

Live-work-scape in Changsin-dong by Jessie Alison Chui, Eunice Seng studio, HKU.

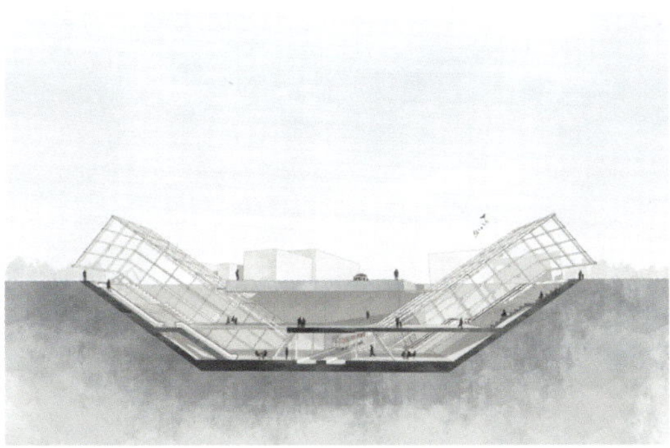

Crossing Boxes at the Euljiro Underground by Jyungryun Shim, Yoonhie Lee studio, Ewha University.

University, and Washington University in St. Louis. In a defining moment, Professor Annie Pedret called for the creation of an *International Studio* "Glossary of Terms." The emerging common vocabulary should bind together the diversity of ideas, focusing the trajectories of research.

For example, Professor Hyungmin Pai, co-director of the Seoul Biennale, brought to the table the idea of a "Synthetic Commons." He argued that while the traditional notion, represented in the now familiar allegory "Tragedy of the Commons," spells out the ultimate depletion of resources from the collective actions of individuals, urban commons actually gain value the more they are used. In fact, they rely on the compounding effect of political, social, economic, and spatial factors working in synchronicity.

Professor Marc Brossa brought forward the resonant term "Missed Modernization." In between and adjacent to the glistening redeveloped areas of Seoul including the DDP, there are regions that are altogether skipped over because of a myriad of complex developmental factors. Their still extant pre-modern spaces contain the potential for a uniquely diverse version of the Commons within the contemporary metropolis. In this light, Professor Dongwoo Yim of Washington University identified the Toy and Stationary Market on the edge of the DDP as a vital area of study. His term "Micro-production" borrowed from North Korean cities like Pyongyang, calls for the integration of small-scale urban manufacturing to reinforce localities. His studio provocatively asks, is there something that liberal economies can now learn from the communist model?

Archiving and making center in Euljiro, Kiwon Jeon, John Hong studio, SNU.

The *Micro-Auditorium* archives the major symposiums of the International Studios.

Similarly, Professor Jorge Almazan brought in the term "Coopetition," a mash-up of the words cooperation and competition. These seemingly exclusive impulses uniquely drive Korean marketplaces. Their spatial repercussions are extended interfaces between inside and outside that aggregate into unlikely common spaces that define districts. A broadening of this idea was Professor Sanki Choe's term, "Traversal City," used to describe the linear spaces of Seoul's modern megastructures such as the 900-meter long Pyeonghwa Market. The building's re-use and misuse generates new auxiliary programs and networks that accommodate what the original architecture failed to provide.

The second major symposium, *Imminent Changsin-dong* held in the DDP, featured professors from Seoul National University, University of Seoul, Hongik University, National University of Singapore, Washington University in St. Louis, Hong Kong University, University of Technology Sydney, Korea University, and the curators of *Production City* for the Seoul Biennale.

Professor Erik L'Heureux started off the discussion with the key question: "How do we not f**k up Changsin-dong?" The inquiry revealed the double-bind of international architectural curriculums: Even as schools require the design of buildings, the professors and students "parachute into a foreign country" for a few days ultimately leaving again with only a "naïve hunch" of the

Technology and fashion lab for Changsin-dong/DDP, Marc Simmons studio, Georgia Tech.

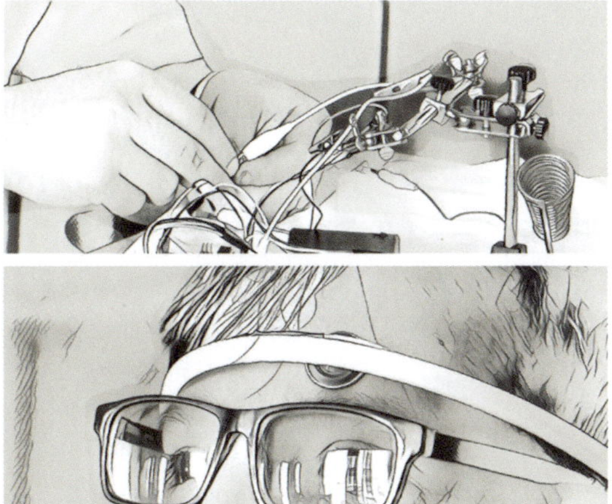

Wearable technology by Mark Freres, Maryam Kouhorostami, Dylan Wells, Kuhn Park studio, Texas Tech University.

actual conditions of the site. Professor L'Heureux continued by claiming that inculcating "love" for a place was the only possible way out of the quandary, demonstrating his point with his students' painstakingly detailed axonometric drawing of the complex micro-scale fabric of Changsin-dong.

In this way, "love" became the theme of the day. The detailed research of the other studios was nothing short of inspiring it. Complex moped delivery logistics, topographic challenges turned to advantages, the sweat of micro-factories, the hidden urban poor, the steam and mist of late night factories: all of these were seen as somehow generating the authenticity of the region. But where the love of a place is usually tied to unique spatial qualities, Changsin-dong love was mixed with images of labor. Somehow, only through the toil of the place was love validated. Instead of fetishizing material patina, the discussion brushed up against a kind of proletarian empathy.

Then, during the roundtable discussions, the Australians brought it all crashing down. Professor Urtzi Grau wanted to problematize love. He shot through what he claimed was the thinly veiled anti-modern focus of small strategic urbanism. Paradoxically, he continued, the proposals still held onto the obsession of the modernist project in the quest to always solve problems. "Is there really something to be solved or is there such a thing as productive conflict that is integral to a place?" In another breath, Professor Gerard

Timeline of *International Studio* public events leading up to the opening of the Seoul Biennale.

Micro-production in Changsin-dong/Dongdaemun, Dongwoo Yim studio, Washington University in St. Louis.

Reinmuth also brought forward another suppressed aspect of love: the fear of gentrification. Rather than assuming we have no control over the "mechanizations that are in place" for urban regeneration, he called for the efficacy of architects engaging in the redirecting of relationships.

For the Seoul Station symposium, *Imminent Connections*, held at Sungkyunkwan University, terms such as "Citizen Participation," "Hybridized Ecologies," and "Anti-masterplan" were brought to the table. Participating schools included Yonsei University, Sungkyunkwan University, University of Bruxelles, and Seoul National University.

Professor Jooeun Sung began the conversation calling for the recognition of social structures as equally important as physical structures. Showing how the average lifespan of buildings in Korea is 19 years as opposed to 103 years in the U.S., she pointed to the preservation of the Seoullo 7017 highway turned linear park as a potentially positive shift in policy. The attitude however needed further interrogation within the realm of participatory urbanism to gain real traction.

Augmenting Professor Sung's question, the collaboration of SKKU and ULB led by Professor

Cosmopolitan Atmospheres, Changsin-dong, Erik L'heureaux studio, Washington University in St. Louis.

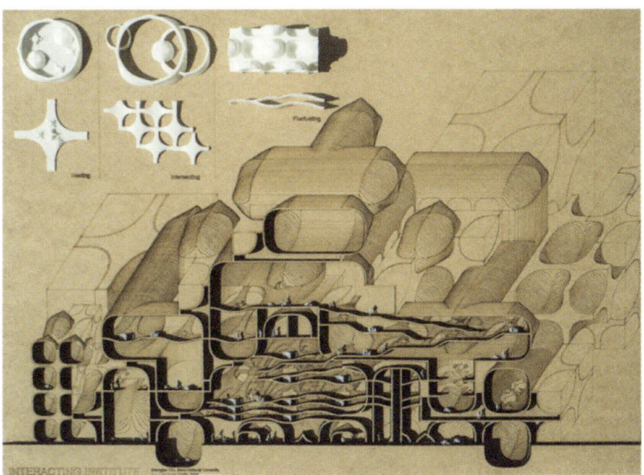

Digitally fabricated *Interacting Institute* for Euljiro by Seungjae Yoo, John Hong studio, Seoul National University.

Interface Pavilion in Donuimun, Jorge Almazan studio, Keio University.

Imminent Dongdaemun symposium, University of Seoul.

Thorsten Schuetze, brought forward the idea of an "Anti-masterplan." Based on urban planning mechanisms that can be gradually accomplished, the idea also called for improvisation along the way. As a kind of psychological warmup to this concept, ULB students in Professors Eve Deprez's and Alain Simon's studios presented a hand-drawn axonometric of the Seoul Station region. As obsessive as the Wash U students in Changsin-dong, the document was equally extreme in the way it mandated a tactile representation of the site in relative, rather than fixed, dimensions. A parallel analysis by the SKKU professors looked at the deep history of the region, how the tracks grew into a divisive barrier between the more affluent eastern section and western side. Uncovering Manchocheon stream was seen as a potential key in introducing a "Hybridized Ecology" of social, landscape, and infrastructural systems to reconnect future development to its surrounds.

Designing Discourse

Like Hyungmin Pai's "Synthetic Commons," design is a combinatory process that gains from layers of more and more synthesis. Unlike raw data, which accumulates almost indiscriminately especially in the digital era, design research requires repeatedly drawing new lines in the sand to define and refine positions. It is analogous to the concept of the "democratic paradox" put forth by cultural theorist Chantal Mouffe: the idea that democracy is inherently agonistic and that a total agreement or final solution signals its demise.

In this way, design research also requires constant discourse and the archive should be a portal to higher levels of engagement. As our symposium participants criticized the modernist project for its search for a final outcome, the changing urbanscape of our cities should also be open to productive negotiation—spatially, cultur-ally, and economically. The task of an archive, therefore, is one of designing discourse: Professor Koon Wee stated during one of our workshops that "there is no innocent delivery of informa-tion." On the other side of this equation, there is also no innocent reception of information either.

In this way, the devolution of the role of the curator into the hands of the visitor requires the design of archives that can be inhabited cre-atively. Michel de Certeau states in his essay "Walking in the City," that the act of choosing one's walking path is not a passive activity, but a creative "appropriation of the topographical system." Similarly, an archive should not passively store information but should inspire an active act

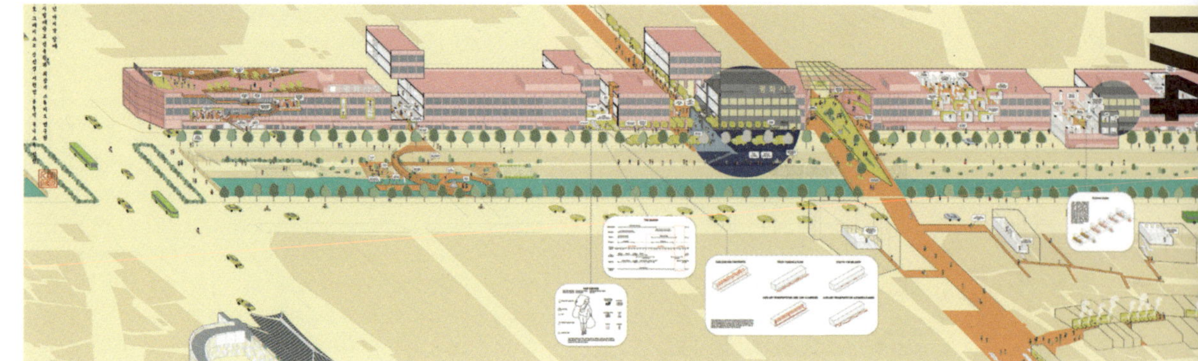

Pyeonghwa Market, Sanki Choe studio, University of Seoul.

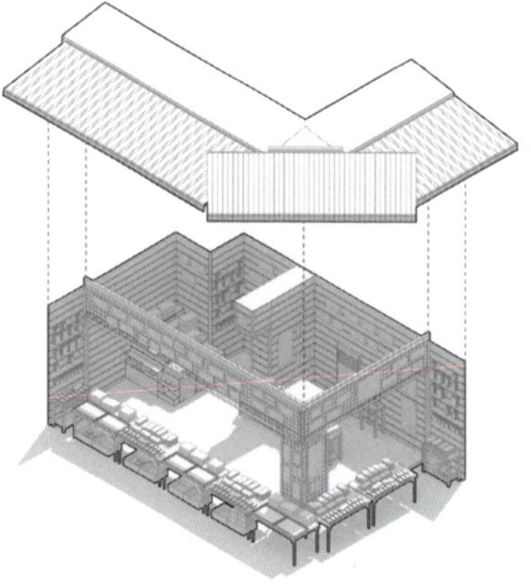

Market interface in Namdaemun by Christopher Pope, Jeffrey Nesbit studio, UNC.

of synthesis on the part of the visitor. Simply put, the role of the *International Studios' Active Archive* is to create creative process. Its design attempts to saturate the visitor with the material, so that she may have enough historical, data-enriched, and aesthetic knowledge to generate a trail of compelling discourse.

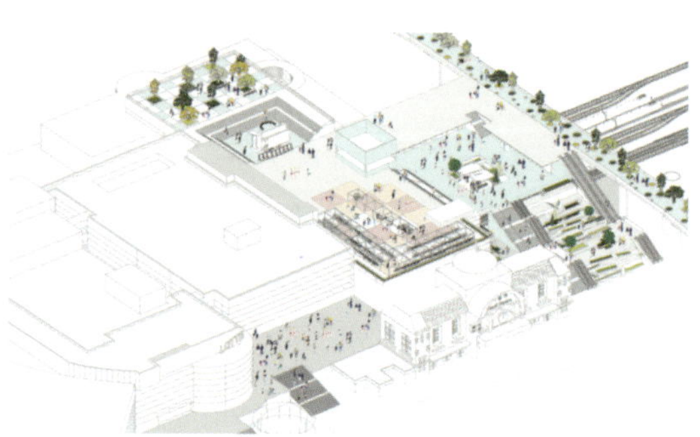

City and Events, Seoul Station, by Nan Zhang, Roberto Cavallo Studio, TU Delft.

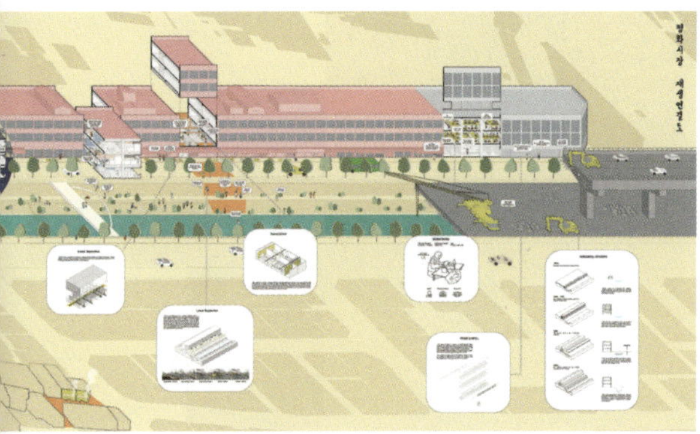

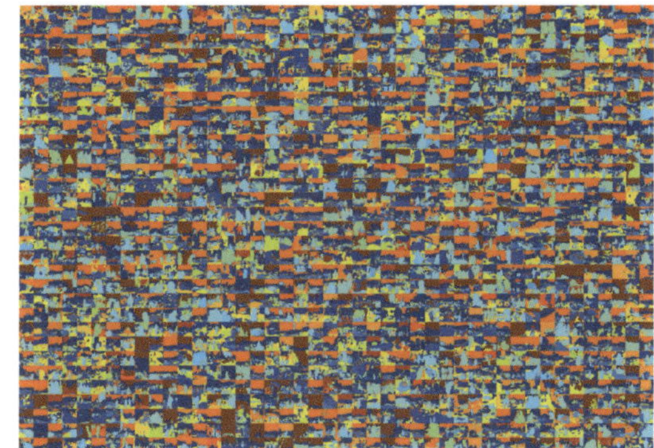

Data mining 5000 Instagram photos of the 7017 project,
Dongsei Kim and Namju Lee.

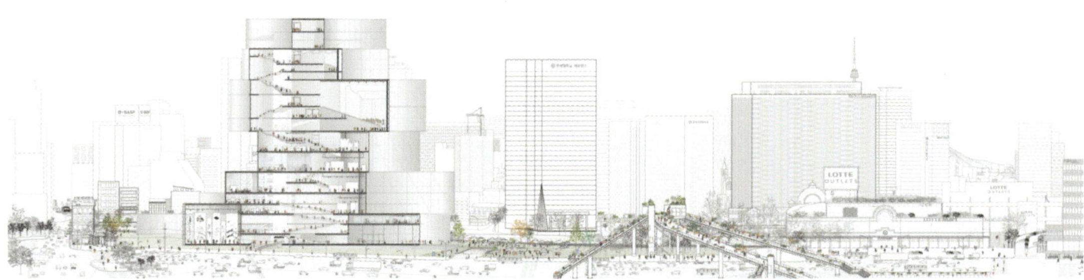

Sites and Sights in Seoul Station by Hana Lee, Gerard Reinmuth / Andrew Benjamin studio, UTS.

Imminent Seoul Station, SKKU/ULB studio.

Exhibition of *Active Archive*, Donuimun Museum Village. Photo: Kyungsub Shin Studio.

COMMON LIBRARY

Lim Kyung yong
*Curator, Seoul Biennale 2017;
co-director, Mediabus*

Logo of *Common Library*. Graphic design: Shin Shin.

At the 2016 Gwangju Biennale, Dora Garcia, a contemporary artist from Spain, featured a restored version of Nokdu Bookstore, which was one of the key venues of the Gwangju Uprising in May 1980. However, instead of merely exhibiting the bookstore the artist sought to make her project function like a real bookstore. As the role of a bookstore is to buy and sell books, her ultimate intention was to actually operate the bookstore at the first floor entrance of the Biennale exhibition hall.

Upon the request of Dora Garcia and the Director of the Biennale, Maria Lind, we put some 1,000 books of The Book Society on contemporary art and architecture, design and literature at the Biennale site, irrespective of the contexts of Nokdu Bookstore or the Gwangju Biennale.

The practice of installing bookstores or archives at a biennale drew attention for the first time at Kassel Documenta in 2012. The Documenta sold books to the visitors by inviting two representative bookstores of Berlin, Pro qm and b-books. The world is witnessing a phenomenon in which bookstores represent the cultural identity of a particular area and play the role of a platform for specific knowledge and activities in the domain of culture and art. The phenomenon has something to with the digital culture that produces and distributes more and more digital contents. As more digital contents are accumulated on the Internet and more people use them, designers and artists have started to use Internet resources for their works, and such works are distributed in a smaller form of publication to art bookstores and art book fairs all over the world. It presents a contrast to the top-down distribution of contents by a few authoritative publishers or online sites. Most of the contents available now are those made and shared by individuals using digital devices and social media services. This type of bottom-up communication is closely associated with the concept of "imminent commons," the theme of the Seoul Biennale 2017.

The *Common Library* exhibition aimed to present the Biennale's core concepts of "commoning" and commons in the context of the contemporary practice of publication. To this end, we took more note of infoshops than bookstores. Started in the squatter neighborhoods in Europe in the 1980s, infoshops now perform the role of bookstores, which produce and distribute

alternative and radical publications or serve as venues for workshops, lectures, screenings and performances. We invited two infoshops that have long been active in Asia. Irregular Rhythm Asylum (IRA), which has been in operation for more than ten years in Shinjuku, Tokyo, defines an infoshop as a "space to share the knowledge and technologies to create lifestyles and culture independent of consumerism and authoritarianism." The founder of IRA, NARITA Keisuke, describes his workplace as follows:

> A half of the IRA space is used for the sale of books on anarchism and social movements, zines, CDs, and T-shirts, with the other half for exhibition, screening events and workshops. Recently, we installed the lithographic printing machine so that anyone can produce print materials at lower prices. On every Tuesday, we open NU-MAN, a sewing meeting, to mend or produce clothes with sewing machines and other needlework devices. On Thursdays, we make woodblocks with anti-war, anti-nuclear messages along with a woodblock society, A3BC. We gain knowledge and inspiration from books and zines, and produce things with our own hands while working with others. (Email interview with Narita Keisuke, 4 August 2017)

We also invited Infoshop Byulkkol based in Seoul, which featured a temporary library, called "an archive."[1] They chose to open an "arctive" library by permitting visitors to the Biennale to establish their own library, not a conventional one selecting and excluding certain books. In fact, many visitors to the exhibition have displayed their own publications at the library during the Biennale. The Infoshop they envisioned is as follows:

> It is not only a place where people get information but also share their own lifestyle, sense, and tastes. Infoshop Byulkkol also operates a DIY (Do it yourself) workshop. We believe, however, that what counts more is to be familiarized with "common senses" rather than to learn specific skills. Infoshop is a place to learn about other values and senses than ours. For instance, it has a tacit rule or an atmosphere or a shared value that disapproves of discrimination against transvestites and hate speech. It is hard to find a place like this in the predominantly patriarchal society of Korea. The word transvestite might be replaced by women, the disabled, the homeless, and other minorities. What should we do

1. "a" refers to numerous beings that remain anonymous until they are uttered or heard. It also represents one personality like a Twitter ID, or it could be a particular space or a moment. "An archive" wants all these beings to record their own voices and to gather and show them to others. Our aim is to create a library that does not yet exist in the world. It is not an archive made of a compilation of existing materials but an archive of minorities which makes and accumulates by itself previously non-existent records on individual(s).

if a person with handicapped hands joins the DIY workshop? We may have to search for another way of operating the workshop, devise a special tool, reorganize the workshop from the very beginning, or hold a discussion again on the very concept of DIY. We can do all of these things with the common sense to "work with others, excluding no one." However, it is hard to find this kind of common sense as people mostly gather just with like-minded people and take the schisms and exclusions for granted. In some cases, even the behaviors excluding or discriminating against minorities are being accepted as cool, as seen in the video clips of collective lynching and sexual assaults uploaded onto the Internet. What should we do to challenge the belief that they can get away with it or the tacit consent of the majority? What we are doing with Infoshop is to find our own answers and share them. One of them is to create an atmosphere and a common sense that helps people never to be submissive to the rule of the majority. (Email and telephone interview, terrapin27@gmail.com, 27 August 2017)

Common Library, as an actual bookstore, had to play the role of an exhibition space hosting various activities, as well. It was composed of three rooms, including a bookstore. One independent space was set for a bookstore, with the other two serving as an archive and an exhibition room. Common Room was entrusted with the task of formalizing the concept and designing the space.[2] It is an architectural practice with a publishing imprint and an exhibition space comprised of architects, architectural researchers, and graphic designers. Knowing that Common Room could fully understand the concepts and practices of Common Library, we commissioned it to design the exhibition space.

They mainly divided the space into two, with one housing a steel bookshelf in the shape of a cross and the other containing a round floor resembling pyeongsang, the traditional Korean wooden bench. By borrowing the concept of the wooden bench, it created a physical platform to share something. At the same time, the ten steel angles rising high within the space signify the notion of exclusion inherent in the concept of "common." They explained their architectural practice as the following:

Conceptually, our design takes a critical stance with respect to the commons. The commons

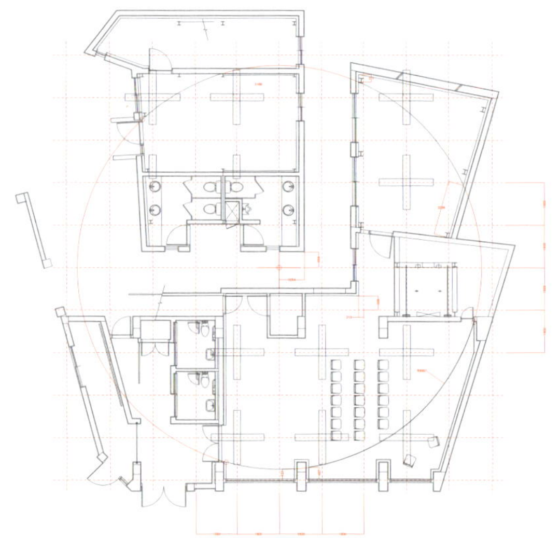

2. Founded in 2006, Common Room is an architectural practice with a publishing house and an exhibition space. Its offices are located in New York and Brussels, and the members are Lars Fischer, Todd Rouhe, Maria Ibañez and Rachel Himmelfarb; architectural researcher Kim Förster; and graphic designer Geoff Han.

is not unconditionally open; it functions only through excluding certain people or groups. The commons always asks the question who may use it and who may not. This is represented by a large circle within the gallery space, defining an inside and an outside. To allow for diversity and be more inclusive, there must then be various commonalities. Such commonalities always exist, never end, and are never closed. The cross structures in our design define space but do not close it off. The two systems, a circle and a cross, stand in contrast to one another; they are schizophrenic, and they are a contraction. They require an on-going negotiation of inclusion and exclusion, between schizophrenia and exclusion. Both systems remain abstract figures in the space. However, the cross structures have the function of defining the display, whereas the circle remains programmatically undefined, setting itself off as an internal boundary geometrically separate from the architecture. (Email interview with Lars Fischer at lars@common-room.net, 25 August 2017)

Common Room wanted to exhibit its interpretation of "common" through space, in which the audience could experience and comprehend the concept physically. Admittedly, all spaces are political to some degree within their own strategies. The characteristics of a large-scale shopping mall or multiplex theaters differ from those of a small SOHO shop or an independent theater, and the difference is exposed in a political way. They inserted the antiquated pyeongsang at the center of their design as a critical commentary on Seoul's spatial politics in which the conglomerates homogenize the cityscape. It is a welcome sight that a pyeongsang is rediscovered as a common space where people can spend time together sharing their thoughts about books.

Meanwhile, Shin Shin, a Korean graphic design duo shaped the identity of *Common Library* and designed the space of the library section, with "modular" bookshelves. This is another example of a productive collaboration between architects and graphic designers.

While *Common Library* is a place for sharing information and the experience of the moment, Cancelled 6/21/90 by Alexander Brodsky and Ilya Utkin, a gigantic book with a collection of architectural drawings existing only on paper, presents the possibility of making past materials come into being in the present through the practice of publication. Russian architects born in 1955, they studied together at MarkHI before working together and spearheading the foundation of an architectural movement, called "Paper Architecture." Though their drawings existed only on paper, not realized as actual buildings, they reveal the utopian aspiration inherent in the practice of architecture. A Finnish publisher, l'Esprit de l'Escalier, published their original drawings in life-size prints.

Another participating artist, EH, is a photographer of city landscapes and buildings. He installed panoramic images of the Sewoon Sangga printed on banners at the exhibition. The images are also reproduced and distributed as postcards, a popular medium to remember cities. In this way, EH examines how a city can be remembered and reproduced by visitors as well as its residents.

Onomatopee, a publishing house based in Einthoven, the Netherlands, has been releasing project-based books. Its books occupy a unique and extraordinary position. How do books produced by artists operate amid contemporary activities of publishing? Their publications may provide an answer to this question.

During the Biennale, *Common Library* conducted four rounds of audience-engaging talks and workshops. Kim Sang-ho, an architectural editor, led the talks on the theme of "Making Architecture Books and Magazines." Focusing on his edited work, "Documentum," he recounted his experience and shared his opinions as an editor specialized in architecture.

Jiro and Yousun of Infoshop Byulkkol, the backbone of *Common Library*, held a zine-making workshop, attended by an open audience. Elementary school students shared their experience of making their own books. Sungmin Lj (director), Gim Ik Hyun (artist), and Hana Oh (editor) shared stories about the "Town and Community Archive," based on their project. Lastly, Jeong Da-young, one of the first curators in Korea specializing in architecture, and now at the National Museum of Modern and Contemporary Art, Korea (MMCA), related her experience of planning and organizing architecture exhibitions at MMCA.

Common Library, Donuimun Museum Village. Photo: Kyungsub Shin Studio.

PROJECTED LIVES: UNDERSTANDING THE CITY THROUGH FICTION FILMS

Choi Won-joon
*Curator, Seoul Biennale 2017; professor,
Soongsil University*

The narrative of a fiction film is often meticulously interwoven with its environmental settings, and we learn much more about the city and its everyday culture through these films than we casually recognize. Jim Jarmusch's *Night on Earth* (1991) invites you to five cities across the globe, to drive through its streets in a cab and witness the way people encounter American and European towns in different manners. In *The Lunchbox* (Ritesh Batra, 2013), a mistake in dabbawala, the unique lunch delivery system of Mumbai, initiates a story of unexpected relationships in the Indian city. Fiction films, or narrative films as they are alternatively called, are attentive to the unique spatial properties and residential culture of each city and region, and capture not only the material features of the built environment but also "the ways people have put meaning on the notions of the home, domestic culture, public spaces, landscapes, monuments, the difference between inside and outside, and so forth." (Jacobs, 2013)

Subplot—Chilsu and Mansu and Seoul: Then (1988) and Now (2017)

Left: provided by Dong-A Export
Right: Choi Won-joon

Park Kwang-su's *Chilsu and Mansu* begins with a shot of the Gwanghwamun boulevard as it was in the late 1980s, unusually empty during a civil defense drill and therefore foreshadowing its later conversion into a plaza in 2009. However, historical records of such monumental areas are abundant, and the true use of fiction films for the understanding of the city can be found in their depiction of lesser known areas and the record of everyday lives that take place in those spaces.

Thus fiction films are a rich source with which we can discover the various aspects of urban space and shared resources throughout the ages, not in abstract theories or academic analyses but in the specificities of the everyday life.

This is why the *Film & Video Program* of the Seoul Biennale of Architecture and Urbanism 2017, in order to reach a broader public audience with this year's theme of "Imminent Commons," engages the popular medium of fiction films. In recent years architecture film festivals have become quite popular across the globe, held in cities such as Rotterdam, Budapest, New York, Santiago de Chile, Istanbul, Johannesburg, and Seoul—now celebrating its ninth year, the Seoul International Architecture Film Festival is our collaborating partner in preparing this program. Whereas the programs of these festivals consist mainly of documentaries, the *Film & Video Program* proposes the strategy of including a larger volume of fiction films. By availing these films as cinematic texts for urban comprehension, the *Film & Video Program* aims to convey architectural and urban issues to an audience beyond an inner community of students, scholars, and practitioners from related professions. Parallel programs of guest talks and fora, inviting renowned filmmakers and architects from Korea and abroad, make these readings readily accessible to the public, and incite further discussions.

Light and the City

The correlation between film and architecture needs no emphasis. The birth of cinema coincided with the historic moment in architecture when its prime language, as suggested by Le Corbusier in his idea of "promenade architecturale" or by Sigfried Giedion in Space, Time & Architecture, was recognized as space and time, which were also the quintessential expressive dimensions of the new medium. These shared dimensions of communication led early silent cinema to a series of city symphonies, from Walter Ruttmann's *Berlin: Symphony for a Great* City (1927) to Dziga Vertov's *The Man with a Movie Camera* (1929), which celebrated the unprecedented dynamism of modern cities in terms of physical environment and the lifestyles it inspires.

Narrative films, which have since become the major form of cinematic production, were also fascinated by the city. Of course, as fiction films offer filmmakers and designers a chance to create imaginary environments, some stories take place in non-places and distant utopias/dystopias. However, the interest of the *Film & Video Program* lies in those films with stories that are intricately connected with the actual realities of a city and its unique way of life. Genres like film noir are inherently linked to the urban environment, and chase scenes, with which the medium of moving images exploited its media-specific capacity in its early years, can act as pretexts for portraying the

In the Gangbuk area, the old half of Seoul, anonymous apartment complexes of enormous scale have replaced many of the shanty towns in hillside areas, where architects often found instances of voluntary cultures of sharing. The overpass, once applied to many busy intersections, has since been demolished, as not only their usefulness in facilitating traffic flow became questionable, but the primary value in urban planning has shifted towards prioritizing spatial quality over functional needs.

distinctive features of cities: San Francisco's *Bullitt* (Peter Yates, 1968), New York's *The French Connection* (William Friedkin, 1971), *To Live and Die in L.A.* of the city of angels (once again Friedkin, 1985), and Paris' *Ronin* (John Frankenheimer, 1998), all make use of each city's unique physical conditions and infrastructures, including hills, narrow alleys, back streets, elevated subway tracks, and inner-city highways.

Some filmmakers are also identified with a certain city: Federico Fellini with Rome; Ozu Yasujiro with Tokyo; Martin Scorsese, Abel Ferrara, Woody Allen with New York; Mike Leigh with London; Wong Kar-wai with Hong Kong; Hou Hsiao-hsien with Taipei; and Michael Mann with Chicago and Los Angeles. (Note the curious absence of a "Seoul director," although there is certainly one known for travelling around the Korean peninsula—Hong Sang-soo sets each of his films in different Korean cities and towns, observantly incorporating their local cultures and environmental features to his formalist depiction of everyday events and relationships.) Most of these filmmakers create work on their own native home towns, but sometimes it takes the distanced, objective, yet affectionate eyes of an outsider to grasp a city's unique features: think of Michelangelo Antonioni's London in *Blow-Up* (1966) or Abbas Kiarostami's Tokyo in *Like Someone in Love* (2012). Because they are fiction, fragmentations, alterations, enhancements, and distortions of reality will happen in the name of "dramatic license," but still it is hard to picture Cleo strolling the streets of Berlin from 5 to 7 in Agnes Varda's 1962 film, just as it is difficult to imagine the mysterious events of *Don't Look Now* (Nicolas Roeg, 1973) taking place anywhere but the canals of Venice. Since these stories are specifically set to the physical characteristics of these respective cities and their unique way of life, none of these films would have the same atmosphere, or even make sense at all, if the setting were moved to another city.

Films featuring a specific city but from different periods will in turn collectively present a chronological record of its historical transformations. In *Rome* (1972), Fellini presented his beloved city as a freewheeling composite of childhood memories, the 1970s, and imaginations for an unknown future, while Paolo Sorrentino in *The Great Beauty* (2014) drew a contemporary portrait of the city with focus on the lives of its cultural upper class. 45 years ago Fellini's film ended with a group of motorcycle gangs storming towards the Colosseum, but in The Great Beauty, the historic monument is visually appropriated from the terrace of a luxury apartment as an extravagant backdrop, exposing how historical heritage, a shared asset crucial for the formation of urban identity, has different presence and social relevance in each era.

Nighttime in Seoul no longer seems to be hours of release, relaxation, and meditation. As the capital of a nation with the longest working hours, Seoul is one of the brightest cities during the night, its use of urban space has expanded considerably over time, giving birth to and being propelled by the proliferation of 24-hour convenience stores. The streets and spaces of the city are also further divided, with minutely articulated functions designated for every inch of space.

Seoul Projections

If we turn our attention to Seoul, Na Hong-jin's first two features, *The Chaser* (2008) and *The Yellow Sea* (2010), can be read as an interesting contemporary diptych. Both thrillers use the physical characteristics of the city, and the cultural norm they gave birth to, to build up the tension of the narrative. In the former, when a shop owner unsuspectingly tells her local customer, who by then the audience identifies as a serial killer, that his narrowly escaped victim is hiding in the shop's back room, the audience's terror is all the more amplified by their knowledge of how suffocatingly confined the spaces of these old-fashioned mom-and-pop stores are. Also, in The Yellow Sea, a contract killing is to take place in a common building type we call geunsaeng: mid-level buildings with floors for rent, and, in this case, topped by the victim's residence. Amusingly one of the floors is rented by an architecture design firm, whose late working hours further add difficulty for the inexperienced killer in finding the right moment to commit his crime in the building's stairway, a space which is both private and public, differentiated through time of use. In addition to further use of typologies such as private residences from the 1970s, apartment block developments, and bus garages as important settings, the way chase scenes are constructed in sharp distinction between the two films—captured by smooth camerawork in the irregularly patterned alleys of Gangbuk (Seoul's old downtown in the north of Han River) in The Chaser and with handheld giddiness in the gridded streets of Gangnam (the southern part of Seoul developed in the 1970s) in The Yellow Sea—attests to Na's keen interest in the features of Korean urban environment. Thus, his narrative is closely linked to the physical and cultural features of a city, and it would not be an overstatement that the tension of these films is much more effective on the Korean audiences who are well aware of the characteristics of these domestic urban typologies and their modes of occupation. Through these narrative settings, we can further grasp not only the physical features but also the cultural implications and meanings we have endowed upon these typologies and our environment at large.

Seoul-based films can also be read from a certain thematic point of view—for instance, the issue of urban commons, the focus of the present Biennale. Bong Joon-ho's *The Host* (2006), one of the most commercially successful films in Korean history, invites the viewer to look into contemporary Seoul in respect to its shared resources and spaces. In the film, the very birth of a creature results from polluting the Han River, the most cherished common resource of the metropolis, and most of the events take place in the shared infrastructures of the city: the riverside parks, sewers, bridges, and plazas. As architect Hwang

Densely lined high-rises casting deep shadows onto the streets, the Taeheran-ro in Gangnam is now one of the busiest streets in Seoul. In the late 1980s, however, it was still a barren landscape. Only two buildings exist in this shot, one being the Renaissance Hotel by the famous modern master Kim Swoo-geun, identifiable by its smooth, fluid corners. Ironically, it is missing in the contemporary photo, as it has been recently demolished—only after a life of three decades—to make way for another large-scale commercial development.

Doo-jin remarked, Bong reconfigurates our map of Seoul and its places through his depictions of these "border spaces," consequently redefining our view of the city and the world. (Hwang, 2006) Such readings can be expanded as we enlarge our scope to other urban objects and broader cinematic texts. *Chilsu and Mansu* (Park Kwang-su, 1988) and *The Day a Pig Fell into the Well* (Hong Sang-soo, 1996), arguably the most impressive debut features from the 1980s and 1990s, present Seoul, its people, and their world views from their respective periods. The former is a bird's-eye-view observation on individual circumstances against a broader social context, while the latter delivers realities of individualist culture ridden with illicit love, abuse, compulsion, and rudeness through fragments of urban sceneries. Certain recurring elements represent the differences in each era's urban perspectives: fast-food franchise restaurants appear as either a romantic place in which one can dream of new—albeit short-lasting— human relations, or a dry, lonely place that an urban nomad can most cheaply but rightfully occupy. Only two to three decades have passed since their original release, but the spaces, densities, customs, and human relations captured by these films are already too different from each other and from today, attesting to the fact that Seoul is indeed one of the rapidly changing cities in the world. By incorporating to our list of films *The Flower in Hell* (Shin Sang-ok, 1958), *Under the*

Sky of Seoul (Lee Hyung-pyo, 1961), *A Day Off* (Lee Man-hee, 1968), *Night Journey* (Kim Soo-yong, 1977), and *Blossom Again* (Jung Ji-woo, 2005), those that concretized the physical and empirical realities of the Korean capital in other periods, we are given a sequential spectrum of incidents with which we can understand how its unique culture of occupation, possession, and use of urban commons, and the general attitude toward urban issues, have changed throughout its modern development, from the postwar years to today.

From the Screen Outwards Towards the City
Cities around the world have created their unique spatial structures and building types over extensive periods, and also their own ways of habitation and cultures of sharing. Today, the accelerated process of globalization threatens to erase such regional differences, but on the other hand it has also created an environment in which we can share our respective wisdoms through a broad network of knowledge, and cultivate a new urban culture through their reinterpretation. Fiction films, whose narratives are generated by careful observations of particular places and how people live in them, enable us to understand in detail the diverse urban cultures of the world. In the words of Korean film critic and director Jung Sung-il, "movies always dealt with people's lives, and those people live within structures set by architecture. Therefore films entered architecture via

The rooftop where the two protagonists accidentally drew the public's attention and ended up holding their unintended protest in the final moments of the film, was located in the Express Bus Terminal area, one of the Gangnam's earliest developments. Although many of the area's buildings survive to this day, many have gone through superficial makeovers. In this particular case, its rooftop is now covered by large walls that make the building seem bigger. Now the name of the building is, quite tellingly, Reborn City.

people's lives, and architecture became the principle to control cinematic space." (Jung, 1996) What we aim to do in the *Film & Video Program* is the reverse: to enter people's lives through cinematic space, to gain a better understanding of their diversity and the possibilities in the culture of sharing that would procure a sustainable future for the city.

Bibliography

Jacobs, Steven. 2013. *The Wrong House: The Architecture of Alfred Hitchcock*. Rotterdam: nai010. p.10.

Jung, Sung-il. 1996. "The Relationship between Movies and Architecture." *PoAR*. October 1996. p.16.

Hwang, Doo-jin. 2006. "The Host: A Reinterpretation of Han River." *Cine 21*. 23 August 2006.

However, these drastic and superficial changes notwithstanding, it is also interesting to observe that certain aspects of the Metropolis have not changed so much over the past thirty years. The CBD area near the City Hall shows two mom-and-pop shops— one a pharmacy and the other a snack bar— still in existence, with the very same name but with much refined signboards. Design styles come and go, but the essential daily circumstances, the everyday life that gives scale and pattern to urban commerce and movements, persist.

EDUCATIONAL PROGRAM

Educational Program of the Seoul Biennale: Reaching Out to the Public

Kim Sunjae
Project Manager

There are many forms of education. It can be a lecture or a workshop, for example. The former is more passive of the two, while in a workshop the participants are expected to have a more active role with direct participation. The educational program of the Seoul Biennale 2017 offered both lectures and workshops.

Lectures

There were four series of lectures: *Open Talks*, *Biennale Lectures*, *Seoul Biennale Talk Series*, and *Curator's Talks on Culture Day*. The first of the lectures in the program began as early as April 2017, while the last was delivered in late October. Lasting seven months, the lecture series was the longest of the Seoul Biennale programs.

What we considered most important in planning the lecture program was making sure that the lectures were suitable for all age levels and backgrounds of the target audience. The other issue was how to approach the diverse themes of the Biennale differently in each lecture series. The main target audience was housewives in their 30s-50s and college students. The diagram below summarizes the distinct characteristics of the four lecture series.

First, nine *Open Talks* were offered from April to August, 2017. True to the series title, the lectures covered a general range of subjects. This series was planned and implemented jointly with the Junglim Architecture and Culture Foundation (http://www.junglim.org). The series was designed to hear experts from various fields address topics on urbanism, society, and Seoul. We asked, what would people expect from general knowledge lectures addressing the theme of architecture and urbanism? We also wanted to make sure that the topics did not overlap with those of the other lectures in the program. In the end, three topics were selected. They were "social capital," "shared wealth," and "local community." Participants were encouraged to share their thoughts on these topics. What are the ways that the citizens of Seoul can take ownership of the urban issues the city faces? What would an urban community based on solidarity of individual citizens look like? What are the ways of

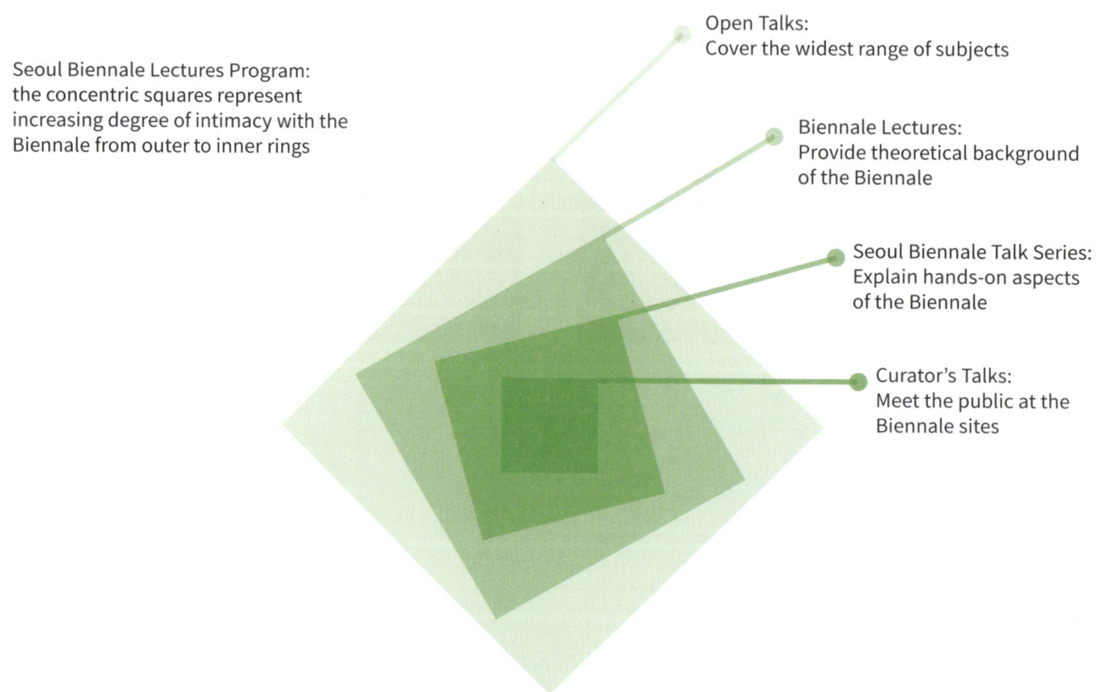

Seoul Biennale Lectures Program: the concentric squares represent increasing degree of intimacy with the Biennale from outer to inner rings

cooperation where voluntary efforts of citizens translate into a new system, or a new form of governance? These were the questions we asked for the lecture series. They were shared with both the lecturers and the public.

Second, like the *Open Talks*, the *Biennale Lectures* also offered nine lectures, and the periods of the two series largely overlapped. However, if the former addressed urbanism and urban issues in Seoul, in general, the latter addressed specific themes on the Seoul Biennale 2017. How does a biennale "exhibit" architecture? What can a biennale of architecture and urbanism contain? Why is Seoul hosting such a biennale? These questions were linked with the four ecology commons (air, water, energy, and earth) and five technology commons (making, moving, communicating, sensing, and recycling) that made up the nine themes of the Seoul Biennale 2017. The nine lectures were not matched specifically with each of the nine Biennale themes. However, the purpose was to raise public interest in and awareness of the Seoul Biennale well before its opening by providing the public an opportunity to familiarize itself with the topics of urbanism, architecture, design, film, and others. The two lecture series in the program (see below), which were offered after the opening of the Biennale, reflected feedback from the first two series.

Seoul Biennale Talk Series: People Who Made the Biennale

The third was *Seoul Biennale Talk Series*: People Who Made the Biennale. It took place while the Biennale was open. The Seoul Biennale was explained most directly in this talk series. This series was originally planned as "curator talks." The plan was changed to include talks from artists, curators, and designers who participated in the Biennale outside of the two main exhibitions, i.e., the *Thematic Exhibition* and *Cities Exhibition*.

In terms of the schedule, too, the series was originally scheduled for Wednesday and Thursday evenings. However, reflecting the feedback from the earlier lecture series, it was changed to Wednesday evenings and Saturday afternoons so as to include more people from diverse age groups. The talks were designed with those who have already seen the Biennale exhibitions as well as potential visitors in mind, and to give them opportunities to learn more about the Biennale. In a series of twelve talks, the audience learned about the curatorial goals and specific works from the Biennale curators and artists, as well as from the designers of the Biennale logo and the

souvenirs. The talks were an opportunity for the audience to have direct and indirect experience with the Biennale. In addition to the Biennale themes, the talks also touched upon the subjects of architecture, design, film, photography, fashion, and exhibition organization in an attempt to reach out to the widest possible population range that might take a sustained interest in the Biennale.

Lastly, *Curators' Talks on Culture Day* provided our program audience the most intimate level of familiarity with the Biennale. There were two talks in this series, each taking place on the last Wednesday of the month marking the "culture day." Unlike the other lectures that took place in conventional lecture venues for one or two hours, the two curator talks took place at the outdoor venues of two Biennale projects for longer hours. This series was designed to complement the more passive lectures in the program, and to give the participants an opportunity to enjoy different aspects of the Seoul Biennale exhibitions apart from the conventional forms of viewing them.

Thus the lecture component of the educational program of the Seoul Biennale 2017 was designed to embrace diverse age groups and a wide range of topics, and to diversify the conventional lecture format. Analyses of the data after the program show a high participation rate of office workers, or young professionals, in addition to participation from the two original population targets, i.e., housewives and college students. Furthermore, unlike our initial expectation of an even dispersion of age groups among the lectures, data also show strong age bias by lecturer. That is to say, depending on the lecturer, the age dispersion was concentrated either in the 20–30s or 40–50s groups. These data provide food for thought on developing and improving future programs. For example, first, more lecture programs should be developed for office workers, or young professionals in architecture and urbanism and in other related fields. Second, publicity campaigns for lecture programs should target specific age groups. Third, programs for over-60 age groups should be developed. Such measures would further enrich the Biennale lecture program in the future.

Workshops Program

The term "workshop" once referred to a working area, or a place where one worked for a living. Today it is more often than not used as an educational term where group consultation and group work takes place. Furthermore, it is a term commonly used to refer to an educational program where teachers and students stand on relatively equal footing, and where greater emphasis is placed on the participation of learners. It was in this context that the Seoul Biennale 2017 prepared a variety of workshops.

The main goal of the workshop program was to "get to know and understand the city we live in." Thanks to the development of transportation and new technologies, many people today are well versed in where to go to find the cheapest hotels in cities around the world, and how to find where the best restaurants are and in what city. But people often do not know much about the city they live in. Our goal was to share with our participants rarely-told stories about Seoul, so that they may take interest in getting to know better the city they thought they already knew but did not. It was decided that workshops, complemented by field trips, would best serve our purpose. The field trips encouraged the participants to express what they saw and felt in the follow-up classes.

We also tried to make our workshops different from those offered by other biennales or museums and analyzed workshops offered by other institutions in Korea and abroad. Our research showed that most programs offer workshops for students from grade school to college age. We decided to expand the age range and included infants and adults in our program. In the case of the workshop organized jointly with the Institut Français in Seoul for infants (age 0–3), we devised a program using foldable mats to enhance their sense of space and touch. For school-age children we organized a field trip to an inner-city neighborhood where their capacity of space perception would expand and where they would newly discover what a city actually looks like. The field trip for the children was organized specifically because such a program is not available as part of their regular school curriculum. For middle school students, few workshop references were available. In the end, considering their age and ability, we gave them a concrete task of building an earthquake-resistant structure. College students were asked to explore the deeper layers of the city; they went to Sewoon Sangga and its vicinity to learn about the historical, social, and cultural backgrounds of an inner-city neighborhood.

Workshops can provide rich educational experiences not available through regular school curricula. Of course, there are limits to how much the students can learn from one or two workshops. However, while it might be logistically possible, it is not a good idea to try to cover too many themes in a single workshop. This is particularly so in the case of workshops dealing with urban neighborhoods. In such a case, it is better to identify a neighborhood, decide what is significant about it, formulate a theme, then develop a workshop program that focuses on that theme. Our workshops were developed around two keywords, "urban regeneration" and "urban manufacturing," and they focused on only two neighborhoods, namely the Euljiro area and Changsin-dong. However, workshops in many other neighborhoods in Seoul can be developed using the same two keywords, or using different keywords. What is important is not that students see and learn about more neighborhoods, but that they see deeper, feel what characterize the neighborhoods, and have a visceral experience of them. It is hoped that future Seoul Biennale educational workshops would offer more such opportunities to the citizens of Seoul.

Workshop on Urbanism: Urban Layers of Time
Jooeun Sung
Curator, Seoul Biennale 2017;
professor, Yonsei University

The vision of the Seoul Biennale is the establishment of Seoul as the "city of humanities." In the past, the terms "city" and "architecture" were synonymous with their physical facilities only. The fact that today there are attempts to understand them from a broader humanities perspective is a sign that Seoul has embarked on a new direction of urban planning, from one that relied on development only to one that respects history and culture. Seoul is a dynamic city with a history that goes as far back as 2,000 years. There are many traditional landmarks that still breathe the city's history and modern structures that fill the city. The more recent, contemporary buildings with atypical shapes boast state-of-the-art construction technologies, while elevated highways are being taken down to make rivers flow and to create more green spaces in the city. What do we see, hear, listen, feel, and share in a city such as this?

In the workshops we organized as part of the Seoul Biennale 2017, we share what the citizens and children of the city see in the development of the city, rather than what the experts see. It is only when the citizens free themselves from the confines of "my house" or "my apartment" and see the city from the perspective of "our neighborhood" or "our city" that the city actually comes alive. Mindful of the alienation and self-centeredness of contemporary life at both individual and many collective levels, our workshops were organized with the goal of opening the doors of communication, of putting into practice citizen participation in the improvement of urban environments.

An American journalist and activist Jane Jacobs said, in *The Death and Life of Great American Cities* (1961), "Cities have the capability of providing something for everybody, only because, and only when, they are created by everybody." Spaces must be organized to respond to the culture and demands of their users, and to that end, participation of users/citizens in the space building process is a must. Long-lasting building are the most environment-friendly solution in a city, not recycling or renewable energy, and not the technologies that make them possible. Architects design buildings, but it is the users who complete them. Citizen participation ensures social sustainability, and a workshop is one of the active ways of participation. Our

workshops were organized to provide a platform of gathering people together. By providing specific programs and venues, it was hoped that people with different backgrounds would gather to communicate and share a common interest, and that ultimately this would contribute to the improvement of the city. More specifically, the workshops were developed in three different tracks so that adults, youth and children could each share their experience in age-appropriate ways.

City Re-readers
For college students and adults
Sewoon Basement
1–4 August 2017

The workshop program for college students and adults was designed as a mini-Biennale with the same theme of "imminent commons." The participants became artist, curator, and reporter and interpreted the Biennale theme from their respective roles. The result was then presented in an "exhibition." According to a city legend from the heyday of Sewoon Sangga, it was said that the manufacturers in the area could make even Mazinger Z, the hero of the popular Japanese super robot manga series by the same names. Indeed, from the time it was built in the 1960s through the 1980s, Sewoon Sangga was the very symbol of modernization. After suffering decades of decay since then, it is now on the threshold of being revived. The basement, once a boiler room, was used as the space for our workshop. Our workshop participants navigated and explored the sangga—the "shopping mall"— without the help of digital devices. Chance encounters led to profound revelations. Participants interpreted the information and organized an exhibition. What do the layers of time at Sewoon Sangga look like to them? In the program pamphlet, Shim Youngkyu and Kim Myoungkyu, the instructors of the workshop describe the program as follows: "'Commoning cities' [is a phrase that] means splitting a city so that the various elements of the city are differentiated and looked at together and up-close. The physical elements of Sewoon Sangga are critically observed and, through the inspiration obtained in the process, reinterpreted. Participants not simply view but participate in the city that they create. Using the surplus resources available from around Sewoon Sangga, participants make an analogue map."

I can feel the change in my child's eyes when she looks around her surroundings. —A parent of a City Explorers participant

It was not like a regular lecture. As a non-specialist, the direct experience was great. —A City Re-readers participant

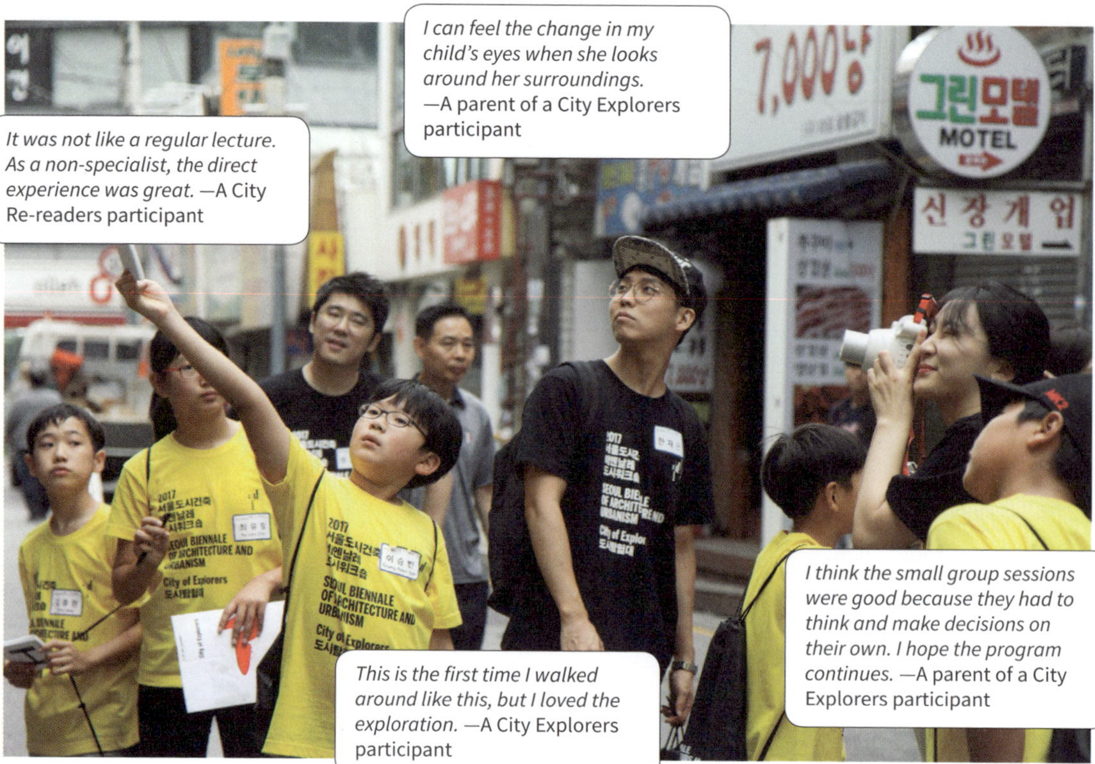

I think the small group sessions were good because they had to think and make decisions on their own. I hope the program continues. —A parent of a City Explorers participant

This is the first time I walked around like this, but I loved the exploration. —A City Explorers participant

The children have such a strong memory of the restaurant. I guess that is the reality of Seoul. —A City Explorers instructor

My child usually does not like unfamiliar environments. It's difficult for him to join a new workshop. But he loved this workshop. —A parent of a City Explorers participant

The teachers were nice, and I made new friends. I learned a lot from them. —A City Challengers participant

It was great because children learned about architecture through various on-site urban experiences. —A parent of a City Explorers participant

City Challengers
For middle school students
Yonsei University
12–13 August 2017

The specific assignment for this workshop was "Withstand the shaking!" More specifically, the students were challenged to understand the principles of earthquakes, and to understand the basic materials and structures of earthquake-resistant buildings. They were divided into small groups and given the assignment of sketching then designing, building, and competing for best earthquake-resistant building. Using a seismic wave simulation device, they tested the actual safety levels of their work. The goal of the workshop was to have the students understand the importance of both the engineering and aesthetics aspects of architecture.

City of Explorers
For grade school children
DDP and the Changsin-dong area
9–30 September 2017

The workshop for children was a program for the children to walk, see, discover, express, and make suggestions on what they saw in the city. The workshops were organized around the three major themes of understanding the city through the alphabet (9–10 September), color (16–17 September), and figure (23–24 September). The children explored the city as treasure hunters, observing urban objects and phenomena according to the task they were given. They took photographs and shared their experience with friends and made suggestions. They explored the DDP and the Dongdaemun areas, the Cheonggye stream, the Changsin-dong area where an urban renewal program recently began, and the trail along the historic City Wall, from where they could see the whole city below them. Various facets of the city would have made small and big impressions on them: the sounds from cars, machines, and people; the smells of food; store signs they did not know existed before; and the microcosm of nature along the Chonggye stream. They would walk, be dazed, and drift. The experience would increase their interest in the city and in architecture. Polaroid pictures were taken, which were used to complete a map by the children. The children made suggestions on the shape (alphabet), color, or figure of an urban object based on their own imagination. They would draw an abstract picture of their exploration of the city, or they would create a three-dimensional object and share their thoughts.

Cultivation of mature citizenship is the ultimate goal of our workshop on urbanism. This may sound old-fashioned, but a more apt expression cannot be found. We live our lives in the city, but we are not taught how to read a city. As an adult and an urbanism professional, we learn by rote. We teach our children music, art, physical education, and social studies. Why should the subject of urbanism and architecture be excluded from the school curriculum? Why should we not connect urbanism and architecture with social sciences? Our workshop on urbanism began with these questions. Thus the focus of the workshops was not on making. The experience gained by the children and its process was more important than what they made in the workshop class. Continuity of such experience, one that accumulates in layers of time and place, is urgently needed. It is hoped that the experience of seeing, listening, expressing, and sharing would have made a positive contribution to the children's attitude toward learning about the city. It is also hoped that our workshop plans would serve as a basic guideline for similar workshop programs in the future, providing opportunities to more citizens, and that their accumulated perceptions would further bring positive changes in Seoul.

IMMINENT COMMONS SEOUL TOUR

Suna Lee (Planning)
Project Manager, Seoul Biennale 2017

Nayeon Kim (Statement)
Project Manager, Seoul Biennale 2017

Cities change and urban landscapes undergo constant transformation. However ordinary citizens do not necessarily keep up with all the changes. *Imminent Commons Seoul Tours* (hereafter "Seoul Tour(s)" or "Tour(s)") were planned to help citizens explore the city's old and new places on foot. The Tours were also organized around the "regenerative city," the heart of the Seoul municipal government's urban planning philosophy that is directly relevant to the "imminent commons" theme of the Seoul Biennale 2017. The city is now being transformed under the direction of an "interactive regeneration" policy that is intended to better embrace all aspects of civic life and all levels of citizenship. At the heart of this municipal program is respect for the distinctive history and culture of various urban places. The Tours were organized to highlight some of the recently regenerated urban sites in Seoul. More specifically, the Saturday Tours were organized around the regenerated sites, while the Sunday Tours were selected based on the four Biennale themes of urban foodshed, urban regeneration, production, and shared resources. A total of twelve Tours was organized.

Saturday Tours

Seoungbuk Art Village
9 September & 14 October 2017, 2–4 pm

Three Tours were organized around the theme of urban regeneration. The first Tour destination was Seongbuk Art Village. Historically, Seongbuk-dong has been a home to many renowned cultural figures and artists. Today, networks of artists and local residents are thriving in the neighborhood, where artists are playing the leading role in the stewardship of and generating public value. Seongbuk-dong sites showcase existing art spaces as well as new cultural spaces created out of the recently regenerated urban spaces, such as the formerly idle public utilities space, as well as a private property that fell into disuse. The tour of Seongbuk Art Village offered the opportunity to learn about the "Seongbuk-dong model," or the regeneration model of urban spaces as venues of public art spaces.

Seoullo 7017
16 September 2017, 2–4pm

The second Tour destination was Seoullo 7017, which is a major urban regeneration project of the Seoul municipal government that was completed only a few months before the opening of the Seoul Biennale. The project transformed an elevated highway cutting across an urban center—completed in 1970—into a pedestrian-only skywalk. There have been mixed responses to the just-opened Seoullo, but the "sky garden" with over 24,000 trees and flowers is becoming an urban oasis of respite from the busy human and vehicle traffic below it. It is also contributing to the regeneration of retail consumer activities around the Seoul Railway Station area, long suffering from decades of urban decay. The installation art work, Yunseul at the Malli-dong Plaza near one end of the sky walk, is one of the must-see highlights of Seoullo. One of the Tour participants said that she did not know about this work before the Tour and that the beauty of the art work alone is enough reason to visit the Malli-dong Plaza, a major entry point of the sky walk.

Embassy of France
21 October 2017, 2–4 pm

The last of the Saturday Tours destinations was the compound of the French Embassy in Seoul, one of the most celebrated works of architecture in Korea best known for its masterly embodiment of modern and traditional aesthetics. It is the work of Kim Chung Up (1922–1988), a pioneer of modernist architecture in Korea. The embassy compound is scheduled for major repurposing work. In particular, the chancery—the office building—will be restored to its original state while two new buildings will be added to the compound. Cho Minsuk of Mass Studies, one of the two architectural firms commissioned for the work, led the tour.

Sunday Tours
The Sunday Tours were organized around the four Biennale and Biennale-affiliated exhibitions: *Urban Foodshed, Regenerative City, Production City*, and Imminent Commons.

Urban Foodshed Tour
3 September & 8 October 2017, 2–5 pm

The *Urban Foodshed Tour* began at the Donuimun Museum Village where the Biennale restaurant and café were located and ended at an urban farming site in Haengchon, a neighborhood north of the Village. The Tour included a trail along the historical City Wall from where the participants had a full view of the old Seoul and the Namsan Tower. The walking was strenuous in this Tour, but the adults and children alike enjoyed the colors of the autumn season and the surprise of finding a farming garden in the middle of the city.

Regenerative City Tour
10 September & 15 October 2017, 2–5 pm

A key destination of the *Regenerative City Tour* was the Oil Tank Culture Park, which transformed an oil storage tank into a cultural space. The tour focused on the Culture Park, but the Seoul Energy Dream Center was also included in the itinerary in consideration of the participants who came as family. In the meantime, a visit to the Nanji Studio—an earlier example of the city government's urban regeneration project—was cancelled due to a schedule conflict. The Tour, in spite of this change, was the most popular Seoul Tour. At Seoul Energy Dream Center, the Tour participants were briefed on the zero-energy system and future fuel cell vehicles. The participants showed keen interests in the Dream Center building, which is a zero-energy building.

Production City Tour
17 September & 22 October 2017, 2–5 pm

The *Production City Tour* was a walking tour of Sewoon Sangga and the Euljiro area, the leading inner-city manufacturing neighborhoods.

Participants started the Tour from DDP, walked along Cheonggye Stream, stopped by an exhibition at MOTOElastico, and weaved through the Gwangjang Market and the narrow alleys in the neighborhood that they did not know existed in Seoul. The old neighborhoods excited the children and the adults were surprised to find the many manufacturing shops still operating in the back streets in the heart of Seoul. The tour also included a visit to the Sewoon Basement where the participants saw a robot arm and an exhibition of its works.

Imminent Commons Tour
24 September & 29 October 2017, 2–5 pm

In the *Imminent Commons Tour*, participants visited the Seoul Upcycling Plaza and its vicinities. The Plaza, which opened in September 2017 with the theme of "commons," or shared resources, focuses on upcycling, not recycling. The Plaza has an exhibition space where visitors view upcycled products created by various designers. Participants also toured the Seoul Sewage Science Museum adjacent to the Plaza. Upcycled products are more widespread than perhaps the general public is aware of. The social value inherent in them, and the aesthetic values they have as designer products, appeal to many people. One designer who made a particularly strong impression on the participants was one who made handbags and wallets out of used fire hoses, which are regularly discarded in massive quantities. The docent explained that the designer's father was a fireman and that, as a child, the designer always played with waste fire hose.

Imminent Commons Seoul Tours took on-line reservations only. It was a popular program, and reservations were closed before the deadlines. The sites chosen for the tour seem to have contributed to this popularity, for it is all too common for anyone living in cities to miss landmark sites near them. As expected, families were the majority of participants, while students and office workers were also visible. For each Tour, an expert on the Tour neighborhood or space accompanied the participants. In their evaluation of the program, many participants said that the Tours helped them to get to know the places better. As already mentioned, some of the Tours were organized around the theme of the Seoul Biennale 2017, namely *Urban Foodshed, Regenerative City* and *Production City*. There were many positive reactions from the participants, with many looking forward to the next Seoul Biennale.

Imminent Commons Seoul Tour, Oil Tank Culture Park, Mapo, Seoul. Photo: Kyungsub Shin Studio.

Letters to the Mayor, DDP. Photo: Kyungsub Shin Studio.

LETTERS TO THE MAYOR

Storefront for Art and Architecture

Letters to the Mayor (hereafter LTM) is an exhibition format first implemented in 2014 in New York City by Storefront for Art and Architecture. Since then *LTM* exhibitions have taken place in fifteen different countries. The project is intended to remind architects of the important role they play in building urban environments. Moreover, architects can represent the collective aspirations of society; they have the responsibility to respond to the voices of the alienated in society. However, contemporary architectural practices today seem to suggest that architecture as a profession is losing sight of its social responsibility. *LTM* provides architects an opportunity to look back on their own role and responsibility while writing and delivering letters—their voice—to the mayors.

It is natural that the Seoul edition of LTM, taking place as part of the Seoul Biennale of Architecture and Urbanism 2017, should consider the social and ethical duty of Korean architects. They cannot avoid embracing the special circumstances of their divided country and the presence of North Korea. Given this un-negotiable reality, their role and responsibility must also reflect their special circumstances. It is in this context that the Seoul edition of *LTM* took the format of writing letters to two mayors.

In the letters to two mayors, the first ever in the LTM history, architects from Korea and abroad wrote letters to the mayor of Seoul or Pyongyang, or to both (in the case of Pyongyang, it would be to the Chairman of the People's Committee of Pyongyang, since the city does not have a mayor). There was no formal requirements or restrictions on the content, and the letters ranged from advice to the mayor to a proposition of a concrete project. For example, architect Kim Jong-seong cites various sites of Seoul and Pyongyang and asks the mayors to take measures to preserve them. Nader Tehrani refers to a new possible project to the mayor of Pyongyang, citing a possibility of inter-Korean exchanges. Another letter by Yi Hyeong-jae suggests exchanges between Seoul and Pyongyang in the vein of the title of the exhibition, *LTM: Seoul + Pyongyang*, while another architect (JI Jungwoo) addresses only the Seoul mayor, reminding him of the problems of the city.

Apart from the letters themselves, the other important elements of *LTM* exhibitions are the tables and the wallpaper. In fact, Storefront considers them two of the three most important elements in any *LTM* exhibition. The tables and the wallpaper not only complement the contents of the letter but they are what distinguish one *LTM* edition from another from city to city. The tables and wallpapers in the Seoul edition were designed by Nameless Architecture, a Seoul-based practice. Eunjoong Na of Nameless calls the work "a series of cross-points" and says that the motif came from the military barricade. One wonders whether the cross-point refers to a border demarcation line or a possibility of creating a new intersection. In the three-vector cross-point that Nameless designed, each vector wears a different color. In general, when two vectors cross each other, the third vector is the balancing element; this seems to tell the story of the future Korean peninsula. For the past seventy years, Seoul and Pyongyang have been running in parallel; it seems that as soon as the two sides cross each other, a certain future must come into play to provide the third balancing element.

The cross-point designed by Nameless has even more interesting stories to tell from the production side. The three vectors come together perfectly to create a single "cross-point" on a computer screen. However, on the production floor, the three vectors cannot so neatly converge on a single point due to certain laws of physics, or certain physical limitations, such as the thickness of the material and the law of gravity. Such might be the reality that Seoul and Pyongyang, or South Korea and North Korea, would inevitably face. While a perfect point of convergence exists in theory, we cannot but ask the fundamental question of whether or not such a point actually exists in reality.

The design work by Nameless is not confined to the tables and wallpapers. The stools, objects, and the letter stand in the exhibition are also part of the design work. They comprise an exhibition method. They also act as a means of directing the visitors to a certain path of movement. The letters themselves, displayed on multiple surfaces, are thus presented in a somewhat loose manner while the contents address serious matters. These various objects greet the visitors at the entrance of the DDP Design Exhibition Hall, the venue for the *Cities Exhibition* of the Seoul Biennale 2017, stoking the interests of the visitors to further explore the *Cities Exhibition* inside the Hall.

The importance of the role LTM plays in the spatial organization of the *Cities Exhibition* is not limited to the fact that it acts as a foyer to the *Cities Exhibition* space. Going back to the Seoul-Pyongyang reference, *LTM* also occupied a 3x3 meter modular space that was adjacent to the foyer and placed between Seoul and Pyongyang within the *Cities Exhibition*. The wallpaper is used only in this modular space, which we, the organizers, conceived of as a figurative Demilitarized Zone (DMZ) which lies between Seoul and Pyongyang. Moreover, it is the most minimal space among the fifty-odd modular spaces that comprise the bulk of the *Cities Exhibition* space. That is to say, just as in the real DMZ along the North-South Korean border, it is the most untouched space. The wallpaper becomes a backdrop, while the tables and stools function more like objects rather than the utilitarian pieces of furniture that they are. The space was designed to make the visitors feel as if they are entering into a picture frame. We found that in this space the visitors actually participated in an exhibition that was not an exhibition.

It is regrettable that we, the organizers of the *LTM* Seoul edition, ultimately failed to persuade architects in Pyongyang to participate in the exhibition. At a certain point during the preparation period, it was difficult to actively solicit the North's participation as inter-Korean relations rapidly deteriorated amidst escalating tensions and hostile words. Our initial hope was to have at least some direct exchanges with Pyongyang. Clearly, those initial plans were not followed through, and the exhibition became one-way communication. There are architects, based outside of Korea, who could write on behalf of North Korean architects. If we solicited them, their letters could have balanced out, at least to a small degree, the total absence of North Korean voices in the exhibition. However, our initial plan was to hear directly from North Korean architects, and to exhibit their letters to the mayors of Seoul and Pyongyang.

The regret was palpable at an LTM-related roundtable talk held at DDP on 17 September 2017. Moderated by Jihoi Lee, the panel of speakers—which included Hwang Doojin, Yehre Suh, Kim Sora and Na Eunjoong—exchanged their thoughts and opinions on Seoul-Pyongyang exchanges from various levels and on how such exchanges might be possible. Na Eunjoong thought that perhaps a cross-point between the

North and South could be set up through LTM design; and Hwang Doojin spoke about the need for new architectural typology in both Seoul and Pyongyang, and about how the two cities should pursue urban planning. Yehre Suh made a presentation on the possibility of a "third way" exchange that involves mapping of the North-South border areas; and Sora Kim delineated the urban characteristics of Seoul and Pyongyang and mentioned the need for exchanges between the two cities. In fact, these are conversations that should continue within the Korean architecture community. It is hoped that the *LTM* roundtable talk we started would only be the first of many such conversations to follow in the future. As it is, one cannot avoid the nagging sense of shouting in the void when it comes to the issue of North-South exchanges.

Perhaps only continued and repeated attempts on the part of South Korean architects would bring a response from the North. In this regard, and ironically, the *LTM* exhibition and the roundtable talk, held amid extremely heightened tensions on the peninsula, could not have been better timed. In the past, architects in South Korea have called for inter-Korean exchanges, only to withdraw from the calls when they were considered inconvenient. That is to say, architects in South Korea can hardly be free from the suspicion that they neglected their responsibility, that not enough efforts were made to engage their counterparts in the North under the pretext of volatile inter-Korean relations. For this reason, I would like to take this opportunity to thank, once again, the architects at the roundtable talk who voiced their strong wishes for renewing efforts for exchanges with the North.

Imminent Commons: Commoning Cities, DDP.
Photo: Kyungsub Shin Studio.

London
Made

A SPACE FOR THE COMMONS

Obra Architects
*DDP exhibition space designers,
Seoul Biennale 2017*

The city is in disarray, too big and too formless, it can no longer be regarded as the spatial embodiment of social order or, as Lewis Mumford would have it, "the crown jewel of human achievement." In the last 50 years, it has gradually become more difficult to think of the city theoretically in any terms other than those of an ideology of relentless production and consumption. If traditionally, the city's representational role had been one of embodying a collective will towards social togetherness, we have found, at some point not too long ago, that it can no longer embody values holding community together.

The Greek Polis found, in the Agora, the urban embodiment of democracy as the ideal of self-governance of a people. Roman Civitas in turn found, in the Thermal Bath for example, an ideal meeting space for the world's first multi-ethnic society, which was enabled by Roman law. It is doubtful that the city of today could ever be able to represent anything of the sort. During the 20th century, the need for a new form of architectural representation was acknowledged by the leading practitioners of the time: starting in the 1920s Le Corbusier, for example, dreamed of the city as the embodiment of a "new spirit" of humanist confidence in advancing technology, and a bit later, Louis Kahn tried to develop a new form of architectural monumentality to give the triumphant values of postwar liberal democracy their physical home in the city.

In our day, perhaps because we now know more about history, we find it more difficult to adopt similar postures of imaginative urban bravado, and tend to take our chances with the continued glorification of new technology as a substitute for fresh urban ideas. Although it would seem the social problems of today such as income inequality, racism, crime, pollution, corruption, etc., are what have caused these urban dysfunctions, it might be that the opposite is true, that the city's functional chaos and disarray are actually the cause of society's pathologies. In other words, the corruption of society did not cause the decline of the city, but instead the decline of the city caused the corruption of society.

It is then very important to try to think the city anew, and the Imminent Commons Biennale—the first architecture biennale of the city of Seoul—offers a great opportunity to do so. We believe the focus on the "commons" already announced in

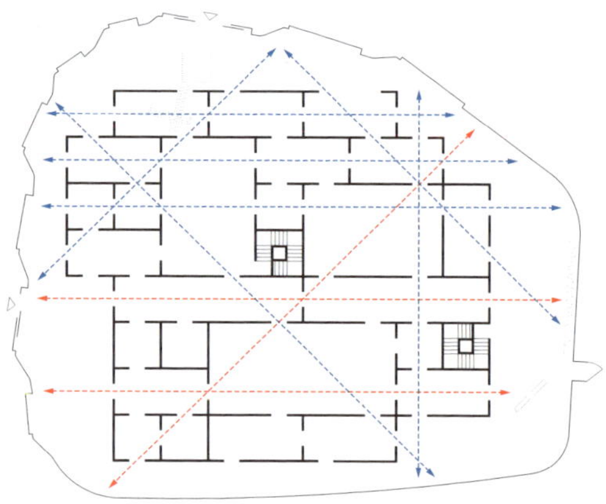

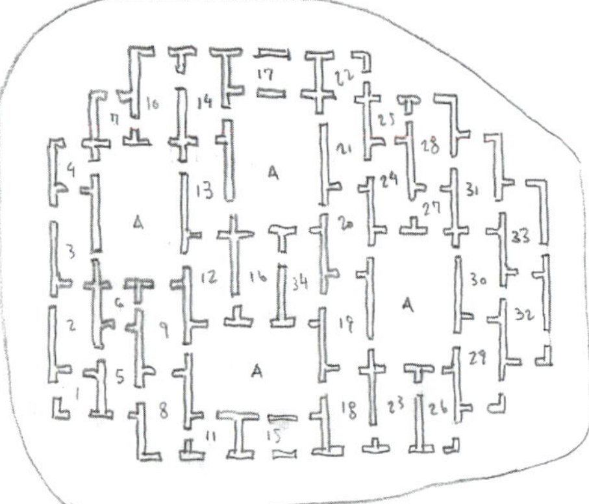

34 GALLERIES   SPACE COUNT

8 SINGLE (9m²)

26 DOUBLE (18m²)

4 COMMONS
LECTURES
INTERACTIVE ACTIVITIES
FILMS
ROUND TABLES
ETC.

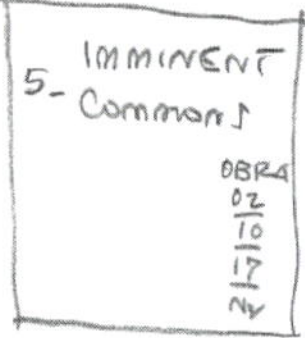

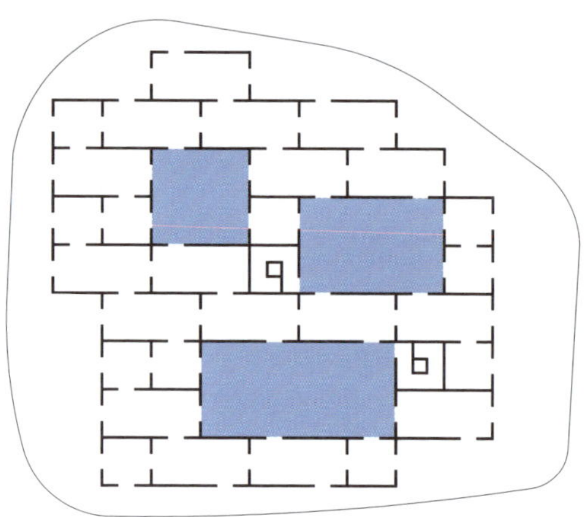

CITIES EXHIBITION COMMON SPACES
SCALE 1:250

the very title of the biennale is a good beginning. The question implied by the title is: who does the city belong to?

Quantitatively considered, most of the city is privately owned, and countless buildings are inaccessible to the public forming a ghostly majority of which we only know very small parts: the random lobby, the place of work, the friend's house, the school building, etc. By virtue of the fact that we don't have access to them, it can be said that in our heads, those private spaces don't really exist and the city remains—at the level of this personal experience of denial—overwhelmingly public while it is experienced as an interconnected sequence of plazas, streets, parks, temples, churches, etc. The city might be technically private, but "phenomenologically," public space still constitutes the glue holding together the images of the city in our heads.

The word "commons" does not only denote public shared space and resources, but in the context of cultural exchange such as the biennale, it also implies the consideration of the opposition and conflict between the ideas of private and public. The underlying notion is of course the idea of private property, perhaps the most momentously fundamental concept for any discussion about anything, not only for the city, but also for society in general. We can say without hesitation that it is perhaps the collision between incompatible understandings of the reach and legitimacy of private property that has always propelled the violent march of history.

To illustrate the range and depth of the contradictions involved, we can mention for example that the word "commons" has historically meant different things. It could refer to a space of social unrest and revolutionary struggle for example, as in the Parisian Commonards of 1871, or, in its medieval assertion, the land that was set aside by the gentry for the modest and controlled use by its subjects, the commoners, who were allowed limited farming, hunting and leisure-related use of the land. The first of these conceptions implies a struggle for public ownership and class equality; the second, basically the opposite, only public access granted with the intention of keeping the social peace and preserving private ownership with modesty alleviating the hardships of life to facilitate submission to the established social order.

Perhaps because of this semantic ambiguity, the word "commons" is used today as a "common ground" word, one that might possibly imply a progressive attitude towards a common struggle for social justice or perhaps, conversely, the consideration of a minimum of social reforms typically adopted with an eye on avoiding class war while we continue to go about business as usual with the world. It has therefore become a safe and fashionable word that can be used for all kinds of events and texts, since in its ambiguity it can point towards the remote possibility of change without necessarily getting budgets defunded by corporate sponsors or event organizers arrested or ostracized by repressive authorities.

But what should the physical form of the "commons" be? In 1915, Le Corbusier considered the issue of public space from a formal point of view while on a trip to Rome. At the Vatican, while making an annotated sketch of Pirro Ligorio's engraving Antiquae Urbis Romae Imago, he theorized on the drawing that the public space loosely contained between the pure geometric forms of Rome's freestanding buildings held the key to the form of the city of the future.

Public space— let's call it the spatial commons—was not, for Le Corbusier, the space of the street as it was in the Medieval City, for example, but it was instead public buildings organized in open space. Some of the most arresting ruins of Ancient Rome are still standing examples of this intuition: the Baths of Trajan and Caracalla, the Colosseum, the Pantheon and the Theater of Marcellus, were all public buildings with unrestricted free access for all the "free men" of the time. They were all also wildly popular, and it is rather ironic that they were built by despots that seem to have understood well the wisdom and political credit accrued in this form of spending of public funds. Our current governments, with all of their supposedly democratic credentials are incapable of building anything remotely like them. This wisdom has been lost; in the United States today for example public space remains a hostage of a vicious cycle of neoliberal denial, as the city's infrastructure crumbles under a tacit prohibition on the spending of tax funds on anything much other than bank bailouts, wars, or incarceration. The reigning myopia of narrow utilitarian ends has obscured from view a city for the people as an end in itself.

What is fascinating about Le Corbusier's observation in confrontation with Rome is that his critique of the street as the key element in the organization of public urban space is really an attack on the building façade, the street's inseparable companion. The façade typically confronts the street "representing" the building behind it, but doing so with potentially absolute independence from the internal organization of the building. An architecture of façades sets the stage for a city of deceptive expression. If this was true in Le Corbusier's time, when Modern Architecture was waging a life-or-death war with 19th century eclecticism, it is even truer today for a society ruled by a state that has retreated from the responsibility of constructing the city and opted instead for subcontracting the task to private developers. Not surprisingly, the result is not only the privatization of public space but also the commodification of architecture's means of expression, which has ceased to embody the aspirations and values of society to become the vehicle for the marketing objectives of private interests.

During the early 1900s, the animosity against façades was connected to a desire to restore "honesty" in architecture. The form of matter was replaced by its absence: space, as the fundamental vehicle of architectural expression. The logic of the significance of architectural space relied on the obvious notion that space could be occupied by free discerning people forever reloading it with changing meaning, and that these people would be able to make their own rational decisions free from rhetorical interference.

Architecture thus shifted early in the 20th century from form to space, but the spatial city was never built. The moment invited a plethora of utopian visions to fill the gap left by the new city's absence. The potential of radically new, more democratic forms of collective inhabitation offered by modern architecture became the stimulant to boundless creativity. The best imagined cities, Ludwig Hilberseimer's High Rise City and Ivan Leonidov's Linear City of Magnitogorsk, offered relentlessly repetitive perfection, as if speculating that, once the ideal formulations for the new city had been found, the city could simply realize itself by their never-ending replication. These absent cities still torment the heart with a beauty that was never to be. Today space has become démodé; as design is being mistaken for architecture, the city's grand sweeping visions have been replaced with modest propositions as humble as urban interventions at the level of new bicycle lanes and randomly dispersed potted plants.

The Imminent Commons Biennale of Seoul 2017 provides the opportunity to rethink the significance and even the very ongoing possibility of the city. The Biennale features the *Cities Exhibition*, which, installed in the main hall of the Dongdaemun Design Plaza, offers the fascinating prospect of more than 50 different exhibits coming from all over the world.

In practical terms, the architectural design of the exhibit focuses mainly on the successful resolution of very specific formal issues related to the complexity of an exhibition designed by a committee of curators working remotely from each other from the four corners of the world. It is this characteristic of the project that suggests the possibility of regarding it as a modest analogical experiment on the city as the organization of vacant spaces available to be occupied by unpredictable content and organized non-hierarchically to invite free movement. These design premises required also a subtle but rigorous structure to prevent the exhibition from descending into a potentially chaotic experience that the collage-like assembly of disparate content might bring about.

As an analogy of urban space, the design of the structure aspires to a normative repetitiveness verging on a potential dissolution of form. Reduced to almost imperceptible rhythms of experience, form will only become legible as an insistence on certain sequences of lined-up doors, some axial and some diagonal. The depth of these sequences is revealed by the doors that, becoming smaller and smaller as they recede in the distance, cut deep into the space of the structure promising potential trajectories open to the visitors. In this way, the architectural design steps aside to give primacy to the exhibited content, while at the same time sustaining it with a measure of discreet order.

The structure, conceived as a large assembly of small galleries, mostly 3 meters wide by 6 meters long, aims to create the atmosphere of repetitive neutrality necessary to contain all the unpredictable collisions of richness the curatorial project proposes. The only exceptions, three larger spaces for public assembly, are created not by adding anything to the project but by subtracting walls and creating larger gaps. The result of the whole is an undifferentiated labyrinth, one in which no proposed sequence of experience is particularly privileged and in which each visitor can trace his or her own personal trajectory having to decide, upon arriving at every new space, to go next to the left or to the right, without ever knowing at any moment in the visit, if they have seen it all or not.

A SPACE FOR THE COMMONS

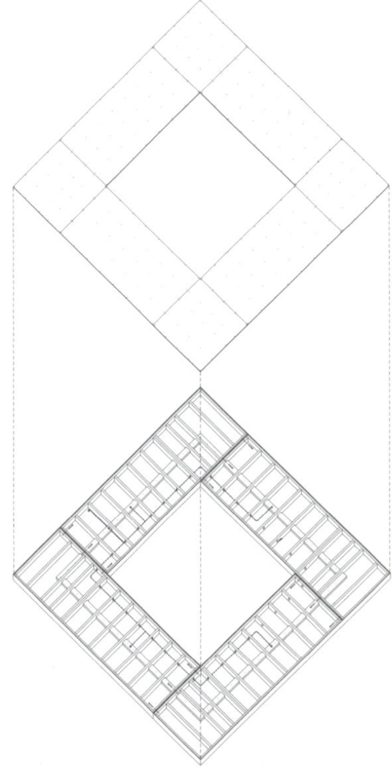

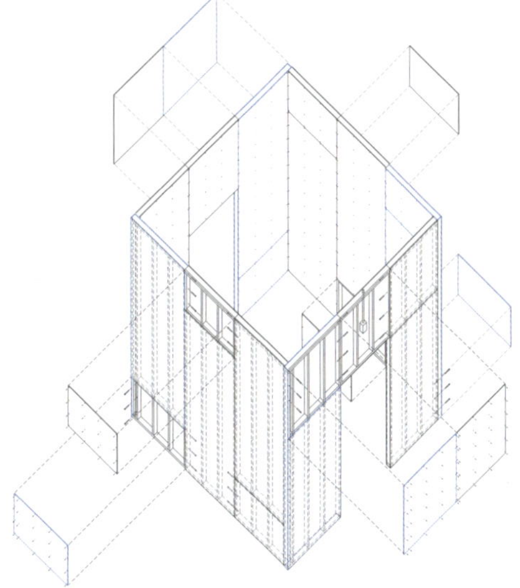

CITIES EXHIBIT
DVLEGIL CONTINUOUS
TABLE
02
20
17
NY

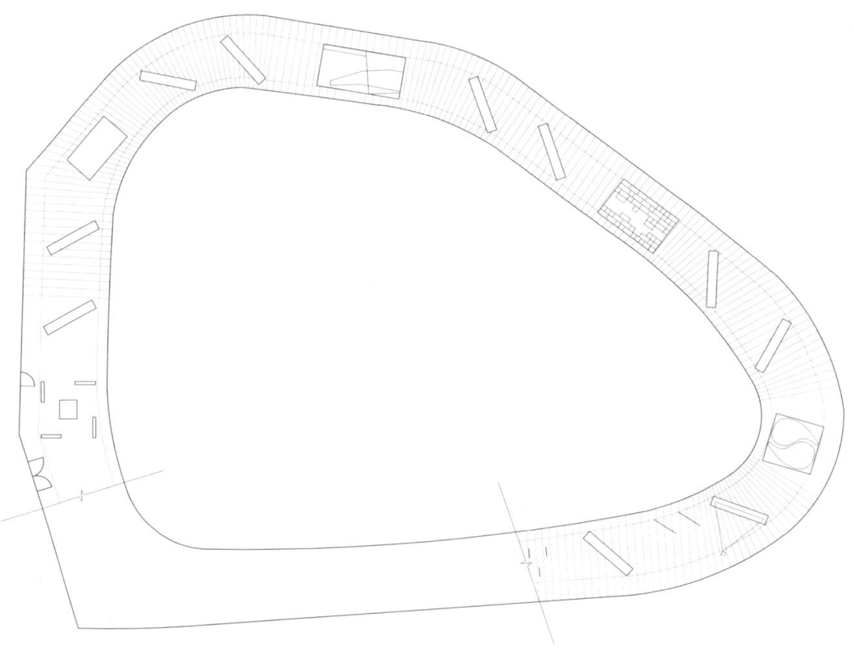

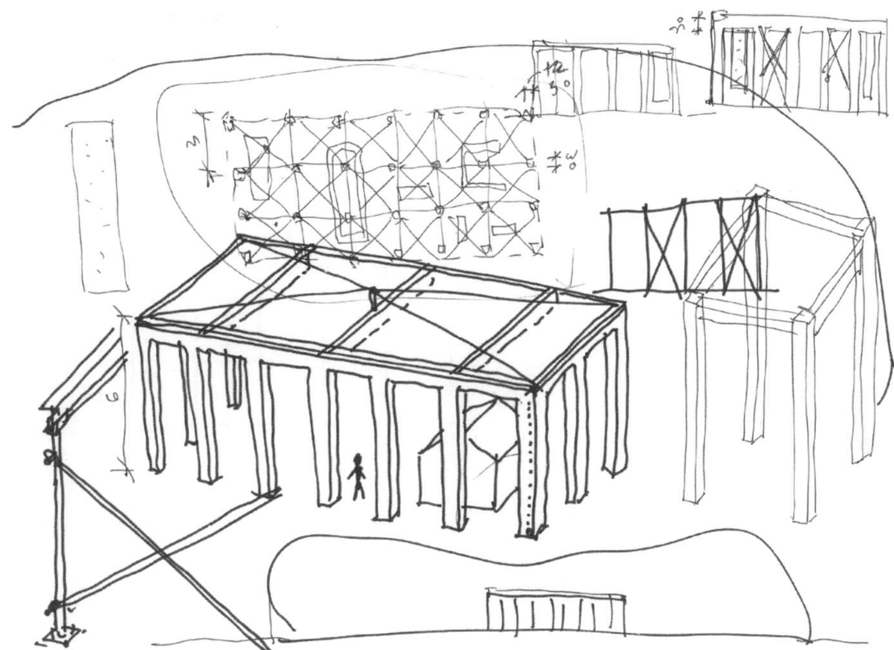

Obra Architects was founded by Pablo Castro and Jennifer Lee in 2000 in New York City. 2013 marked the inception of their third outpost in Seoul, following the opening of their Beijing office in 2011. Obra's efforts span the realms of architecture on all scales, from international masterplanning and institutional work to the scale of interiors, furniture, and public art. The work of Obra has been exhibited widely, and has been featured at the Museum of Modern Art, PS1 Contemporary Art Center, the Solomon R. Guggenheim Museum, the National Art Museum of China, the Deutsches Architekturmuseum, and Rhode Island School of Design, and most recently at Architektur Galerie Berlin. Obra Architects was selected for the 2005 Architectural League Emerging Voices and the 2006 Winner of the PS1 MoMA Young Architects Program with its installation *BEATFUSE!* which opened to the public in June of that year. Obra participated in the US Pavilion at the 2014 & 2016 International Architecture Biennale in Venice, Italy and received the 2014 Kim Swoo Geun Preview Prize as well as a 6th AIA NY Design Award the same year. Obra is appointed as one of Seoul City Government's Public Architects and is a selected NYC Department of Design and Construction Design Excellence contract architect.

Imminent Commons: Commoning Cities, DDP.
Photo: Kyungsub Shin Studio.

Imminent Commons: Commoning Cities, DDP.
Photo: Kyungsub Shin Studio.

藍
すし
乃池
小林静山堂
菊まつり

Imminent Commons: Commoning Cities, DDP.
Photo: Kyungsub Shin Studio.

정자
OPEN RAIL

Imminent Commons: Commoning Cities, DDP.
Photo: Kyungsub Shin Studio.

CREDITS

HOSTED/ORGANIZED BY

Seoul Metropolitan Government
Won-Soon Park (Mayor)

Co-Directors
Hyungmin Pai, Alejandro Zaera-Polo

Biennale Steering Committee
Seung H-Sang (Chair), Young Joon Kim
(Vice-chair), Minsuk Cho, Hyug-jae
Jang, Hee Seon Jin, You Seung Jung,
Hak-Jin Kim, Inje Kim, Tae Hyung Kim,
Chang-Hyun Lee, Jiyoon Lee, Keun
Lee, Ok-sang Lim, Hyungmin Pai,
Soh Yeong Roh, Jeong Hyup Thomas
Seo, Dong-gyun Yoo (Members)

Urban Space Improvement Bureau of
Seoul Metropolitan Government
Tae Hyung Kim (Director-General),
Jae-Hyuk Ahn (Director), Jae Jun Choi
(Team Leader), Young-moo Kim, Mijin
Park, Siwon Park (Managers)

Seoul Design Foundation
Keun Lee (CEO)

Division of the Seoul Biennale of
Architecture and Urbanism
Soik Jung (Director), Myeongju Keum,
Green Kim, Nayeon Kim, Sunjae Kim,
Junyoung Lee, Jina Lee, Suna Lee,
Sobaek Oh, Hye Seong Park,
Myeongcheol Shin, Ri Jin Yoo (Project
Managers). Thanks to: Jun Hui Byun,
Yunji Hwang, Hyemin Jeon, May Jieun
Jeong, Inkoo Kang, Hannah Kim,
Hoyoung Kim, Eunjee Ko, Young Joo
Ko, Ji Young Lee, Seungjae Lee, Yujin
Lee, So Hyun Park

Biennale Advisory Committee
Sang-soo Ahn, Barry Bergdoll, Yung Ho
Chang, Hyo-joon Choi, Yong-Woo Lee,
In-Ho Song

Directors Advisory Committee
Ricky Burdett, Rahul Mehrotra, Carlo
Ratti, Saskia Sassen

THEMATIC EXHIBITION

Curator
Youngseok Lee, Jeffrey S. Anderson

Project Manager
Jina Lee

Intro

Nine Commons: Filmic Introductions
Liam Young

Air

Yellow Dust
C+ arquitectos, In The Air (Nerea
Calvillo with Raúl Nieves, Pep
Tornabell and Yee Thong Chai).
Sponsors: Acción Cultural Española

Seoul On-Air: Augmented
Environments for Urban Activism
Maider Llaguno-Munitxa, Biayna
Bogosian, Elie Bou-Zeid, Scott Fisher,
Youngryel Ryu. Research Collabo-
rators: Abdulghafar Al Tair, David
Radcliff, Arman Atoyan, Arman
Zakaryan, Jongmin Kim, Jeehwan Bae
and Zhan Chen. Sponsors: Princeton
University, USC, Acción Cultural
Española

The Aerocene Explorer
The Aerocene Foundation, Tomás
Saraceno

Water

Underworlds
Carlo Ratti, Newsha Ghaeli, Wonyoung
So, Mariana Matus, Shinkyu Park, Eric
Alm

The Ocean Commons and the
Culture of Seaweeds
MAP Office

Fire

Energy is Everywhere and Nowhere
Forrest Meggers, Dorit Aviv, Andrew
Cruse, Kipp Bradford, Salmaan Craig,
Kiel Moe, Marcel Brülisauer. Sponsors:
Princeton University—CHAOS Lab,
Andlinger Center, School of
Architecture

Do We Dream Under the Same Sky
Nikolaus Hirsch, Michel Müller with
Rirkrit Tiravanija. In collaboration
with: Hannah Bürckstümmer, Michael
Grund, Richard Harding, Martina
Hüber, Hermann Issa, David Müller,
Guido Olbertz, Ralph Paetzold, Pavel
Schilinsky. Sponsors: Merck, Kolon,
OLEDWORKS, OPVIUS, Goethe Institut

The Anthropocene Style:
The Architecture Collection
Philippe Rahm architects. Sponsors:
ARTEMIDE (Lighting Italy)

Invasive Regeneration
Raad Studio, Sun Portal. Sponsors:
Sun Portal

Earth

Beyond Mining—Urban Growth
Dirk E. Hebel, Philippe Block. Project
Team: (Zürich) Matthias Rippmann,
Tomas Ignacio Mendez Echenagucia,
Juney Lee, Alessandro Dell'Endice,
Andrew Liew, Noelle Paulson, Tom Van
Mele, Mariana Popescu, (Karlsruhe)
Karsten Schlesier, Felix Heisel,
(Singapore) Nazanin Saeidi, Alireza
Javadian, Philipp Müller, Adi Reza
Nugroho, Robbi Zidnallman,
Erlambang Adjidarma. Sponsors:
Department of Architecture at ETH
Zürich, ETH Global at ETH Zürich,
Karlsruhe Institute of Technology
(KIT), Future Cities Laboratory (FCL)
Singapore-ETH Centre

CELL·O: New Balance between
Urban Lifestyle and Nature
Jonghyun Baek, JYGG

Thermal Mass
Stoss Landscape Urbanism (Elaine
Stokes, Katherine Harvey, Amy
Whitesides, Chris Reed)

Plug-In Ecology: Urban Farm Pod
Terreform ONE, Mitchell Joachim,
DJ Spooky

Seoul Agro-City in 2050:
Proposal on Food Security in Seoul
Turenscape (Kongjian Yu, Stanley
Lung). Project Team: Longfei Qiao,
Cathy Dao, Jiesi Luo, Yufei Wang,
Yawen Jin, Xiaoxuan Lu. Sponsors:
Qinhuangdao Yaohua FRP Ltd, Yetu
Culture & Landscape Architecture
Frontier, MIX Design Studio, the
University of Hong Kong

Making

Strange Weather
Ibañez Kim (Mariana Ibañez, Simon
Kim). Sponsors: USG, AutoDesk Build
Space

Cyclopean Cannibalism
Matter Design (Brandon Clifford, Wes McGee), Quarra Stone (Jim Durham). Mural and Book Design: Johanna Lobdell. Illustration: Joshua Longo. Structural Consultant: Caitlin Mueller. Research Team: James Addison, Daniel Marshall, Mackenzie Muhonen. Fabrication Leads: Eric Kudrna, Alex Marshall, Ali Seyedahmadian, Brian Smith. Fabrication Team: Ryan Askew, Eddie Banderas, Ramsey Bartlett, Frank Haufe, Jesse Kauppila. Sponsors: Quarra Stone, MIT HASS Fund, MIT Sloan Latin America Office

Adaptive Assembly: Collaborative Robotic Reuse in Construction
Greyshed (Ryan Johns), Jeffrey S. Anderson. Sponsors: Universal Robots. Assisted by: Ayesha Ghosh

Growmore
Sine Lindholm, Mads-Ulrik Husum. Sponsors: Danish Art Foundation, The Danish National Bank's Jubilee Foundation, Beckett Fonden, Space 10, Embassy of Denmark

Moving

The Logistical City:
Artifacts, Processes and Projections
Clare Lyster. Sponsors: College of Architecture, Design and the Arts, University of Illinois at Chicago

Architectures of Fulfillment
Jesse LeCavalier. Project Team: Jedy Lau, Zach White. Sponsors: New Jersey Institute of Technology, StrongArm Technologies, Inc.

Moving Parts: How the Design of Vehicles Shapes Cities
Philipp Rode. Sponsors: LSE Cities

The Dabbawala:
Informality Leveraging Formality
Rahul Mehrotra, Michael Jen. Sponsors: Architecture Foundation

Driver Less Vision
Fake Industries Architectural Agonism, Guillermo Fernandez-Abascal, Perlin Studios. Sponsors: Acción Cultural Española, Ocular Robotics, Rice University, UTS. Collaborators: Daniel Perlin, Max Lauter, Robert Crabtree, and Dan Taeyoung

Communicating

Transurban Love:
The Architecturalization of Romance
Andrés Jaque (Office for Political Innovation), Miguel Mesa. Sponsors: Acción Cultural Española

The City of Social Media
Beatriz Colomina with Evangelos Kotsioris and Weiwei Zhang, Princeton University. Display: Andrés Jaque (Office for Political Innovation). Sponsors: Princeton University (School of Architecture, Mellon Initiative in Architecture, Urbanism & the Humanities, Department of East Asian Studies), Acción Cultural Española

An Architecture for Outcomes
Dark Matter Laboratories (Indy Johar). Sponsors: Future Cities Catapult

Gig Faces, Gig Spaces
Pablo Garcia

Sensing

Autonomous Architectural Robots
Axel Kilian

Chronosphere
Jason Kelly Johnson, Nataly Gattegno (Future Cities Lab, San Francisco). Project Team: Jason Kelly Johnson and Nataly Gattegno Ho with Emily Saunders, Jeff Maeshiro, Joel Frank, Carlos Sabogal, Nava Haghighi. Sponsors: Machinic LLC, CCA Digital Craft Lab (California College of the Arts)

Control Syntax Songdo
Mark Wasiuta, Farzin Lotfi-Jam with Jean Im. Design and Production Assistants: Sharif Anous, John Arnold, Joachim Hackl. Sponsors: GSAPP Columbia University, The Graham Foundation for Advanced Studies in the Fine Arts, Samsung Electronics

SmellScape Seoul 2017:
Inside ⇄ Outside
Sissel Tolaas. Sponsors: IFF Inc. USA, Office for Contemporary Art Norway (OCA), Post Poetics Seoul

Twin Mirror
The Living. Sponsors: Columbia GSAPP, Viss Display Co., Ltd.

Recycling

Three Ordinary Funerals
Common Accounts (Igor Bragado, Miles Gertler) with Jihoi Lee. Intern: Nowk Choe. Performer: Dasol Han. Alkaline Hydrolysis Consultants: Supreme Thermal Instrument. Sponsors: Spanish Embassy in Korea, STI (Supreme Thermal Instrument), Ryerson Design Fabrication Zone

Trash Peaks
Design Earth (El Hadi Jazairy, Rania Ghosn)

States of Disassembly:
Territory, Electronics, and Toxicity
Lateral Office. Project team: Lola Sheppard, Mason White, Brandon Bergem, Jason McMillan, Kearon Roy Taylor, Genevieve Simms, Zaven Titizian, YouBeen Kim, Joo Boung Park

A Back-to-the-City Movement:
Some Proofs and Potentials of New Eco-Villages in American Cities
Sarah Mineko Ichioka. Exhibition Concept Consultant: ANNEX A / Architects. Exhibition Designer & Producer: Chai Yun Ray Chung. Graphic Design Concept: Benjamin Critton Art Department. Illustrations: Victor Ichioka. Films: Fair Companies, Streetfilms, Urban Treehouse. Photographs: The Los Angeles Eco-Village community. Toys: Hugg-A-Planet. Sponsors: Graham Foundation for Advanced Studies in the Fine Arts. With special thanks to: Lois Arkin, Jieun Chang, Alexis Cornejo, Kirsten Dirksen, Robert Forenza, Fritz Haeg, Hyewon Lee, Michael Pawlyn, Michelle Provoost, Cassim Shepard, Jack Stiller, Jeong-reung Professor's Village, Seong-dae-gol Village, Seowon Village, Sungmisan Village, and the caretaker of Acro River Park.

Computational Hug in Digital Fabrication
Yusuke Obuchi with Deborah Lopez and Hadin Charbel. Project Team: Mika Kaibara Portugaise, Ruta Stankevičiūtė, Shuntaro Nozawa. Computational Support: Shuta Takagi. Structural Support: Jun Sato, Furuichi Shohei. Sponsor: CEMEDINE CO., LTD. Management and Organization of the Building Process Laboratory, the University of Tokyo

CITIES EXHIBITION

Curator
Helen Hejung Choi

Associate Curators
Donghwa Kang, Hyoeun Kim

Project Manager
Ri Jin Yoo

Coordinator
Dasom Gong

Fabrication
Jonghyeok Shin, Seonug Youn, Youan Lee, Junseok Jeong

Curatorial Production Assistants
Seohui Woo, Ji Hyun Yoo

Support/Collaboration
COAM—Official College of Architects of Madrid, IAAC—Institute for Adavnced Architecture of Catalonia, IBA Vienna, Tijuana, IMPLAN—Instituto Metropolitano de Planeación, MIT Civic Data Design Lab, SEGRO, Samuel Tak Lee MIT Real Estate Entrepreneurship Lab, Gauteng Provincial Government, Keio University, Space (journal), Gwangju Biennale Foundation, Grupo Tecma Red S.L., South African Local Government Association, Designog arkitektur Norge (DogA), Ministry of Foreign Affairs, Norway, New London Architecture, The Office of the NSW Government Architect, Jeju Institute of Architects, The Store Studios, UddC—Urban Design and Development Center, Alfred Herrhausen Gesellschaft, Deutsche Bundesstiftung Umwelt, Greater London Authority, Rome City Council, Corporation Amigos Parques del Rio, Municipality of Madrid, Marie-Laure Fleisch, Future Architecture Platform, Future Earth MENA Regional Center(FEMRC), Barcelona Metropolitan Area (AMB), TU Wien, University of the Witwatersrand, Fine Arts Center University of São Paulo, San Diego State University, Urban Regeneration Centre for Seoul Station Area, Seongbuk Cultural Foundation, Seoul Housing and Communities Corporation, Storefront Art & Architecture, CURB—Center for Architecture and Urbanism, Stratasys Korea, University of Technology Sydney, Singapore University of Technology and Design, Agora Biennale de Bordeaux Métropole, Iceland Disign Fund / Icelnad Design Center, EYDAP, Anna University, Bibliotheca Alexandria, Department of Planning and Sustainability in City of Amsterdam, AIR LAB—Architectural International Research Laboratory Design Institute, Whydesign, University of Johannesburg, European University of Madrid, InKo Centre, Jeju City Government, Institut Français de Russie, Korean Cultural Centre UK, Goethe-Institut Korea, Istituto Italiano di Cultura Seul, Embassy of France in Korea, Institut français de Séoul, Changwon Institute of Registered Architects, Changwon Regeneration Centre, Changwon City Government, Carto, The Cyprus Institute, Time+Architecture Journal, Tehran Urban Innovation Center, TOINAD Co., Ltd., Tongji University, Institut français de Paris, Atelier FOR YOU, COLEF—El Colegio de la Frontera Norte, Chinese University of Hong Kong, Foresco (Exhibition space sponsor)

Urban Age
LSE Cities (Ricky Burdett, Aron Bohmann, Peter Griffiths, Emily Cruz), Alfred Herrhausen Gesellschaft (Anna Herrhausen, Elisabeth Mansfeld, Quentin Newark, Matthew Hannah), Squint/Opera (Ollie Alsop, Toño Slon)

From the "Functional City" to "Total Function": Modern City Planning 1925–1971
Annie Pedret, Huyoung Eom, Jae Ho Lee, Ju Hong Park, Fatemeh Rezaee, Jeemin (Jasmine) Sohn, Kristina Dziedzic Wright

Gwangju—Cultural Landscape of the City: Gwangju Folly
Hongguen Park, Donggeun Lee, Seonjeong Kim, TaeYoung Yang, Mijeong An, Hyeongkie Choi, Dongchul Cha, Hyunjin Cha, Uiyeong Cheon, Usang Yoo

Nicosia—Climate Change Hot Spot: Future's Extremes
Melina Nicolaides, Manfred A. Lange, Georgios Artopoulos, Theodoros Christoudias, Panayiotis Charalambous, Colter Wehmeier, Charalambos Ioannou, Charis Iacovou, Harry Varnava, Adriana Bruggeman, Katerina Charalambous

Tokyo—Common Matters
Keigo Kobayashi, Christian Dimmer, Ryuta Fujii, Chen Jiahui, Junko Kawabata, Wataru Kitaoka, Ayano Kumazawa, Shun Kuronuma, Wataru Nakanishi, Hyeok Namkung, Nozomu Shiotani, Haruka Uemura, Hayate Watanabe

EM/MENA—Connecting Cities: Commonalities and Challenges
Melina Nicolaides, Manfred A. Lange, Georgios Artopoulos, Theodoros Christoudias, Charalambos Ioannou, Charis Iacovou, Harry Varnava, Panos Hadjinicolaou, Jonilda Kushta, FEMRC Regional Institutional Partners from: Alexandria, Amman, Athens, Beirut, Kuwait City, Muscat, Tehran, Rabat, Tangier, Tunis

Dubai—Projected Futures for the Commons in Dubai
George Katodrytis, Maryam Mudhaffar, Kevin Mitchell, Mi Chang, Meitha Al Mazrooei, Fortuné Penniman, Hatem Hatem, Rama Husamdine, Noor Abdelhamid, Dunia Abu Shanab, Naji Mahmoud, Warith Zaki, Rami Al Otaibi, Talin Hazbar, Andreas Alexandrines, Katayoun Lazar, Eric Tan, Leon Lai, Sharmeen Inayat, Reyan Hanafi, Noora Al Awar, Fatima Al Za'abi, Khalda El Jack

London—London Made
We Made That (Sam Brown, Oliver Goodhall, Melissa Meyer), Joe Almond, Dan Hayhurst, Edward Maddison, Alfie Maddison, Alice Masters

London, Annex—Place, Spaces, Work
Alex Arestis, Cecily Chua, Myrna D'Ambrosio, Nick Green, Charlotte Lord, Raja Moussaoui, Lucy Musgrave, Jacob Neville, Oliver Riviere, Victoria Wägner

Reykjavik—The Hot Pot as Political Arena
Brynja Baldursdóttir, Thomas Forget, Kjersti Hembre, Kathrine Lagethon Lunøe, Arna Mathiesen, Harpa Fönn Sigurjónsdóttir

Rome—The Theatres of Culture: Ephemeral Projects for the Eternal City
MAXXI (Pippo Ciorra, Alessandra Spagnoli, Chiara Castiglia), Luca Galofaro, Federica Fava, Rome City Council (Luca Montuori)

Madrid—DREAMadrid
José Luis Esteban Penelas, María Esteban Casañas, Álvaro Galmés, Fernando Gonzaéz Piris, James London Mills, Juan Ramón Martin Salicio, Marisol Mena Rubio, Santiago Porras Álvarez, Óscar Rueda, Daniel Valle

Macao—Macao Shaped by Use: Formalizing the Vernacular Customization of the City
Nuno Soares, Teresa Brito da Cruz, Tiago Patatas, Andreia Soares, Inês Paiva, Kevin Lam, Vincent Chan, Filipa Simões, Hermana Heong

Medellín—A City for Life
Jorge Pérez-Jaramillo, Sebastián Monsalve-Gómez, Latitud Taller de Arquitectura y Ciudad (David Mesa, Lina Flórez, Sebastián González), New Media Publicidad, Aníbal

Gaviria-Correa, Carlos Pardo-Botero, Corporación Amigos de Parques del Río (Juan Pablo López), Giovanna Spera-Velásquez, Horacio Valencia

Messina—Messina Waterfront Polycenter: A Socio Economic and Cultural Catalyst
Claudio Lucchesi, Andrew Yau, Anna Liuzzo, Carmela Notaristefano, Caterina Sposato, Franco Giordano, Giacomo Villari, Leonardo Santoro, Renato Accorinti, Salvo Fiorello

Mexico City—A Living Laboratory to Prototype: The Future of the Cities We Want
Gabriella Gómez-Mont, Laboratorio Para La Ciudad, Clorinda Romo, Alejandro Ruiz

Mumbai—The Bench-Ladder Conversations: Between Systems and Madness
Rupali Gupte, Prasad Shetty, Vinit Dharia

Barcelona—Mixed Use, Mixed Time, Mixed People
IAAC—Institute for Adavnced Architecture of Catalonia, IBA Vienna (Vicente Guallart, Marta Milà, Laia Pifarré), Barcelona Metropolitan Area (AMB) (Noemí Martinez, Xavier Segura, Luisa Solsona, Ramon Torra)

Bangkok—Street Food: A Common Canteen
UddC—Urban Design and Development Center (Niramon Kulsrisombat, Piya Limpiti, Adisak Guntamueanglee, Wantaphan Tappayuthpijarn, Victor Hazan)

Berlin—Die "Laube" in the City Garden: Architecture as a Trigger Towards a Co-produced City
Diego Aracil, Christian Burkhard, Marco Clausen, Florian Köhl, Philipp Misselwitz, Laura Ordoñez, Tim Sawford

Beijing—Code City
Yung Ho Chang, Zheng Tan, Yemo Li, Hao Li, Xiaotian Duan, Pin Lu, Xiang Li, Maowen Luo, Xing Xia, Chenyue Cheng

Vienna—The Vienna Model
Michael Ludwig, Wolfgang Förster, William Menking, Sabine Bitter, Helmut Weber, Michael Rieper, Werner Taibon

São Paulo—Food Circuit in São Paulo
Anderson Kazuo Nakano, Antonio Rodriges Netto, Bruna Belfiore, Denise Xavier de Mendonça, Denivaldo Pereira Leite, Ivan Alves Pereira, Jaime Martin Vega Rocobado, Letícia Aguida Medeiros, Rodrigo de Moura, Viviana Lumi Okazaki, Equipe LIS

Shanghai—The Other Factory: Late-Industrial Organization and Form
H. Koon Wee, Eunice Seng, Darren Zhou, Lam Lai Shun, Wen Chen, Matthew Chan, Alessandro Ronga, Ksenia Dyusembaeva, Pan Di'an, Chu Laijing, Nancy Chen, Angell Yao, Lin Yimeng, Judy Bong, Kim Kyung Min, Boo Eun Bin, Jackie Xu, Janice Chu, Lau Bo Yee, Sharon So

San Diego/Tijuana—Living Borders
Tito Alegría, Mónica Fragoso, Denise Luna, Jungmook Moon, René Peralta, Alberto Pulido, Alejandro Ruiz, Alejandro Santander, Elías Sanz

San Francisco—At Home Together
Neeraj Bhatia, Antje Steinmuller, Clare Hacko, Shawn Komlos, Bella Mang, Zhongwei Wang, Zizheng Wu, Eric Rogers (Commune Governance), Jason Anderson (AR Consultant)

Seoul—Sectioning Seoul
Sora Kim, Junha Jeon, Taejin Lee, Gyeongoh Chung

Participating artists: VW Lab (Seungbum Kim), Sekwon Ahn, Urbanplay (Jooseok Hong, Dongkil Lim, Taejoon Yeop), Onionskin (Jihyun Park), Dongwook Hwang Invited artists: Terminal 7 Architects, N.E.E.D Architects, E_Scape Architects/ Taek Bin Kim+Yongsoon Chang, Modo Studio, KCAP Architects & Planners, MVRDV, SoA, Hyupdongone, PMA+Soongsil University+UIA, RoA_rchitects+Seogoo Heo, Mass Studies, MMK+, Kyungsub Shin

Seoul, Seongbuk—Seongbuk Art Commons
Wesuck Kang, Sharing Seongbuk Round-Table Conference, Kyoung-woo Kwon, Jiinn Park, Youjung Jang, Woongkie Kim, Design Studio Pigeon of Seongbuk-dong, Stone Kim, Seyeong Jeong, Jin Park, Jang-Oh Hong

SH Corporation—Seoul Housing and Community Movements 1: Towards Open Communities
Jieun Kim, Taejin Lee, Gyeongoh Chung, Jongbeom Lim, Yoonchae Yoon, Hongkyu Jang, Jaewon Shin, Gyeongseok, Jaebeom Oh, Jungho Shin

SH Corporation—Seoul Housing and Community Movements 2: Landscripts for New Communities: Seoul via Vienna
Hae-Won Shin, Mladen Jadric, Seung H-Sang, SungMin LJ, Anna Wiktoria Tutakiewicz, Camilla Vässmar Frick, Gizem Dokuzoguz, Nico Hillen, Simon Groihofer, Anna Aichberger, Cosma Grosser, Team TU Wien, Kim Eunha, Hyae-myung Lee

Seoul + Pyongyang—Letters to the Mayor
Storefront for Art and Architecture (Eva Franch i Gilabert, Carlos Mínguez Carrasco, Jinny Khanduja, Project Projects), Dongwoo Yim, Calvin Chua, PRAUD (Jung Min Kim, Hye Soo Oh), NAMELESS Architecture (Eun Jung Na, So Rae Yoo)

Shenzhen—Shenzhen to PRD Method
Jason Hilgefort, Merve Bedir, David Li, Joseph Grima, Martina Muzi, Shaun Teo, Adeline Tou, Rita Wang, Katrine Hesseldahl, Victor Strimfors

Sejong—Zero-Energy Smart City Development
National Agency for Administrative City Construction, Korea Land & Housing Corporation

Sydney—Spatial Frameworks: City Strategy in the 21st Century
Gerard Reinmuth, Kim Ohrstrom, Maria Vittorelli, Peter Poulet, Ben Hewett, Diana Snape, George Savoulis, Stephanie Morison, Tobin Lush

Singapore—White Space
Chong Keng Hua, Calvin Chua, Felix Raspall, Carlos Banon, Kenneth Tracy, Christine Yogiaman, Michael Budig, Felix Amtsberg, Tshui Mum Ha, Joshua Camaroff, Oliver Heckmann, Trevor Ryan Patt

Athens—From Antiquity to Tomorrow: The People's Water Project
Melina Nicolaides, EYDAP (Lambrini Tzamourani, Giorgos Sachinis, Sonia Tzimopoulou, Eftihia Nestoridou)

Alexandria—After Past & Present: Determining the Future
Melina Nicolaides, Salah A. Soliman, Riham Abd Elhamid, Sahar Hamouda, Mohamed Mehaina, Mina Nader, Ahmed Sabry, Essam Barakat

Amsterdam—Amsterdam Approach
Eric van der Kooij, Rick Vermeulen, Karla Gutierrez, Bastiaan Woudenberg, Emma Diehl, Julia Krick, Thomas Galesloot

Yeongju—Multiple System of Urban-Rural Integrated City: Yeongju's Public Architecture Masterplan
Yeongju City (Changju An, Wookhyeon Jang, Shingu Jung, Jaechan Park, Byunggyu Seo, Miji Shi) SPACE(Semi Park, Seungtae Choi, Efrain Mendez, Sungjin Park)

Oslo—Edible Oslo
Transborder Studio (Øystein Rø, Espen Røyseland , Fredrikke Frølich, Gauthier Durey, Margrete Bjone Engelien, Tuva Øvsthus Maire), Soyoung lee (Illustration)

Johannesburg—Shifting Borders and Building Bridges
Alexandra Parker, Christina Culwick, Christian Hamann, Samkelisiwe Khanyile, Gillian Maree, Ngaka Mosiane, Mncedisi Siteleki, Eben Keun, Hester Viljoen, Richardt Strydom, Lanita van Niekerk

Jakarta—Micro Practice and Macro Perspective for Building Resilience of Urban Kampung
Ellisa Evawani, ikhael Johanes, Amira Paramitha, Inesa Purnama Sari, Gadisha Amelia Febrianti Rahayu, Anwar Bahir, Endy Subijono, Akiko Okabe, Tomohiko Amemiya, Akira Hirano

Jeju—Dolchanggo: Between Home and Nomadism, Jeju Rurbanism
Seong-Cheon Ko, Gun Yang, Young Joon Kang, Seoung Weon Kim, Chang-Hun Oh, Ki Wook Hyun, Kwang Taik Hong, Yong-Kwon Jin, Kyung Roh, Jung Hyo Kang, In Ho Lee, Hee Jong Cheon

Chinese Cities—Ghost Cities: Understanding Patterns in Chinese Urbanization
Sarah Williams, Chaewon Ahn, Kyuchul Ahn, Zhekun Xiong, Ege Ozgirin, Xinhui Li, Wenfei Xu

Changwon—Three Cities: Assemblage Urbanism
Jin Seok Park, Hyunsu Kim, Jungseok Seo, Changhyun Ryu, Dongwan Gimm, Jinho Park, Jinkyung Chong, Minsik Moon, Seojun Yang, Jonghun Jang

Chennai—At the Cross-Rivers: Reconnecting Chennai
Raghuram Avula (Studio RDA), InKo Centre (Rathi Jafer), S Naresh Kumar, Anna University (Ranee Vedamuthu, R Rajeswari, C B Cibi, P Yuvaraj), Kumarappan Balaji, K R Viswanathan

Tehran—Cultivating Tehran
Amin Tadj, Nashid Nabian, Shima Roshan Zamir, Sahar Barzani, Parnian Pezeshki, Sima Sarkar, Avisa Yazdani, Sina Zibakerdar, Mahdi Najafi

Paris—Réinventer Paris
Pavillon de l'Arsenal

Pyongyang—Pyongyang Salim
Dongwoo Yim, Calvin Chua, Jung Min Kim, Kahyun Kim, Jae Hoon Jang, Kyuyeon Park, Youngha Cho, Rafael Luna, Hye Soo Oh, Denise Lee, Gabi Quek, Sam Tang

Hong Kong / Shenzhen—By-City / By-Product
Peter W. Ferretto, Doreen Liu, Chinese University of Hong Kong

Humanity, Cities and the Environment
Seoyeon Park, So Hwa Ahn, MiMi Kim, BokEum Yoo, Ahra Jo, JiHyun Hong, Myung Joo Kim, Jihye Lee

A Three-Way Dialogue
InYoung Yeo, Jong Wook Choi, Eui Seok Seong, Felix Nybergh, Euntaek Lee, Jane Yoo, Sujit Kumar Mallik, Greta Granderath, Till Wolfer/N55, Bike Party Seoul / Vincent Themba Liptrot

Emergent Tokyo: Five Spontaneous Urban Patterns
Jorge Almazán, Kevin Canonica, Javier Celaya, Naoki Saito

Towards a (Dis)-Educating City: The (Dis)-Educational Workshop
Giuseppe Stampone, Pablo Castro, Eleonora Filiputti, Marie-Laure Fleisch, Pietro Gaglianò, Jennifer Lee, Davide Sottanelli

Homo Urbanus
Bêka and Lemoine, Agora Biennale de Bordeaux Métropole

LIVE PROJECTS

Urban Foodshed

Curator
Hyewon Lee

Associate Curator
Yunsu Yi

Project Manager
Myeongcheol Shin

Advising Architect
Seowon Oh

Photography
Suyeon Yun

Installation & Technology
Sungil Lee, Kyungcheol Lee,

Curatorial Production Assistance
Hyein Hwang, Hyunkyung Han

Biennale Restaurant Project Manager
Yunha Kim

Themed Dinner Manager
Yelim Seo

Themed Dinner Coordinator
Youngkyung Kim

Exhibition Coordinator
Seungkyung Lee

Events Coordinator
Jiyeon Kim

Booklet Editors
Hyemin Kim, Hyunseung Lee

Social Media Outreach
Minji Ha

Plants Caretaker
Chungsuk Lee

Participating Artists, Activists, Chefs & Lecturers
S. A. Anbalagan, Chef, b. Vengaikal, India, 1976; lives and works in Chennai. Biennale Restaurant.
Venkateshi Aparna, Restaurant owner, b. Madras, India, 1963; lives and works in Chennai. Biennale Restaurant.
Amita Baviskar, Sociologist, b. Bombay, 1965; based in Dehli. Themed Dinner Talk: "Consumer Citizenship: The Social Life of Industrial Foods in India," 21 October.
Jieun Chang, Environmental activist, b. Busan, 1984; based in Seoul. Café Talk: "Environment & I," 23 September; "Environment vs. Economy?," 14 October; "Going Beyond Alternatives," 4 October.
Gwangho Choi, Entomologist, b. Busan, 1970; lives and works in Jeonju. Restaurant Talk: "Silk Worms and Edible Insects Research in Korea," 20 October.
Meehyang Choi, Urban farmer, b. Busan, 1957; lives and works in Seoul. Food preparation for Urban Herbivores, Themed Dinner, 14 October.
Yongsu Choi, Entomologist, b. Masan, 1973; lives and works in Jeonju. Restaurant Talk: "Bees and Future of

Agriculture," 15 September.

Yunkyung Choi, Seed librarian, b. Seoul, 1963; lives and works in Seoul. Themed Dinner Talk: "Urban Farming for Seed Saving," 7 October.

Gyuhwa Chung, Agrobiologist, b. Jinju, 1954; lives and works in Jinju. Themed Dinner Talk: "The Origns of the Soybean and Wild Soybeans as Genetic Resource," 23 September.

Courtney Dehn-Gurbacki, Environmental activist, b. New York, 1989; lives and works in Katima Mulilo, Namibia. Agri-connexions Africa, an interview video, 2017.

Savvas Hadjixenophontos, Inventor of Fornellia, a solar oven system, b. Lithos, Cyprus; based in Nicosia, Cyprus. Portable solar oven-cooked food tasting: 31 August, 1 September, 2–10 September.

Guiyoung Hwang, Artist, b. Masan, 1983; based in Seoul. Future Mart.

Ahmed Imam, Entomologist, b. Cairo, 1972; lives and works in Cairo. Pest-Control Using Parasitoid Bracon Brevicornis, an exhibition.

Rathi Jafer, Director of InKo Centre, b. Madras, 1964; based in Chennai. Hosted Multi-National Dinner, a Themed Dinner, 21 October.

K. Jayakumar, Chef, b. Keermangalam, India, 1963; lives and works in Chennai. Biennale Restaurant.

Heesik Jeon, Farmer, b. Hamyang, 1958; lives and works in Jangsu, South Jeolla Province, Korea. Restaurant Talk: "GMO and Food Sovereignty," 30 September.

Byunghwa Kang, Botanist, b. Sangju, 1947: based in Seoul. Themed Dinner Talk: "Wild Plants and Soil Regeneration," 16 September.

Ayoung Kim, Landscape designer, b. Seoul, 1972; based in Yongin, Korea. Honey Bee Diary, an exhibition.

Jisuk Kim, Ecologist, b. Miryang, 1971; works and lives in Jeonju. Honey Bee Diary, an exhibition.

Wangechi Kiongo, Environmental activist, b. Nyeri, Kenya, 1994; based in Nairobi. Plastic Ban in Kenya and Rwanda, video.

Kwon Byong Hyon, Former Ambassador of Korea to China (April 1998–August 2000) & currently President of Future Forest, b. Hadong, Korea, 1938: based in Seoul. Desert Storm: From Kubuqi to Beijing and Seoul, an audio installation.

Hyukdae Kwon, Head of China Headquarters, Future Forest, b. Seoul, 1970; lives and works in Beijing. Masks from Beijing, a photo exhibition.

Manfred Langer, Formerly Professor in Geophysics and Director of the Institute for Geophysics at the University of Münster, Germany; currently Director of the Energy, Environment and Water Research Center of the Cyprus Institute; b. Potsdam, East Germany, 1950; lives and works in Nicosia, Cyprus. Café Talk: "The Water-Energy-Food Nexus in the MENA Region, Scientist, Water and Energy Challenges in EM/MENA Region," 2 September.

Donggun Lee, Inventor, b. Seoul, 1969; lives and works in Seoul. Environmental Monitoring System, a device and system installation.

Dongyong Lee, Artist, b. Gimpo, 1960; based in Gimpo, Korea. Seed Library and Water Feeders for Bees.

Lim Young Soo, Forest engineer, b. Seoul, 1977; lives and works in Seoul. Air Bang Talk: "How to Prevent Yellow Dust," 17 October.

Antti Lipponen, Researcher (Finnish Meteorological Institute), b. Kiuruvesi, Finland, 1984; lives and works in Kuopio, Finland. Temperature Anomalies Arranged by Country 1900–2016.

Jeongryang Mok, (One Pixel Gardening), b. Busan 1984; lives and works in Seoul. Mangwon-dong Dust Sensor Project.

Carlos Giovanni Ruiz Moreira, Environmenal activist, b. Quito, Equador, 1994; based in Quito. Social Media Activism for Biodiversity in Ecuador, an interview video

Nicolas Netien, Farmer, b. Lyon, France, 1979; lives and works in Solea Valley, Cyprus. Atsas Olive Oil Tasting, 31 August–2 September; Café Talk: "Let Thy Food be Thy Medicine," 2 September; Themed Dinner Talk: "Going Beyond Sustainable: The Global Case for Agro-ecology," 3 September.

Melina Nicolaides, Independent curator, b. Washington D.C., 1972; based in Nicosia, Cyprus. Curator, EM/MENA Project.

Jihyun Park, Ocean activist, b. Seoul, 1973; based in Seoul. Trolling and Desertification of the Ocean, an interview video.

Kyung-bum Park, Farmer, b. Gimcheon, 1964; lives and works in Gimcheon, Korea. Themed Dinner Talk: "Bees, Melons & Terminal High Altitude Area Defense (THAAD)," 28 October.

Sunmi Park, Game designer, b. Seoul, 1975, lives and works in Uijeongbu, Korea. World Digital Map of Deserts.

Daphnis S. Panagides, Agro-scientist, b. Limassol, Cyprus, 1929; works and lives in Limassol. Importance of Seed Saving

Subhadra Raju, Restaurant owner, b. Hyderabad, 1966; lives and works in Chennai. Biennale Restaurant

G. Sarvanan, Chef, b. Vaniyambadi, India, 1981; lives and works in Chennai. Biennale Restaurant.

Boyan Slat, Inventer and entrepreneur, b. Delft, the Netherlands, 1994; based in Delft. The Ocean Cleanup, video.

Wontae Seo, Filmmaker, b. Seoul, 1977; based in Cheonan, Korea. Human Trees and Monsanto Out

Youngjae Shin, Graduate student (Landscape Design), b. Iksan, 1991; Lives and studies in Seoul. Honey Bee Diary.

Wonyoung So, Programmer, b. Seoul, 1986; lives and works in Singapore. IBWA Water ATM, installation.

Salah A. Soliman, Toxicologist and Professor of Pesticide Chemistry Toxicology, Alexandri University (1986 –present), b. Souhag, Egypt, 1944; lives and works in Alexandria, Egypt. Café Talk: "Food Crisis in Egypt," 2 September.

Imbong Song, Municipal official (Urban Farming Manager), b. Seoul, 1961; lives and works in Seoul. Themed Dinner Talk: "Urban Farming in Seoul," 14 October.

Hojun Song, Artist, b. Gwangju, Korea, 1978; lives and works in Seoul. Water Monitoring Duckboat and Mangwon-dong Dust Sensor Project, installation.

Michael Sorkin (Terreform), Architect, b. Washington D.C., 1948; lives and works in New York. New York City (Steady) State: Home Grown.

Jamuna Thiagarajan, Environmental activist, b. Tirupathur, India, 1934; lives and works in Ambalur, India. Water Activism in Ambalur Village.

Aparna Venkateshi, Restaurant owner, b. Delhi, 1968; lives and works in Chennai. Biennale Restaurant.

Yongtae Yu (One Pixel Gardening), Programmer, b. Busan, 1983; lives and works in Seoul Mangwon-dong Dust Sensor Project

Suyeon Yun, Artist, b. Seoul, 1972; based in Suwon. Seoul Guerilla Farmers and Asia's Climate Refugees: Guo & Lee.

Mushon Zer-Aviv, Artist, b. Tel Aviv, 1976; based in Tel Aviv. IBWA Water ATM (2017).

Indian Night:
Biennale Pre-Opening Reception
TAAN, a percussion quartet from Ahmedabad, India.

Translation and Interpretation
Alice S. Kim, Kyunghee Lee, Taekyun Lee, Yeseol Woo, Sujin Park, Raehyun Lee, Taeho Sung, Sungmin Lee, Yongjun Kim, Jiyoung Yun, Younsoo Ko

Supporting Farms and Restaurants
Eden Vegetarian Restaurant(Chennai), Santorini Restaurant (Seoul), Ham's Heirloom Beans, (Jeonju), Atsas Organic Farm(Cyprus), Gyuhwa Chung's Wild Soybean(Jinju, Korea), Dongyoung Cho's String Beans (Suncheon, Korea), Yongkyu Lee's Organic Apples, (Cheolwon, Korea), Jinwoong Hwang's Heirloom Rice (Gongju, Korea)

Embassies, and Institutions, NGOs
InKo Centre, National Institute for Agricultural Science (Korea), Indian Embassy, German Embassy, Egyptian Cultural Center, UNCCD (United Nations Convention to Combat Desertification), Desert Research Center (Egypt), National Geographic, Future Earth, Ministry of Agriculture (Rural Development and Environment, Republic of Cyprus), EYDAP, Gangdong-gu Seed Library, Environmental Research Center (Alexandria Library), futureforest.org, localfuture.org, savegreekwater.org, right2water.ie, detroitwaterbrigade.org, eatschottsandroots.org, Na Terra East Timor

Production City

Curators
Yerin Kang (SoA), Jie-Eun Hwang

Associate Curators
Stephanie Seungmin Kim, Isak Chung

Project Manager
Green Kim

Assistants
Sungkwang Choi, Young Keum Choi, Inho Kim, Jiyeong Kim, Eunhee Ko, Jee Eun Lee, Kyungjin Lee, Jiung Yoo

Project Seoul Apparel Assistants
Suji Han, Sung-Jin Kang, Smin Lee, Tian Long Lee

Designers
Eun Joo Hong, Na Kim, Bong-kyu Song

Participants
AMP—DK Osseo-Asare(LOWDO), AMP—Yasmine Abbas(Panurban), BARE, B.A.T, Seoyeon Cho, Stylianos Dritsas, Koo Young Han(Urban Hybrid), HENN + Technische Universität Darmstadt,

Digital Design Unit, Dongwook Hwang, Pil Joon Jeon, Heeyoung Jung, Chanjoong Kim + Hyesun Lee, Na Kim, Hyungchul Kwon (ETH Zurich, Digital Building Technologies), Jieun Lee, Lifethings, Marie Maisonnueve, MOTOElastico, Optical Race, Jongkwan Paik, Hyun Parke, Bong-kyu Song (BKID), Luke Stevens, Sunshine Underground, TechCapsule

Co-hosts
The Seoul Institute, Seoul Design Foundation, Sewing Industry Support Team, British Council ("UK/KOREA 2017–18." Connected City), Seoul Jung-gu Office

Sponsors
Altair Korea, ABB Korea, Wooyang Foundation

Partner Institutions
University of Seoul, Slow Slow Quick Quick, garmSSI, Art and Disaster, Finding E-Waste, URBANPLAY, Spaceba, PRAG, Nahoson Elektrik

Advisors
Sook-Ok Chun, Eunjin Regina Shin, Royal College of Arts Fashion Programme

Special Thanks
OOUNIVELAB, Changsin-dong Sewing Factory ACE, Kanghyuk Choi, Sena Gu, Dongwon Jo, Taewook Kang, Myoung-Rye Kim, Sejung Kim, Hyoung-gul Kook, Jeonghoon Lee, METAA, Plus Plastic, Jaeyoung Ryu, SamhanC1, Seed:s, Historic City Center Regeneration Division of Seoul Metropolitan Government, Cultural Convergence Economy Division of Seoul Metropolitan Government, Sewoon Governance (Sewoon OO), Sindang-dong Sample Room ELISABETH, TIDE Institute

Walking the Commons

Curators
Soo-in Yang, Kyung Jae Kim

Project Manager
Hye Seong Park

Project Research
Bomi Kim, Hyeonji Kim, Jiwon Shin, Yugyeong Yi, Sohyeon Park, Hyewon Kim, Jisu Ha

Sponsors and Supporters
British Council Korea, the Seoul Metropolitan Government Urban Renewal Support Center of the Seoul Station Area, Producer Group DOT,

Seoul Walk, the Cloud Lab at the Columbia University Graduate School of Architecture, Planning and Preservation (GSAPP), Watershed, Musicity

Brainwave Flaneur
Artists: Mark Collins, Toru Hasegawa | Data Analysis: David Jangraw | Images: TJ Choe | Operation: Yugyeong Yi | Workshop (18–20 July): Seong-gyu Choi, Jong-wu Kim, Jiyonn Kim, Hiju SI, Seong-gyu Choi, Gyeong-ho Park, Seung-jae Yu, Ji-hye Na, Yeon-woo Yi, Jin-gyeong Choi, Jun-su Park, Gyeong-eun Go, Yeong-geum Choi, Ye-ji Kim, Hye-rin Kwon, Hyo-min Baek | Pedestrian Playground (3 September–5 November): Kyung Jae Kim, Sohyeon Park (graphic design), Sohyeon Park, Seong-gyu Choi, Tae-eun Kim, Yeong-jin Kim (operations), Taesu Eom (Video), Gyeongmin Yi, Hyeon-hak Yi, Gangmin Bae, Sol-min Be, Jong-seok Kim, Su-yeon Park, Ji-yeong Jo, Yun-a Lee and 1 other, Bo-hye Jeong and 1 other, Ju-hyeon Oh, Jinsu Park, Nagyeong Lee, Deok-min Lee, Haechan Kim, Subin Han, Seon-yeong Myeong, Seon-hee Kim and 1other, Sang-yun Bae, Si-hyeon Jeong, Jae-yeon Lee, Su-yeong Kim, Hyejin Lee, Sang-yun, Su-yeong Kim, Hye-jin Lee, Sang-yun Bae, Seung-hye Park, Su-jeong Ok, Ha-rin Kim, Tae-yeon Kim, Dong-wook Han, Hyeonmi Lee, Suik Jang, Jae-won Jang, Hanna Lee, Yeong-jin Kim, Eun-chan Ju, Hye-jin Lee, Hyo-jin Park, Sua Kim, Su-jeong Jeong, Seo-yul Shin, In-gu Han, Bok-ran Yi, Jong-wook Ha, Seong-jin Jeong, Ha-hyeon Kim, Sang-muk Yi, Tae-hyeon Kang, Alexandra, Ju-hyeon Oh, Yeong-su Pyo, Jae-ha Pyo, Jae-in Pyo, Jae-won Yu, Eunji Lee (participants)

Soundlines
Artist: Kayip (Woojun Lee), Gang Il Yi | Program Development: Sewon Ahn, Donghoon Yi, Gang Il Yi, Kayip(Woojun Lee) | Visual Design: Sewon Ahn | Sever Programming: Umur Gedik | Playwright: Yesol Han | Accompanying event: Pedestrian Playground | Kyung Jae Kim, Sohyeon Park (graphic design), Sohyeon Park, Sunjae Kim (Operation)

Musicity:
5 October–5 November 2017 | Curator: Nick Luscombe | Producers: Jisun Park, Suna CHOE, Byong-Jin Yoo | Artists: Neon Bunny, Hannah Peel, JANG Young-gyu, Steve Guy Hellier, Music Group NaMu, Gabriel Prokofiev, Kayip (Woojun Lee) | Musicity Tour:

Urban Poetry Flaneur (27–29 October): Kyeonghwa Song, Minki Kim, Taeyun Kim, Harim Lee, Seonsuk Kim, Romantic Vagabond

Playable City
27–29 October 2017 | Producers: Clare Reddington, Hilary O'Shaughnessy, Victoria Tillotson, Byong-Jin Yoo | Game Development Collaboration: Simon Johnson | Game Mentor: Nolgong | Artists: Borahm Kim, Sun Kim, YANG Sookyun, Eunkyoung Lee, Minji Kim, Strangers at Honja Factory (Eunju Hitchcock-Yoo, IM Do One), Rosie Poebright | Operation: Kim Jongwon, Park Shinhye, Byeon Jaesin, Yu Hyeyeon, Yi Yujin, Im Seongho, Jo Yuto

Connected City
27–29 October 2017 | Hosted by: British Council Korea, Seoul Metropolitan Government, Seoul Design Foundation | Organized by: Producer Group DOT, the Seoul Metropolitan Government Urban Renewal Support Center of the Seoul Station Area, Seoul Walk, the Seoul Biennale of Architecture and Urbanism 2017 | Creative Producer: Jisun Park | Program Producers: Suna Choe, Byong-Jin Yoo, Bongmin Choi, Seongjin Jeong | Project Manager: Gyu Choi, Eunsil Lee, Hye Seong Park, Minha Kim, Green Kim, Seonguk Choi | Operations: Minkyung Kim, Hyeyeon Kim, Seungho Yeo, Yeram Jeong, Aram Jang, Gijang Han, Eunjeong Jeong, Seungmi Kim

PUBLIC PROGRAMS

Director
Soik Jung

Seoul Libre Maps

Curators
E Roon Kang, Wonyoung So

Artists
Minkee Bae, Hanbyul Jo, Listen to the City (Eunseon Park, Cheolhun Baek, Choonggeun Yoon, Hyunwook Jang), Dan Phiffer,

Project Manager
Hye Seong Park

Operation Management
Yoo Kyung Lee

Designer
Moonsick Gang

Editor, Translator
Achim Koh

Video Documentation
Sunshine Underground

International Studios

Curator
John Hong

Assistant Curator
Youbeen Um

Project Manager
Myeongju Keum

Designers
Youngju Lee, Seungjae Kang, Jinwook Jang, Hyun Jei Lee, Hyein Kim, Kiwon Jeon, Daye Kim

Studios
Chinese University of Hong Kong | Professors & Advisors: Peter W. Ferretto | Students: Chan Tik Chun Zion, Chan Wai Sum Sam, Ha Chui Ying Gloria, Lam Jeun Diane, Lam Joshua Wai Hon, Lam Man Yan Milly, Lau Kin Keung Jason, Lie Cheuk Lam, Tam Wing Yee Winnie, To Wai Kin Ric, Yue Ka Hin Jasmine

Delft University of Technology | Professors & Advisors: Roberto Cavallo, Maurice Harteveld, Steven Steenbruggen, Valentina Ciccotosto | Students: Maurits van Ardenne, Juul Heuvelmans, Jessica Admiraal, Adrian Richter, Reinier van Vliet, Malon Houben, Virginia Santilli, Seunghan Yeum, Jingsi Li, Erik van der Valk, Xiufan Mu, Anaïs Sarvary, Eline Verhoeven, Ailsa Craigen, My My Ngo, Nan Zhang

École Polytechnique Fédérale de Lausanne | Professors & Advisors: Dominique Perrault, Juan Fernandez Andrino, Ignacio Ferrer Rizzo, Richard Nguyen | Students : Maud Clara Abbé-Decarroux, Lucie Audrey Alioth, Maxim Andrist, Pauline Ayache, Lucas Balet, Amélie Alexandra Marie Bès, Audrey Marie Billy, Alexandre Maxime Bron, Lena Brucchietti, Tanguy Romain Caversaccio, Alexis Guillaume Louis Corre, Camille Laura Ehrensperger, Anthony Felber, Marine Solène Gigandet, Florence Virginie Louise Gilbert, Michael Göhring, Mégane Anouchka Hänni, Era Këri, Delphine Pia Klumpp, Fanny Lucrezia Marianne Ladisa, Sébastien Wilfried Guy Léveillé, Pedro Maiurano, Jeremy Morris, Tanguy Mulard, Kimberlyne Nguyen, Alex Orsholits, Arnaud Blaise Pasche, Guillaume

Charles Pause, Rida Perret, Stéphanie Pitteloud, Laura Primiceri, Merlin Sydney Jacques Rozenberg, Laura Sacher, Alizé Lilou Océane Soubeyran, Louis Stähelin, Paul Emmanuel Trellu, Lisa Virgillito, Raphaël Vouilloz, Olivia Louise Wechsler, Manuel Zuloaga

Ewha Womans University | Professors & Advisors: Yoonhie Lee | Students: Kyunghwa Bang, Hyunsoo Cho, Sungyeon Choi, Yejin Choi, Jooyeon Choi, Taehee Kim, Suejeong Kim, Eunbee Kim, Seungwon Lee, Jiye Lee, Chanseo Park, Minji Park, Sehyun Shin, Jyungryun Shim

Georgia Institute of Technology | Professors & Advisors: Marc Simmons | Students: Samuel Shams, Alexandria Davis, Nicole Schmeider, Paul Steidl, Paul Petromichelis, Coston Dickinson, Sun Yifeng, Chao Dang, Roberto Bucheli, Vincent Yee, Matthew Forsell, Jeffrey Olson

Harvard University Graduate School of Design | Professors & Advisors: Niall Kirkwood, Francesca Benedetto, Sangyong Cho (Studio Consultant) | Students: Taylor Baer, Johanna Cairns, Ellen Epley, Siobhan Feehan, Sophia Geller, Dana Kash, Ho-Ting Liu, Soo Ran Shin, Diana Tao, Lu Wang, Boxiang Yu, Junbo Zhang

Hongik University | Professors & Advisors: Sooran Kim, Jae Yong Chung | Students: Soohong Kim, Ryong Min Rho, Seo Yong Yang, Kyung Hwa Chung, Yeong Han Choi, Taewoo Ha, Jinseol Nam, Kwunhee Lee, Eva Jastrezebski, Elia Molinaro

Keio University | Professors & Advisors: Jorge Almazán | Students: Kotaro Sato, Reika Hara, Azusa Nagata, Alexandre Paul, Hana Sakurai, Yuichi Tatsumi, Kyoko Suganuma, Gaku Inoue, Naoki Saito, Kevin Canonica, Roberto Roel

Korea University | Professors & Advisors: Chongkul Yi, So Young Park | Students: Dong Rim Hahm, Jin Ha Bak, Jin Sik Kim, Jigjid Battulga, Se Mi Lee, Su Jin Ahn, Jae Ho Lee, Ha Nuel Oh, Hyue In Song, Ho In Han

National University of Singapore | Professors & Advisors: Peng Beng Khoo | Students: Bernard Heng Jia Chuin, Espanol Daniel Aguinalde, Kang De Yuan, Khong Jia Xin Valerie, Jo Hee Lee, Nur Afiqah Bte Agus, Siow Yee Ning Eunice, Tan Jing Min, Vincent Phoen Yusheng, Zachary Kho Ming Hui

Princeton University | Professors & Advisors: Alejandro Zaera-Polo | Students: Ying Qi Chen, Benjamin Vanmuysen, Samuel Clovis, Taylor

Cornelson, Leen Katrib, Wan Li, Gillian Shaffer, Ji Shi

Rhode Island School of Design | Professors & Advisors: Rafael Luna | Students: An Huang, Chun Qiu, Madison Kim, Kyunghwa Kang, Yun-Wen Hwang, Lingfei Liu, Xing Wu, Qi Zhao, Jiahui Yang, Madeleine Devall, Peihan Wang, Hyekyung Won, Ananya Vij

Rice University | Professors & Advisors: Urtzi Grau, Guillermo Fernández-Abascal | Students: June Deng, JP Jackson, Sai Ma, Yu Kono, Isabella Marcotulli, David Seung Jun Lee, Keegan Hebert, Evio Isaac, Alina Plyusnina, Natalia O'Neill Vega, Haley Koesters, Daria Piekos

Seoul National University | Professors & Advisors: John Hong, Hangman Zo | Students: Camila Botero, Emilio Granda Caicedo, Kiwon Jeon, Jungho Kwon, Seungjae Yoo, Younghyun Kim, Yerim Yoo, Yeon Park, Hyunjei Lee, Changsuk You, Junghoon Nam, Hahun Choi, Dongwon Lee, Hyeyoung Park, On Sim, Callan Green, Siyoung Lee, Clara Asperilla Arias, Yeonjoong Jung

Sungkyunkwan University | Professors & Advisors: Thorsten Schuetze, Wonsuk Lee, Suejin Sung, Geunpoong Lim, Yoonhee Cho, Hyeonseok Kang | Students: Dongjin Seong, Sang Hyun Ahn, Hyun Soo Ra, Sung Hwa Hong, Seung Geon Baek, Kyeong Lae Lee, Chao Zhang, Yuxiang Liu, Kyoyoung Hwang, Junhyung Je, Seokgil Jang, Eunju Jeon, Gihoon Lee, Jimin Lee, Ira Kwak, Suyeon Kim, Jiyeon Lee, Minji Ava Kim, Tal Ohayon, Gal Kapon, Emanuele Martinangeli, Min Jung Choi, Kang San Kim, Ju Heum Ryu, Bo Wang, Heng Gao, Jae Hong Kim, Nayoon Yang, Kiho Min, Mi Jeong An, Woo Sung Jeong, Jin Su Kim, Woo Jin Ou, Pill Soo Go, Hae Ram Kim, Soo Suk Park, Eun Ho Cheon, In Young Ho, Song Mee Han, Ji Soon Kang, Seung Ho Choi, Tae Hyun Nam, Dae Hyun Kim, Hyun Woo Park, Jiangping Si, Run Chen, Hye Bin Park, Hee Gun Chong, Ah Hyun Chung, Ji Hye Seo, Jun Seok Kim, Il Sup Jung, Won Woo Choi, Jae Hyoung Choe, Ji Hong Bae, Seon Gyu Han, Sung Kyung Lee, Xiuchen Lyu, Ga Young Shin, Hyeon Nyeong Kim, Gi Hoon Seo, Javier Espinosa Quintana, Jiawei Wang, Jorge de la Vega Albinana, In Ji Jeong, Jun Kyu Bang, Jae Seung Lee, Seung Won Yang

Texas Tech University | Professors & Advisors: Kuhn Park | Students: Alan

Escareno, Angela Li, Bobby Brown, Carolina Aguilar, Chas Gold, James Taylor, Jonathan Matz, Romina Cardiello, Rosalie Perez, Ruwaida Albawab, Savannah Salazar, Tristan Snyder, Cinthya Berrocal, Karla Murillo, Ismael Rivera, Mark Freres, Dylan Wells, Maryam Kouhorostami

Università IUAV di Venezia | Professors & Advisors: Sara Marini | Students: Egidio Cutillo, Alberto Petracchin

Université Libre de Bruxelles | Professors & Advisors: Alain Simon, Eve Deprez | Students: Rodrigo Oliveira Rodrigues, Teodor Dan, Fyona Yahiaoui, François Lamblin, Hadrien Nicora, Ronny Campos Pereira, Charlotte Gyselynck, Valentin Colleony Gorchkoff, Nicolas Colman, Alessandro Perlaux, Ramatoulaye Keita, Safrina Mougamadou, Kim Lefebvre, Driss M'rini, Jean-Baptiste Rigal, Garance Poëzevara, Valentine Pelletier, Kevin Dabeedin, Axel Ricbourg, Teodora Andreea Tiron, Louis Ville, Carlos Zavala Aranda

Università degli studi di Camerino | Professors & Advisors: Silvia Lupini, Daniele Rossi, Pippo Ciorra | Students: Giacomo Attardi, Yiwen Qian

University of Hong Kong | Professors & Advisors: Koon Wee, Eunice Seng | Students: Timothy Wong Chum-Hin, Johnny Tse Chun Lai, David Wong Ka Wai, Connie Yeung Man Ki, Canossa Chan Yuet Sum, Andres Antolin Sanchez, Anderson Chan Cho Fai, Haydn Lo Hei Ting, Tracy Yeung Tsz Wing, Jessie Alison Chui, Justin Kong Sze Wai, Thomas Lee Bing Him, Montserrat Guierriez, Charlotte Chan Cheung Kei, Gabriel Chan Yat Him, Khaitan Ashara, Joyce Leung Mei See, Irene Wei Yuxi, Veronica Cheung, Arnold Wong, Jessical Wong

University of Melbourne, Harvard University Graduate School of Design | Students: Dongsei Kim, Namju Lee

University of North Carolina at Charlotte | Professors & Advisors: Jeffrey S. Nesbit | Students: Merrick Castillo, Sejdiu Bekim, Jonathan Warner, Brittany Battaile, Douglas Cao, Christopher Pope, Ibha Shrestha

University of Pennsylvania | Professors & Advisors: Simon Kim | Students: Michelle Ann Chew, Wooyoung Choi, John Dade Darby, Ricardo Arturo Hernandez-Perez, Chang Yuan Max Hsu, Jieming Jin, Dawoon Jung, Ritika Kapoor, Han Kwon, Hadeel Ayed Mohammad, Mengjie Zhu

University of Seoul | Professors & Advisors: Marc Brossa | Students: Shin Young Park, So Yeon Kim, Seok Jae Shin, Su Heon Song, Seung Hee Cha, Tae Huei Lee, Nikola Macháčová, Inn Sarin Ronnakiat, Napat Assavaborvornvong, Sofia Latherington

University of Seoul | Professors & Advisors: Sanki Choe | Students: Jangho Gal, Hyumin Seo, Juik Song, Jinkyoung Kim, Grace Shin, Eunice Yi, Jean Lin

University of Technology Sydney | Professors & Advisors: Gerard Reinmuth, Andrew Benjamin | Students: Andreas Ian Anggabrata, Hana Lee, Lachlan McLean, Abbie Thoi Yen Ngo, Daniel Sagurit, Anna Spaggiari, Lucy Wang, Shuang Wu, Ian Tran, Kimberley Angangan

Washington University in St. Louis | Professors & Advisors: Dongwoo Yim | Students: Ce Huang, Ruicong Tang, Ye Fu, Heng Gu, Yuqing Zou, Qi Yang, Xingguang Li, Xuan Chen, Jialong Lao, Jingyi Tan, Daniel Adams, Chenghui Nan

Washington University in St. Louis, National University of Singapore | Professors & Advisors: Erik L'Heureux | Students: Gregory Barber, Yi Ding, Xinyi Du, Biying Li, Siyang Liu, Amanda Malone, Chenghui Nan, Mengqiao Sun, Lige Tan, Yang Wu, Zezhong Yu, Muhong Zhang

Yonsei University | Professors & Advisors: Jooeun Sung | Students: Dehao Kong, Han Byeol Oh, Ignatius Morgen Chombo, Jinchul Yeon, Khin Moe Pyayt, Kwonhyuk Lee, Tsz Yui Ngan, Seo woo lee, Yeganeh Panahijoo, Yuanyuan Che

Common Library

Curator
Lim Kyung yong (The Book Society)

Project Manager
Jina Lee

Participating Artists
Alexander Brodsky & Ilya Utkin, common room(Space Design), EH, Infoshop Byulkkol, Irregular Rhythm Asylum, Onomatopee, Shinshin(Graphic Design, Bookshop Space Design)

Installation
Cho Sung-tae, Aram Jung

Film & Video Program (Special Section of Seoul International Architecture Film Festival)
Fiction/Non-fiction: Working, Sharing, Loving in the Cities)

Curator
Choi Won-joon

Project Manager
Oh Sobaek

Programmers
Hwang Hei-rim, Seol Suan (Metaplay)

Host
Seoul Metropolitan Government, Korea Institute of Registered Architects

Co-host
Seoul Design Foundation, Seoul Museum of History

Sponsors
Italian Cultural Institute, JinJin Company, Ambassade de France en Corée, Agora Biennale de Bordeaux

Venues
Seoul Museum of History Yajugae Hall (4–10 September)
Arthouse Momo in ECC, Ewha Womans University (11–17 September)
Oil Tank Culture Park (22–24 September)

List of Films
The Amateur (Maria Mauti, 2016, Italy)
Chilsu and Mansu (Park Kwang-su, 1988, Korea)
Comrade Kim Goes Flying (Kim Gwang-hun, Nicholas Bonner, Anja Daelemans, 2012, North Korea/ Belgium/UK)
The Day a Pig Fell Into the Well (Hong Sang-soo, 1996, Korea)
The Great Beauty (Paolo Sorrentino, 2013, Italy/ France)
A Journey Around the Moon (Ila Beka, Louise Lemoine, 2016, France)
The Lunchbox (Ritesh Batra, 2013, India /France/Germany)
Rohmer in Paris (Richard Misek, 2013, UK/ France)
Roma (Federico Fellini, 1972, Italy)
The Tree, the Mayor and the Mediatheque (Eric Rohmer, 1993, France)
Uncommon Sense: The Life and Architecture of Laurie Baker (Vineet Radhakrishnan, 2017, India)
Plus 23 more films in the regular section

Forum/Guest Talk Participants
Landscape as Urban Cultural Foundation (5 September): Benjamin Joinau (Professor, Hongik University), Kim Jung-hee (Professor, Seoul National University), Michèle Laruë-Charlus (Town-planning Head Manager at Bordeaux Métropole/General Delegate for Agora), Pai Hyungmin (Director, Seoul Biennale of Architecture and Urbanism/ Professor, University of Seoul), Élizabeth Touton (Deputy Mayor for Town-planning, Housing and Transportation, Bordeaux Métropole)
Comrade Kim's Pyongyang (8 September): Yim Dong-woo (Architect/Professor, Hongik University)
Films Contained in Seoul (9 September): Choi Won-joon (Professor, Soongsil University), Han Sun-hee (Producer/Professor, Busan Asian Film School), Hwang Doojin (Architect), Jeong Jae-eun (Filmmaker), Jung Ji-woo (Filmmaker/Professor, Soongsil University)

Educational Program: Lecture

Project Manager
Sun Jae Kim

Support
Junglim Foundation

Lecturers
Opening Talk: Jeon Hyo Gwan, JEONG Seok, Lee Jae-Joon, CHUN Eun-ho, Park Haecheon, REIGH Young Bum, HA Seung-woo, Shim Bo-Seon, Eunseon Park (Listen to the City)
Biennale Lecture: Hyungmin Pai, Helen Hejung Choi, Sora Kim, Song Bongkyu, Jiwon Yu, E Roon Kang, Wonyoung So, Optical Race (Hyungjae Kim, Park Jaehyun), Hyewon Lee, Jie-Eun Hwang, Won-joon Choi
Talk Series: Annie Pedret, Jooeun Sung, Sulki and Min (Sungmin Choi, Sulki Choi), MMMG (Suyel Bae, Miyoung Yu), Jeong Jae-eun, Isak Chung (Jongkwan Paik, Jieun Lee, Heeyoung Jung, Seoyeon Cho, Koo young Han), Suyeon Yun, John Hong, Soik Jung, Dongwoo Yim, Minkee Bae, Soo-in Yang
Curator's Talk on Culture Day: Yerin Kang, Jie-Eun Hwang, Woojun Lee(Kayip), Gang il Yi

Educational Program: Workshop

Research
Jooeun Sung, Jaeyune Kim, Hanul Kim, Dongeun Hwang

Project Manager
Sunjae Kim

Supporting Institutions
Yonsei University Office of Research Affairs and University-Industry Foundation (UIF), Korea Architects Institute

City Re;Readers
Lecturers: Shim Youngkyu, Myoungkyu Kim | Students: Chang Sungjin, Hong Jinwook, Jeong Gyu Yeong, Jung Chanho, Kim Jiyoon, Kim Soobin, Kim Soonyoung, Kim Ye Ji, Jeeseon Kwon, Lee Jihoon, Lee Siwon, Lim Choi, Lim Gyeong Hyeon, Park Jesang, Park Jooeun, Park Minhyuk, Park Sooyeon, Seo Wonji, Yoon Jiwoon | Support: Yonsei University Office of Research Affairs and University-Industry Foundation (UIF), Korea Architects Institute

City Challengers
Lecturers: Jun Hee Kim, Jaeyune Kim | Assistant Lecturers: Hak Jong Chang (Researcher), Ha Yeon Lee, Kun Hyuk Lee, Sang Hoon Lee, Young Seo Park, Ki Seon Yoo | Students: Ahn Taekul, Baek Jo-Yeol, Bai Hyeonjin, Chae Hoon, Cho Yunseo, Chun Semin, Im Ji hyo, Gyun Tae Kim, Kim Sehoon, Kim Taekhun, Kim Yongchan, Lee Kyungjo, Lee Sona, Park Sohyung, Shin Hwarang | Support: Yonsei University Office of Research Affairs and University-Industry Foundation (UIF), Korea Architects Institute

Extra! 1
Lecturer: Fanny Millard | Support: Institut Français

Extra! 2
Lecturer: Fanny Milard | Support: Institut Français

City Explorer 1
Lecturers: Giuseppe Stampone, Soontak Joo | Assistant Lecturers: Jae Geun Han, Inyoung Jang, Dawn Jung, Saerom Kim, Myoung Joo Ko, Se Eun Park, Juyeon Sohn | Students: Jayden Baek, Sung Jun Byeon, Byun Jiho, Hyunwoo Cho, Yu Lim Choi, Jun Choi, Samuel Han, Seung Jae Hwang, Soojin Kang, Hae Yul Kim, Jenny Kim, Terry Kim, Theo Kim, Lee Hwa Jun, Geon Lee, Seoui Lee, Seung Been Lee, Eunjin Lee, Luke Lee, Jae Won Lee, June Liu, Yoonseo Moon, Yoonjoo Park, Sungwon Shin, Taerin Sohn, Erica Yoo, Hyun Woong Yoon | Support: Yonsei University Office of Research Affairs and University-Industry Foundation (UIF), Korea Architects Institute

City Explorer 2
Lecturer: Soontak Joo | Assistant Lecturers: Jae Geun Han, Inyoung Jang, Dawn Jung, Saerom Kim, Myoung Joo Ko, Se Eun Park, Juyeon Sohn | Students: Ahn Uijoo, Byun Jiho, Chen Bailong, Jun Choi, Han Jung Won, Samuel Han, Hong Joseph, Seung Jae Hwang, Hyun Heejo, Jung Yoojin, Kang Chang Hee, Kang Chang Hwa, Soojin Kang, Kim Dong Ha, Kim Kyoung Hwan, Kim Min Sung, Kim San, Terry Kim, Theo Kim, Kim Yeri, Eunjin Lee, Geon Lee, Lee Hwa Jun, Luke Lee, Seoui Lee, Seung Been Lee, Lee Sihoo, Park Seo Yul | Support: Yonsei University Office of Research Affairs and University-Industry Foundation (UIF), Korea Architects Institute

City Explorer 3
Lecturer: Jinoh Lee | Assistant Lecturers: Jae Geun Han, Inyoung Jang, Dawn Jung, Saerom Kim, Myoung Joo Ko, Se Eun Park, Juyeon Sohn | Students: Byun Jiho, Jun Choi, Yu Lim Choi, Go Byungjoon, Go Jun Seo, Samuel Han, Hong Jeseph, Seung Jae Hwang, Hwang Wonjoon, Kang Joonmo, Soojin Kang, Kim Audrey, Kim Donghoon, Kim Dong Hyun, Kim Min Kyun, Seohyun Kim, Terry Kim, Theo Kim, Eunjin Lee, Geon Lee, Lee Hwa Jun, Lee Jung Yeon, Luke Lee, Lee Sang Ha, Seoui Lee, Lee Sihyun, Lee So Jung, Park Sang Hyun | Support: Yonsei University Office of Research Affairs and University-Industry Foundation (UIF), Korea Architects Institute

Imminent Commons Seoul Tour

Project Manager
Nayeon Kim, Sun-A Lee

Exhibition Contractor
I PRO, Hyun-Kyung Cho

Special Thanks to (Individuals)
Young Joon Kim (City Architect, Seoul Metropolitan Government), Minsuk Cho (Head, Mass Studies), Eun-Mi Ko (Curator, Kimchungup Museum), Green Kim (Project Manager, Production City

Special Thanks to (Institutions)
Sewoon Electron Plaza, Seoul Upcycling Plaza, Seoul Sewerage Science Museum, Seoul Energy Dream Center, Culture Tank, Haneng Chon Gong-teo

EVENTS, 2015–2017

2015 Seoul International Biennale of Architecture and Urbanism Symposium
26–27 October 2015, Seoul Museum of History, Auditorium

Symposium Director
Alejandro Zaera-Polo

Participants
Josep Acebillo, Aaron Betsky, Miree Byun, Chang Heum Byeon, Minsuk Cho, Myung Rae Cho, Mack Joong Choi, Beatriz Colomina, Joseph Grima, Weiwen Huang, Sarah Mineko Ichioka, Indy Johar, Mi Gyeong Kim, Jewon Lee, Kuniyoshi Naoyuki, Hyungmin Pai, Jorge Pérez, Francisco Sanin, Saskia Sassen, Katja Schechtner, Seung H-Sang, In Ho Song, Hans Stimmann, Yehre Suh, Mark Wigley

Seoul Lab: Seoul Workshop 1: Urban Map Commons
9 May 2015, Dongdaemun Design Plaza, Academy Hall

Participants
Jaehyun Bahk, Miree Byun, Min Choi, Rupali Gupte, David Hong, Soik Jung, Hyungjae Kim, Sangwook Lee, Erik L'Heureux, Sey Min, Hyungmin Pai, Hyoung-June Park, Cuz Potter, Young Bum Reigh, Florian Schaetz, Yehre Suh, In Ho Won, Dong Kun Yim

Seoul Lab: Venice Roundtable
19 May 2016, Università Iuav di Venezia (IUAV)

Participants
Aldo Aymonino, Alastair Donald, Enrico Fontanari, John Hong, Franco Mancuso, Hyungmin Pai, Vicky Richardson, Finn Williams, Alejandro Zaera-Polo

Seoul Lab: London Roundtable
3 June 2016, Korean Cultural Centre UK

Participants
John Hong, Indy Johar, Soik Jung, Torange Khonsari, Andreas Lang, Robert Mull, Lucy Musgrave, Hyungmin Pai, Hae-Won Shin

Seoul Lab: Venice-London Exhibition
7 May 2016, Università Iuav di Venezia (IUAV), Korean Cultural Centre UK

Curator
John Hong

Photographer
Kyungsub Shin Studio

Video Documentation
Tapio Snellman

Exhibition Team
Younghyun Heo, Hyelim Jang, Eunhye Kim, Hyein Kim, Geonil Lee, Hyun Jei Lee, Youngju Lee, Sewon Min, Dongwan Roh

Sponsors
SH Corporation, British Council, Università Iuav di Venezia (IUAV), Korean Cultural Centre UK, London Festival of Architecture

Seoul Lab: Seoul Workshop 2 Project @Seoul
17 June 2016, Seoul Design Foundation

Participants
Kim Seong-woo, Kim Yeong-uk, Young Joon Kim, Kim In-su, Kim Tae-hyeon, Tae Hyung Kim, Park Hyun Chan, Hyungmin Pai, Kwan Seok Seo, Seung H-Sang, Yi Jae-joon, Lee Chung-Kee, Jo Jin-man

Seoul Lab: Live Projects International Workshop
18 November 2016, MIT Media Lab

Participants
Eric Howeler, Greg Lynn, Hyungmin Pai, Carlo Ratti, Jeffrey Schnapp, Soo-in Yang, Meejin Yoon, Liam Young, Alejandro Zaera-Polo

Seoul Lab: Themes Research International Workshop
22 November 2016, Storefront Art & Architecture, New York

Participants
Emily Abruzzo, Elvira Barriga, Adam Frampton, Eva Franch i Gilabert, Soik Jung, Jimenez Lai, Laura Y. Liu, Hyungmin Pai, Alejandro Zaera-Polo,

Publicity Tour of "Book 1": Imminent Commons: Urban Questions for the Near Future

New York
David Benjamin, Beatriz Colomina, Winka Duddleman, Keller Easterling, Mitchel Joachim, Laura Kurgan, Jesse LeCavalier, Maider Llaguno-Munitxa, Mark Wigley, Alejandro Zaera-Polo | Partner/Sponsor: New Lab, Terreform 1, Cosentino

London
Mario Carpo, Jennifer Gabrys, Rory Hyde, Hyungmin Pai, Alejandro Zaera-Polo | Partner/Sponsor: Victoria & Albert Museum, Cosentino

Hong Kong
Ole Bouman, Jason Hilgefort, Christian Lange, Hyungmin Pai, Valerie Portefaix, Nasrine Seraji, Eunice Song, Chris Webster, Alvin Yip | Partner/Sponsor: Department of Architecture at the University of Hong Kong

Opening Forums / Pre-opening Reception: "Indian Night"
1–2 September 2017, Dongdamun Design Plaza, Academy Hall

Speakers
Barry Bergdoll, Ricky Burdett, Kyu Choi, Yongwoo Lee, Rahul Mehrotra, Hilary O'Shaughnessy, In-ho Song

Hosted by
Embassy of India in Korea, InKo Centre

Co-hosts
British Council, Urban Regeneration Centre for Seoul Station Area

Opening Ceremony
2 September 2017

Artistic Director
Eun-Me Ahn

Directors
Younggyu Jang (Music), Jinwon Lee (Video), Youngsoo Choi (Technical), Kijae Kim (Stage), Younghoon Oh (Sound), Jinyoung Jang (Lighting)

Production/Management
Younzee Kang, Eunji Park, Soree JungKim, Sang Lee

Props
June Kim

Costume Design /Production
Eun-Me Ahn, Yoonkwan Design (Production)

Sponsored by
GS Caltex

Opening Ceremony Part 1 (DDP)
Master of Ceremony: Jayoung Min | Performance: Ahn Eun-Me Company and Friends (Hyunwoo Nam, Hyeokyoung Kim, Youngmin Jung, Sihan Park, Jihye Ha, Jaeyun Lee, Yeji Yi, Kyoungmin Kim, Jeeyeun Kim, Sunmin Lee, Yeonhee Cho, Eunkyung Lee, Boram Kim, Kyeongmin Jang, Eiseul Lee, Beomgeon Lee, Bongsu Kim, Seunguk Song, Jaeyoung Lee, Hyuk Kwon, Jeongyun Yeom, Joohyun Lee, Chaeyeon Kang, Kwanzi Kim, Haram Jang, Soyeon Kim, Jeongmin Son, Jihyun Park, Donghun Go, Haneul Jung) | Tap Dancers: Tapper Joker, Soeun Kim, Seihyun Chung, Dera Shin, Kiwoong Eom, Kisuk Hwang, Seonghun Lee, Seongkwang Kim, Sumi Kim, Gyeol Han, Yul Han, Yoonha Jang, Kotbyul Kim, Mick, Seonmi Song, Leeseul Song, Donghyung Kim, Jonghyun Lee, Deokhoe Cho, Seongsoo Heo | Soriggun (Traditional Vocal Artists): Choonhee Lee, Heemoon Lee, Heeyoung Kim | Chang Chang: Heeyoung Kim, Seungtae Shin, Yiho Ahn, Sukki Yoon, Eunhye Jung | Creative Dandi: Eusook Ahn, Jeejeong Kim, Mari Kang, Minyoung Lee, Doori Choi, Sunah Oh | Taepyeongso: Seongdae Chun | DJ: Bagagee Viphex13

Opening Ceremony Part 2 (Donuimun Museum Village)
Moderator: Soik Jung | Performance: Ahn Eun-Me Company and Friends (Hyunwoo Nam, Hyeokyoung Kim, Youngmin Jung, Sihan Park, Jihye Ha, Jaeyun Lee, Yeji Yi, Kyoungmin Kim, Jeeyeun Kim, Sunmin Lee, Yeonhee Cho, Eunkyung Lee, Boram Kim, Kyeongmin Jang, Eiseul Lee, Beomgeon Lee, Bongsu Kim, Seunguk Song, Jaeyoung Lee, Hyuk Kwon, Jeongyun Yeom, Joohyun Lee, Chaeyeon Kang, Kwanzi Kim, Haram Jang, Soyeon Kim, Jeongmin Son, Jihyun Park, Donghun Go, Haneul Jung) | Gyeonggi Minyo Singers (Traditional Vocalists): Heemoon Lee, Seungtae Shin, Gaye Kim, Joohyun Kim, Jihyun Lee, Kyoungok Lee, Hyunjoo Park, Eiseon Hwang, Meeran Park, Moonsook Choi, Eire Lee, Jongsook Park, Hyunjoo Hwang, Jinho Kim, Geumsook Choi, Namsook No, Myeongsook Lim, Sunyoung Yoon, Bongsoon Shin | Music Performance: Hangyul Park | Lecture: Namsoo Kim, Jeongtae Eun, Youngjun Lee, Wooyong Jeon | Invitation Performance: Lukas Gabric Jazz Trio

City Architect Forum
3 November 2017, Donuimun Museum Village

Curator
Francisco Sanin (Syracuse University)

Assistant Curator
Eungee Cinn (Incheon National University)

Project Manager
Sobaek Oh, Jina Lee

City Architects
Alejandro Echeverri (URBAM at EAFIT University, former Director of the Empresa de Desarrollo Urbano of Medellin), Vicente Guallart (Guallart Architects, former Chief Architect of Barcelona), Young-Joon Kim (City Architect of Seoul), Peter Poulet (New South Wales Government Architect), Michele Zaoui (Architecture, Heritage and Public Space Advisor, Cabinet of the Mayor of Paris)

Panel
Jun-Bae Cho, Helen Hejung Choi, Soojeong Seo, Chun Gyu Shin

Graphic Design
Taesan Choi

Operations
Jina Lee (Seoul Architects Forum)

PARTNER PROGRAMS

Sharable City

Director
Soh Yeong Roh

Project Manager
Mihong Kim

Curator
Yelin Park

Production
Jae Young Kim, Jeong Hwan Kim, Ho Man Kwon

Tech
Yeong Hwan Kim, Young Ho Lee

Design
Studio Mentum

Participants
Urban Terrain Lab of Seoul National University GSES (Suh Yehre, Chae Hae In, Park Kyung Sun, Song Ara, Im Bumtaek, Kang Sang Hyun, Choi Kay), Zero boundary (Yoo Jae Hyeong, Arai Rika, Bae Young Soo), Sinpa City (PaTI) (Lee Jaeok, Lim Gowoon, Lee Jung Eun, Kim Jina, Lee Tae Yeon, Ahn Jihee), Institute for Global Social Responsibility (Lee Yumi, Choi Su Young, Ren Yiwei, Shim So Hui, Shim Chae Eun, Choi Yeujung, Lee Gwang Eon, Bae Sangyoon), City Profiler (Lee Sangwook, Han Kooyoung), Seojin Ceci Kim, Sangcheon Kang

**Retrospective Futures:
Seoul Regeneration**

Curator
Sang Hoon Youm

Associate Curator
Hanuy Park

Exhibition Design
Ja Kyung Kim, Seung Youp Lee

Exhibition Graphic Design
Hye Min Song

Researchers
Jun Youn Cha, Jinchul Yeon, Sukoung Lee, Khin Moe Pyayt, Se Won Kim, Hangyeol Kim

Construction
Joosung Design Lab

Models
Seongmin Moon, Jun Youn Cha, Dahn Gyu Cho, Zhishi Cui, Callie Diong, Yu Lim Heo, Seong Won Jeon, Jae Suk Kang, Chae Young Kim, Soyoung Kim, EunJi Kim, Seunghyeon Ko, Byoung Joo Kwak, Seojin Park, Eugene Um, Hyung Mo Yang

GIS DATA
Dong-Wook Sohn, Ji Hyun Ok, Hyun Suk Song, Jinchul Yeon, Sukoung Lee, Khin Moe Pyayt, Se Won Kim

Participants
Regeneration Story: Jisu Choi, Heeseon Kim, Sangwha Hong
Regeneration Video: Jae-Hee Chung, Signature Film (Daehoon Kim, Jaehyeong Yoo, Sunghwan Moon, Seunghwan Jeon, Jihoon Yoo)
Regeneration Agent: Amateur Seoul, Hyunjin Cho, Hyunjin Choi, Hanadori, Huijun Han GoRyong Kang, JJaJJi, Dawun Ju, JinRyol Jung, Jiyae Kim, Doori Lee, Hana Lee, Thinking Bus, Urban Play, InYoung Yeo, Hyein Yoo
Layered Connection: E_SCape (Taekbin Kim, Yongsoon Jang, Sango Lee), Jong-Ho Lee, MVRDV
Process: Band of Nodeul, Changshin-Soongin Urban Regeneration Support Center, Sojung Cho, Youngbae Go, Donghwan Jung, Jung-bin Kim, Minsuk Kim, Jaesun Lee, Taewok Lee, Hyunsong Lee, Maellomangs, Mint Paper, Sunbin Park, Yooil Pyun, Myeonho Seo, Studio MMK (Pilsoo Maing, Jihoon Kim, Donghwan Moon) + Taehyung Park, The KOXX
History: Terminal 7 Architects, K-Chan Zoh, Miwok Choi, Kangil Ji, SulA

Baek, Jinhyun Jun, Youngjun Cho, Minkyung Song
Memory: Green Kim, Junglim Foundation, Changshin-Soongin Urban Regeneration Support Center Juhung Kang, Hyein Yoo, Architecture Farm, SGHS, Studio Plat
Architectural Welfare/ Residential Welfare: KDDH, VJO

Supporting Institutions
Changsin-Sungin Urban Regeneration Support Centers, Haebangchon Urban Regeneration Support Centers, Jangwi-dong Urban Regeneration Support Centers, Amsa-dong Urban Regeneration Support Centers, Shinchon-dong Urban Regeneration Support Centers, Sungsu-dong Urban Regeneration Support Centers, Sangdo-dong Urban Regeneration Support Centers, Garibong-dong Urban Regeneration Support Centers, Mok 2-dong Urban Regeneration Support Centers, Suyu 1-dong Urban Regeneration Support Centers, Chang 3-dong Urban Regeneration Support Centers, Bulgwang 2-dong Urban Regeneration Support Centers, Cheonyeon-Chunghyeon-dong Urban Regeneration Support Centers, Nangok-Nanhyang-dong Urban Regeneration Support Centers, British Council, Urban Regeneration Centre for Seoul Station Area, Ikseon-dong Urban Regeneration Support Centers, Haengchon-dong Urban Regeneration Support Centers, Janganpyeong Urban Regeneration Support Centers, PMA

Namsan Cluster

The Angel, Tenuously Named
29 August–3 September 2017, The Drama Center of Namsan Arts Center | Director: Hyun-Suk Seo | Hosted by: Seoul Metropolitan Government | Organized by: Seoul Foundation for Arts and Culture, Art Sonje Center | Produced by: Namsan Arts Center, Art Sonje Center

A Three-Way Dialogue
Organizer: Space One | Curator: InYoung Yeo | Photo & Video Documentation: Jong Wook Choi, Eui Seok Seong, Felix Nybergh | Photo & Video Assistant: Chanmin Jeong, Seunghui Sim | Design: Jina Eom | Coordinator: Yena Ku | Volunteers: Alicia Wang, Daniel Icaza Milson, Ester Lee

A Three-Way Dialogue: Present In Presence (Exhibition)
3 September–1 October 2017, Space One | Artists: Sejin Kim, Gustav Hellberg, InYoung Yeo (Video: Jong Wook Choi, Eui Seok Seong, Felix Nybergh / Sound: Euntaek Lee)

A Three-Way Dialogue: A Cycling Loop (Performance + Installation + Video)
3 September 2017, Space One / Shinheung Market / Goethe-Institut Seoul / DDP | Curator: InYoung Yeo | Performance: Bike Party Seoul, Greta Granderath, Vincent Themba Liptrot, Sujit Kumar Mallik, Jane Yoo | Installation: Till Wolfer/N55 "Co-"

A Three-Way Dialogue: Communities and Solidarity in Flux (Panel talk)
4 September 2017, Goethe-Institut Seoul | Participants: Marzena Chilewski, Lipika Singh Darai, Suparna Surabhita Das, Greta Granderath, GwangYa Han (Hansol Lee, Ester Lee), Sandeep Hota, Sejin Kim, Jihoi Lee, Sujit Kumar Mallik, Till Wolfer, InYoung Yeo | Partners & Sponsors: Seoul Metropolitan Government, Seoul Design Foundation, Goethe-Institut Korea, UTSHA Foundation for Contemporary Art, IPCA Foundation, Yongsan GU, Haebangchon Urban Regeneration Center

Pyongyang Sallim Program

Symposium: Revisited Pyongyang
1–2 November 2017, National Museum of Modern and Contemporary Art Korea, B1 (Multi-Project Hall) | Organized by: Urban Regeneration Headquarters, Seoul Metropolitan Government, Seoul Design Foundation | Co-Organized by: National Museum of Modern and Contemporary Art Korea, Seoul | Participants: Chang-mo Ahn, Benoit Bertherley, Nick Bonner, Koen De Ceuster, Hee Sun Choi, Valérie Gelézeau, Owen Hatherley, Marsha Haufler, Young Sun Jeon, Benjamin Joinau, Sung Ha Joo, Inha Jung, Keunsik Jung, Hyun Soo Kim, Michael Kim (Ilguk Kim), Yu-hwan Koh, Jean H. Lee, Frédéric Ojardias, Carey Park, Heejin Park, Annie Pedret, Jelena Prokopljevic, Andre Schmid, Dong Sam Shin, Yehre Suh, Robert Winstanley-Chesters, Dongwoo Yim

North Korean Film Festival
2–3 November 2017, National Museum of Modern and Contemporary Art Korea, B1 (MMCA Film and Video) | Organized by: Urban Regeneration Headquarters, Seoul Metropolitan Government, Seoul Design

Foundation | Co-Organized by:
National Museum of Modern and
Contemporary Art Korea | Curator:
Nick Bonner

OTHERS

**CI, Graphic Design, Website,
Publication, Photograph**

CI & Graphic Design
Sulki & Min

Exhibition Signage Design
Sulki & Min, Kwon Youngchan,
Gunjung Lee

Website
E Roon Kang (Math Practice)

Publication
Workroom, ACTAR, Mediabus

Editors
Hyungmin Pai, Alejandro Zaera-Polo,
Ramon Prat, Soik Jung, Hwalsung
park, Kyunghee Lee, Junyoung Lee,
LIM Kyung yong, Helen Hejung Choi,
Jeffrey S. Anderson

Translators
Kyunghee Lee, Soonik Cho,
Translation Cooperative, Yong-bom
Kim, Alice S. Kim, Eun Ah Shin

Book Design
Sulki & Min, Workroom, Ramon Prat

Photographer
Kyungsub Shin Studio

Publicity

Domestic
Press and Online outlets: Rainbow
Communications (Hyo Sun Lee, Bi Chi
Lee, Gippeum Kim, So Jin Lee, Hye Su
Noh) | KBS Arts Vision (Joo Sang Park,
Sung Kyu Choi) | Special Thanks to:
Hye Won Ji, Min Hee Kim, Ha Rim Lee,
Jiae Lee, Hye Sun Park, Nae Seon Park

International
urbanNext (Ramon Prat Homs, Ricardo
Devesa)

Operation Management

Project Agency
Ipro Communications (Hyungyeong
Jo), Windmill Communications
(Jaebak Kim)

Managers
Minwoo Park, Hyungmo Goo,
Wonseop Lee

Staff
Soyeon Ahn, Yoona Cha, Hyerin Chae,
Soyeon Cheon, Hyeonhee Choi,
Hyoseung Choi, Yerin Choi, Yoojin
Choi, Yoonji Ha, Minna Han,
Seonggyeong Han, Eunhye Hwang,
Hyeonjong Hwang, Jieun Hwang,
Seunghwan Hwang, Dongseong Jang,
Inye Jang, Seongwoo Jang, Haein Jo,
Sangho Jo, Dahee Jung, Hyeyoon
Jung, Yongtaek Jung, Hyeyoung Kang,
Leena Kang, Dongkyu Kim, Eunchae
Kim, Heujae Kim, Hyeri Kim, Jeongmin
Kim, Jineun Kim, Jingyeong Kim,
Mingyeong Kim, Minseong Kim,
Minwoo Kim, Sangjeong Kim,
Seohyeon, Kim, Seongyeong Kim,
Seungbeom Kim, Seungho Kim,
Sinyeoung Kim, Sujin Kim, Yein Kim,
Yejin Kim, Yeongman Kim, Yeonjoon
Kim, Yoogyeong Kim, Yoojin Kim,
Yoonhwan Kim, Taemoon Kim,
Taewan Kim, Iyeong Kwak,
Seongyeong Kwon, Deabeom Lee,
Gaeun Lee, Haejeong Lee, Hajoon Lee,
Hwajin Lee, Hyewon Lee, Jaeho Lee,
Jeongyeon Lee, Jieun Lee, Jihyeon
Lee, Jinseon Lee, Jinsol Lee, Jiyeon
Lee, Meil Lee, Miso Lee, Sanggul Lee,
Seula Lee, Seulbi Lee, Seounghye Lee,
Seungcheol Lee, Seunghwan Lee,
Seungsoo Lee, Yejae Lee, Yoonmi Lee,
Bokgi Min, Jonghyeon Nam,
Hyeoncheol Oh, Soobin Oh, Soomin
Oh, Boeun Park, Eunhae Park, Goun
Park, Jisoo Park, Junbeom Park,
Mingyeong Park, Minwoo Park,
Sohyeon Park, Wonwoo Park,
Wooyeong Park, Gyeongmin Ryu,
Saniya, Dongjae Seo, Minjoo Seo,
Joon Seok, Hyeonho Shin, Gyuseoung
Sim, Wongyeong Son, Byeongjin Woo,
Hyemin Yim, Hansol Yong, Sooyeong
Yoo, Heeseon Yoo, Heewon Yoon,
Taekhan Yoon, Yeji Yoon

Docents
Yoonseo Cha, Joohyeon Cheon,
Hyemin Jeon, Jinyeong Jeon, Sejin
Kim, Seolhee Yim, Seul Kim, Soobin
Kim, Yeongmi Kwan

Volunteers
Seungwon Ahn, Harim Choi, Mina
Hwang, Hyeonjeong Jo, Seonhee Joo,
Gyeongah Jye, Gyeongchan Kang,
Byeongsoo Kim, Gyodeok Kim, Hyein
Kim, Gunsil Park, San Yoon

Custodians
Eusook Cha, Myeongsook Kim, Hyorye
Yoon

Guards
Seonghwan Choi, Jeong Kim, Jaewoo
Lee, Yonghwan Shin

Assistants
Hyemin Jeon, Yeongjoo Ko

Supporters

Educational Supporters
An Sujin, Choi Jaeeun, Choi Yeonjae,
Jeong Leerang, Kang Minkyung, Kim
Jongwoo, Kim Minseon, Lee Suhyun,
Min Jihye, Woo Jihyun

Recording and Video Team
Han Sooji, Jeon Hyojin, Kim Hangyeol,
Kim Jiyeong, Lee joohee, Park
Donghan, Park Sooyeon, Shim Juyong,
Shin Insoo

Student Reporters
Cho Eunhyung, Hong Jeeeun, Jeong
Jongwon, Kwag Minjun, Park Jihye

Management Agency

Consortium
KBS Arts Vision (Yeon Sun Jung, Joo
  Sang Park, Sung Kyu Choi, Hyun
  jung Lee)
RISHIYAGI Co.ltd (Richard Yang, Ji
  Young Seo)

Graphic Design
Hyun Jung Park

Space Design
Young Jin Hong, Jae Hoon Choi

Operation
Hye Na Koh, Bo Ra Son, Jung Sik Shin

Production/Installation
Cheil Architerior, June Design, IZY
Design, Mido Design, ERE Rental

Design Street, DDP. Photo: Kyungsub Shin Studio.

S
EPFL
Unde
Urba
by Pr

DDP. Photo: Kyungsub Shin Studio.

Imminent Commons: Live From Seoul

First published by
Seoul Biennale of Architecture and
Urbanism, Actar Publishers, 2017

Editor-in-Chief
Hyungmin Pai

Managing Editors
Kyunghee Lee
Junyoung Lee

Editors
Kyunghee Lee
Park Hwalsung
Hyungmin Pai
Soik Jung

Translation
Kim Yong-bom, Jeong Hye Kim,
Hyeonju Shin, Junyoung Lee

Proofreading & Copy-Editing
Kyunghee Lee
Helen Elizabeth Gyger
Hyungmin Pai
Vanessa Kamp

Design
Sulki & Min

Distributed by
Actar Publishers
440 Park avenue South, 17th Floor
New York, NY 10016
T +1 212 966 2207
F +1 212 966 2214
salesnewyork@actar-d.com

Barcelona
Roca I Batlle 2–4
08023 Barcelona
T +34 933 282 183
salesbarcelona@actar-d.com
eurosales@actar-d.com

ISBN 978-1-945150-92-0
Library of Congress Control Number:
2017952491
A CIP catalogue record for this book
is available from the Library of
Congress, Washington D.C., U.S.A.

Cover: Sewoon Sanga. Photo: Kyungsub Shin Studio.